I dedicate this book to all those
who have gone through similar struggles.

Rayco Saunders

Blessed
Or Cursed

My First 35 Years

By RAYCO SAUNDERS
As told to JOHN V. AMODEO

1st WORLD
PUBLISHING

BLESSED OR CURSED

By Rayco Saunders

As told to John V. Amodeo

© Rayco Saunders 2010

Published by 1stWorld Publishing
P.O. Box 2211, Fairfield, Iowa 52556
tel: 641-209-5000 • fax: 866-440-5234
web: www.1stworldpublishing.com

First Edition

LCCN: 2010939370
SoftCover ISBN: 978-1-4218-9180-4
HardCover ISBN: 978-1-4218-9181-1
eBook ISBN: 978-1-4218-9182-8

Dear reader of this book, I proclaim that everything you are about to read in this manuscript is the truth, the whole truth and nothing but the truth!

If anyone wishes to dispute anything that is written in this book, I, Rayco Saunders, am willing to submit to a polygraph examination to quash any and all disputes, providing that the individual being disputed, first submits to a polygraph examination on any issue of my discretion!

ACKNOWLEDGMENTS

This endeavor would not have been possible without the support and cooperation of Rayco Saunders. I had the opportunity to travel to Pittsburgh, PA on several occasions to meet with him, his sons, grandmother and family, all of whom contributed to make *Blessed or Cursed* possible.

Rayco and I would like to thank Tom Tousey for editing the manuscript.

To my family and friends in both New York City and upstate Mechanicville, a special thanks is needed.

—John Amodeo

I want to thank:

—John Amodeo for recording history and for recognizing the need for this story to be told.

—My brothers Raymont Saunders and Wachi Turner who made my experience of being a big brother enjoyable in the new millennium.

—My sisters Bonnie, Mia and Paris — because of you I respect all women.

—To my grandma, Helen Saunders, who is my mother; It is because of you that I've never given up even at the lowest moment of my life.

—To my brothers from another mother: Melvin Dunbar, I appreciate everything you taught me; Gerard Hardrick, I hold you right there with Melvin, and Isaiah "Manny" Paillett, my evil twin, you inspire me in your own special way.

—Chuck Senft for introducing me to the boxing world and showing me a left jab- right hand-left hook. Thank you

—James Gus Charles Jones, without you, my story would not be as amazing as it is.

—Rayco Saunders

INTRODUCTION

I pledge allegiance to the flag of the United States of America and to the republic for which it stands, one nation under God, indivisible with liberty and justice for all. For All, For ALL, FOR ALL......

21 July 1974, I was born "Rayco Lashon Saunders". I don't remember much good about my childhood. The things that I do remember, I remember them as if they occurred yesterday.

I was never given any guidance while growing up as a child. I was only taught to hate myself. My mother died when I was almost 12. The guy who slept with my mother and conceived me was never a part of my life. So, the streets became my life.

My story is one of few, but one of many. I say this because many "Afrikans born and raised in the United States of America" have similar stories, but only a few, like myself, Triumph. With all of my accomplishments in this life, some times I feel blessed. But with all of my tribulations, at times I feel cursed. This is the first 35 years of my life:

CHAPTER 1

Changes in our lives can be both good and bad, a blessing or a curse or a life-altering event. For Constance Patricia Saunders, life was about to change dramatically. The 17 year old recent high school graduate was about to give birth. A birth she had not planned. Like most 17 year olds, the unplanned pregnancy was the result of a love affair that went too far between two young people who never thought of the consequences. "I never thought it would happen to me," she remarked to her sister. A brief encounter that got out of hand. Too far for a young man, Arthur Evans/Turner, who wanted nothing to do with the responsibilities of facing reality. A child! Arthur couldn't and wouldn't hear of it. He would walk away from the scene and leave young Connie and her family with the task of raising a child. Arthur Evans/Turner was symptomatic of many young men who would walk away from the scene. No responsibility. No consequences. No problem for him. No "Maury Povich" challenging him with DNA. Just walk away! Don't look back and move on – what paternity? It didn't matter to him. He was out of the picture. Forget about caring, love or wanting to bond with Connie. He knew the deal. Child support or government intervention would now rule the roost.

But, it was different in 1974. Arthur knew he was the father. There was never any question. He knew it, Connie knew it, their families and friends did as well. Yet Arthur, like many young, rebellious men, was frightened off with the responsibilities of fatherhood. It was not in his game plan and it played no part in his grand design. He got what he wanted and fled the scene, leaving a gifted young woman vulnerable and in need. A beautiful, looks-could-kill teenager named Connie. Always noticed whenever she set foot from her home.

"She was a diving champ. I have all of her trophies from high school.

She had the grace of a swan and could show anyone up in the water," recalls her mother, Helen Saunders. Yes, the unexpected and unwelcome pregnancy turned everything upside down for Connie.

Changes and challenges. And now this! Changes! The stress of her pregnancy, the acceptance of being an unwed teenage mom weighed heavily on her mind. "What do I do, will I have the support I need?"

Many young women faced the situation and by 1974 had alternatives from which to choose. The year before, the Supreme Court had rendered its controversial decision in Roe v. Wade. That decision made it easier for a woman to terminate a pregnancy. It started a firestorm with the religious right, the Catholic church and would subsequently be the topic of talk shows, presidential debates and state litigations contesting its constitutionality.

Connie could have taken advantage of the nation's highest court and aborted her fetus. But that was out of the question. "I want to have this child." She knew it wouldn't be easy. She would need a support system to guide her. She didn't have to look too far. All Connie had to do was to reach out to her family. Unlike, many young girls in her situation, she had a loving and caring extended family. Indeed, she didn't have to look too far. She had her family: mother Helen Saunders and her eight sisters and brother. A big bunch, no doubt. But sisters Diane, Helen Jr., Gail, Shirley, Rose, Brenda, Bernita, Carol and sole brother Bill made up the Saunders brood. They would be there for her, as they had been during her early years in the gritty neighborhood of Northview, one of Pittsburgh's poorer areas. Family mattered most to Connie and they would be there for her in her most vulnerable state. They wouldn't fail her. A support network emphasizing love and concern. Now, she was ready to meet the challenge. Like it or not, Connie, unlike her former boyfriend, was not afraid but ready to face life head-on. She wouldn't run away from challenges, but met them head on. She was strong and up to the task. Like most young women in her situation, she took charge and was in control.

"I'm due about the middle of July," she announced to sympathetic friends and family members alike. She bore her pregnancy well for a young woman who would be otherwise college-bound in any other circumstance. She carried her baby well and when July came, she knew she was full term and ready. By the middle of the month, she knew her time had come.

"A few kicks here and there and I knew the baby wanted out."

She didn't have to wait very long.

The contractions started to occur more often the morning of July 21st and she knew it was time to get to the hospital. Arriving at the maternity ward, she was ushered into a waiting area and her vitals were checked and she was prepared for delivery. The attending nurse smiled and prepped her for the event to unfold telling her: "You'll be just fine. Just follow me through and I'll be here." Connie was relieved to see this middle-aged woman who calmly went about the room getting an assortment of utensils. Placing them near Connie's bed, she again smiled, wiping her brow in the hot maternity ward. Within a few minutes, Connie was surrounded by attending nurses and the physician ready to deliver what she hoped would be a natural, healthy child.

She knew she had to perform and perform she did to ensure that the precious cargo inside would be healthy and strong.

From the expressions on the doctor's and attendants faces, she knew the only way to accomplish this was to push and push. "You're doing fine, honey," one of the younger nurses remarked. The smile on her face made all the difference to soon-to-be young mother of Northview Heights. The barren hospital walls sent no message, no pictures or still-life or pop-art. No feeling of warmth or coziness. Just barren walls. Its bare walls were a testament to the task at hand. Like thousands before her, Connie would have to do much of the work to make for a smooth and clean delivery. Her nose detected a familiar odor. Indeed, added to the mix was the peculiar hospital odor that always seemed to suggest that someone had just applied a generous supply of Ajax or Lysol to the room. Such were the quarters that Connie found herself in, surrounded by a few sympathetic and reassuring attendants who told her it was just a matter of time now. "Keep pushing, keep pushing," one young attendant kept repeating, casually looking at the delivery physician. Yet, what seemed like hours in actuality was a smooth, natural birth that produced a healthy young male, weighing in at 8lbs. 7ozs.

Like most new mothers, she forgot about the hot steamy days carrying her baby. She forgot about the pain that every young mother experiencing a first-time birth undergoes. She forgot about the contractions and the pushing and the feeling that this ordeal would never end.

Forgetting the pain of the contractions and the sweating and pushing, her precious cargo was finally in her arms. The blank walls of the hospital and the smell of disinfectant were history. She delivered well, accomplishing the miracle of birth and allowing a new chapter in her short life to begin.

She had in her arms a beautiful new bundle. The one nurse that was with her, a forty-ish white haired woman, patted Connie and said: "You have a healthy, beautiful son, honey."

"I'm calling him Rayco," she uttered almost inaudibly to the staff. "I always liked the sound of that name."

She remembers another nurse, younger and also smiling, carefully, wiping her still sweaty forehead, remarking: "A nice name. A real nice name."

"He looks too white!", his aunt remembers saying to her mother. Helen Saunders, a woman who bore ten children, took one look at her grandson and reassured her daughter, "No way. His balls are black. He's black, don't you worry!"

The birth of Rayco Saunders on July 21, 1974, was one of several that hot summer day at Pittsburgh's Mercy Hospital, the main facility of the University of Pittsburgh Medical Center, located in the Uptown section of the city not far from today's Mellon Arena. It prided itself as the first chartered hospital in the Steel City, founded by the Sisters of Mercy in 1848. Today, it has merged with UMPC and has taken on the name of UMPC Mercy.

Mercy's mission, since its antebellum founding in 1848, declares that it "welcomed all and served all who are in need of services over the years." The tough Steel City needed a repository of hope for those workers who spend hours in the city and nearby Homestead at the iron works. These were 'salt of the earth' people – immigrants from Eastern Europe, Russians, Poles, Slovaks as well as Italians, African Americans and more recently, Asian and Spanish speakers from Central and South America. Like all new comers, they wanted to better their lot and would need a place like Mercy for their needs from cradle to grave. Mercy prided itself as having seven core values that include: reverence for each person, community support, justice for all, commitment to the poor, stewardship, courage and integrity. Such lofty goals! Yet, these were core values that Connie would need as she looked with love and awe at her precious bundle. For young Connie Saunders and her family, that mission would serve her well. As it had for a century, it gave Connie relief. It took some of the tension and allowed her some comfort in the knowledge that her child, like the thousands before, would be welcomed into the world and provided with all the care needed. Such was the case in 1974, as the young teenage mother brought her new baby into an uncertain future.

Young Rayco Saunders' entry into the world occurred during the summer of Watergate and the impending crisis that toppled the presidency of Richard M. Nixon. While the hearing played out daily in the press and the nation sat riveted to the ongoing drama on TV, young Connie Saunders' concern was to be there for a new, young son. Each of us have our own agenda and concerns. For Connie Saunders, the events unfolding in Washington were of no consequence to the events that were about to unfold in her own young life. Not totally unaware of the tension that rocked the nation and the rest of the world, Nixon's resignation a few weeks later had little impact on the challenges that awaited Connie and young Rayco Saunders. Her life was changed forever and her mission was to raise her young son. She had a job to do and she was determined to fulfill it. Her entire focus was to be there for her young son and no one would stop her.

The father, Arthur Evans/Turner, the young city neighborhood youth, upon finding out about Connie, was nowhere in sight. Not a player. Even when told of the birth of his son. Walking away and no where to be found, he was already a person in the past to Connie and her family. She would not even dignify him by giving her young Rayco the last name of Evans or Turner. "No way was he to carry the name Evans or Turner," she told her mother. Her son, her baby was now her life and not with someone who abandoned her at the most vulnerable time. He would be named Rayco Saunders and cloak the mantle of the Saunders family. A family she was proud of who and had been there throughout this ordeal. Mother, sisters, cousins and friends were there for her. But Connie was also a realist. She knew the deal. It was up to her to raise the young son and make sure he became more of a man that his biological father ever hoped to be. A man who ran away when the circumstances called for sacrifice and unselfish and unconditional love. She would show him the real world and never lose sight of the little things that mattered so much – the manners, values and love that stems from a solid family structure. So, what was left for Connie was the responsibility of raising a son as a young, single mom.

Single young mom! "I know sometimes we make the wrong choices and have to live with the outcome," she remarked to her sister. That's what life had given Connie – the choice to raise Rayco or the choice not to. There was never any doubt once she held that baby in her arms.

Her own goals no longer mattered. Her son needed her attention and she would be there for him.

Yet, events would eventually overwhelm even Connie's good intentions. Events that, as she held her precious young baby, never occurred to her would ensue. Stroking the baby's face, everything seemed to be in perfect harmony and it was for the present. Yet, there was a price to pay for the young, unwed mother. She was, after all, still a young 17 year-old mother. She would find out just how difficult it was to rear a child while trying to make it in the world. The real test of Connie's Saunders life was about to unfold with consequences that would test her every fiber. It would impact upon her family, especially the young baby in her arms. For Connie and her son, life's event were ultimately to be a challenge beyond anyone's imagination.

CHAPTER 2

Young Rayco who came into the world found a loving family beset by problems that would have lasting effects. Problems that would linger and stay with him from a young age to adulthood. Problems began with his mother. As with any young, single parent challenges ensued. Children having children and not yet grown up to devote their entire energy to their young. Connie was a good mother, but she had her needs too.

By the time he was attending school, Rayco was now staying with his mom on a limited basis. The situation for Connie had become more difficult. Bad choices. First, the bad choices came in her selection of boyfriends. Then, the shoe dropped, as drugs came onto the scene. An environment rife with tension, constant worry and apprehension. No place for a five year old just starting out and in need. Boyfriends and friends who wanted her attention at the expense of her sons. Bad choices. Added to the mix was the responsibility of raising her two-year-old, Raymont.

More often, his grandmother, Helen Saunders, provided the safety net that was needed for the young men. She and his many aunts and uncle provided that special niche that was soon to be tested to the extreme. Surrogate parents, loving household and a safe haven. All seemed so real, so much better.

Young Rayco grew up in the extended household and was soon a favorite of his grandmother.

"He wasn't fussy. He ate just about anything I prepared," recalls his grandmother. "Whenever the smell of hot food was in the air, he'd be at the stove, inquiring, 'It sure smells good in here.' He ate well and was not a problem when it came to food – meat, potatoes, vegetables and of course, my pies. But times were tough for us." Things were getting out of hand for Connie, Rayco's mom. The family was facing a major crisis. Crisis mode started to develop as Connie got deeper and deeper into the drug scene and started her downward spiral. It affected everyone, especially her young sons, Rayco and Raymont.

Tough times. For some, that means financial challenges – just getting by, paying rent and gas and trying to save a few bucks. For others, it's more personal and emotional – a bad relationship, a pending divorce, the loss of a loved one through death. For still others, it's a matter of feeling wanted and searching for a cause. Looking for something or someone, but not sure where to navigate. Meeting people who turn out to be users and leaving you withdrawn and hurt. Anger, depression and the need to be alone are the results. Feelings of hopelessness. Wanting someone, anyone to make you feel you're special, yet suspicious of even the slightest good intention. For Rayco, it would all come to a boil as a young elementary student. The problems began as early as the third grade.

"He knew his mother had problems and he didn't like what he saw," recalls his grandmother.

Except for his Uncle Bill, there was no male figure – a role model to emulate. Young Rayco started his school years, a troubled young man. Shifted about because his mom was in need herself, Rayco stayed with his grandmother more frequently. He was searching and in need. A man in search of identity. A lot of challenges for a 5 year old. Changes were occurring in the life of the young man. Not all good changes. He started to respond and the results weren't always good.

"I had a bad temper. No one could touch me physically, I mean no one." He would push anyone away, withdrawing into a insolent, irascible and angry young man. Rayco's attitude was one of a rebellious young man who felt that life had dealt a bad blow to him. In part, this was the result of his being shifted from his grandmother's to his mother's house and back again. He also saw the steady decline in his mother's condition.

Introverted, tense and suspect of other's intentions set in.

"Those days made me realize that I had to be tough to survive. Even at age 8, I was aware that life wasn't going to control me. It made me strong mentally and toughened me up."

He was young but knew the situation. His mother was getting into the drug scene and it wasn't controllable. He and his family couldn't be there for her 24/7. Soon, others were getting the attention that her young son craved. Not the kind that served Connie's interest. It wasn't easy for him or the family. "He started to react," his grandmother noted, "and the results weren't pretty."

A parade of suitors, so-called friends and party hanger-ons soon took over Connie's life.

Rayco had developed a temper. He was moody and angry. He knew that events at his mom's house were getting worse with this seemingly endless cast of so-called friends and men who seemed intent on getting affection at the expense of Connie. "They were just using her and nobody cared," he recalls saying. Mistrust of strangers and a sense of people to watch out for started to set in for the young man. A mix of not feeling totally at home and seeing his mother's condition worsen, made the young man very rebellious. He started acting out and it was soon apparent that he was in need himself.

"I started to mistrust people." He stayed more often with his grandmother and aunts and they noticed that the young man was becoming more introverted.

"His temper got in the way and he often just sat alone," recalls his aunt.

"We thought it would be best to let him just get it out of his system, but the pain was deep, too deep," she added.

Rayco's mom had delved into the drug scene, the result of making poor decisions with the boyfriends that came and went. She couldn't devote all her attention to her son and it soon began to show. She loved her son and wanted his affections, but, as with most habits, the addiction started to control events. Slowly, then more gradually and finally a crisis.

By the time he was 7 and in the second grade, the young, aloof and often mercurial Rayco found himself in trouble. That trouble began in school. The school and its administration proved to be of little help as well. The consequences would stay with him and further cement a feeling of resentment to authority and power that would stay with him and shape his character.

"People in charge who should have known better didn't step up to the plate. In fact, they became the problem and made it worse," he recalls.

"I had this crazy teacher, Ms. Barr. I mean she was something else," he explains, shaking his head as if it were yesterday. Brushing his hand as if to dismiss the incident, he began to explain the problem with this teacher.

What Rayco and the other students were exposed to was nothing short of abuse from a supposedly responsible adult – his teacher.

"I was put up to the third grade in certain classes because I was far more advanced than the other children in the second grade. I remember my third grade math teacher the most though.

"She was abusive not only to me but also the other kids. I wouldn't put up with it. When we asked for permission to go to the bathroom, she refused, saying sarcastically just 'pee in your pants!' She would take her nails and dig them deep into my neck and shoulder area!" Behavior of this nature from a teacher solidified Rayco's mistrust of authority figures to the point that his grandmother often appeared in the principal's office, asking for an explanation.

"We're being called too often to come in and have a conference," his grandmother recalls.

"All I got from those conferences was the feeling that everything wrong was my fault," Rayco recalls.

Like most concerned guardians, Helen Saunders listened to the principal and the teacher who explained the incorrigible young man needed special attention. Forget the fact that the administration did nothing to investigate the actions of the teacher. This episode further eroded and contributed to the mistrust that Rayco now saw in authority figures.

Neglected by his teacher, feeling alone and insecure, he started to 'act out.'

Introverted, tense and always feeling that someone was about to 'spring' something on him added to the mix.

The trouble began soon afterwards.

"I started getting into fights and missed school due to suspensions.

"That third grade teacher really messed me up to the point that I didn't want to go to her class, even though I tested well and should have been accelerated. But it was not to be. The worst thing I can reflect upon today is that no disciplinary action was ever directed to the teacher. It was always us, the kids in the class."

The classroom, normally a refuge of learning and fun, became a hostile environment. One to avoid. The mental anguish took its toll. Now, with the onset of childhood asthma, an equally serious situation set in. And he would think of what was going at his mom's home and it made him more reclusive and ill.

Abuse takes many forms and for Rayco it was very personal. Coming from his teacher, the sensitive young man was made to feel that he was the cause of the problem.

"I was always clean, neatly dressed and ready for school, but to have that teacher tell us to piss in our pants and not bother her to get a bathroom pass, was too much. How else was I going to respond?" With no supportive services to assist, Rayco acted out more often than not.

The lack of respect on the part of his teacher had lasting effects.

What should've been a productive, learning experience became for him a place to avoid controlled by an uncaring person who had no interest in molding him into a young adult.

Under these circumstances, he became more introverted and had a problem with anyone who tried to touch him.

"I don't know but no one, I mean, no one could touch me!"

The situation meanwhile with Connie Saunders, his young mother went from bad to worse.

Soon, his mother, started having more drug difficulties that would haunt him and the family. A family that had now grown with the addition of yet another child, a daughter named Paris.

During this period, young Rayco's mother was often with her boyfriend or boyfriends and it was hard for him to come to terms. He wanted attention, craved attention and 'acted out' whenever it wasn't there. Shifted from various elementary schools in the Pittsburgh school system, his mistrust of authority figures only got worse. Adults in his life, such as his grandmother, aunts and mother were there; however, when dark events started to unfold it was Rayco who felt left out.

It began with his young mother. So it was that a young, vulnerable and in-need youngster was slipping through the system, transferred in a few short years to schools from St. Clair Village to Northview and back again to St. Clair's. Transfers that didn't help. Transfers that couldn't probe into the psyche of the young man. Transfers that alleviated the problem for one school without a follow-up and neglected a custodial need. Rayco's life was troubled and he was hurting. Then it happened.

In 1986, Connie Saunders died of an overdose. Her son, Rayco was the person who found her in the bathroom.

There are few seminal events in our lives that stay with us. Good and bad times are remembered and absorbed into our psyche and we recall the event and move on. Some never leave us completely. But, for a young 11 year old angry, young man it was the worst possible situation. The horror of discovering his young, beautiful mother dead of an overdose only sealed his fate. It would be an event that would change him further and further into the abyss of the unknown.

CHAPTER 3

It happened so quickly. One moment, the family was talking and laughing. Yet, young Rayco felt something was wrong. Very wrong. It was a day that would change him, shatter his family and leave the vulnerable young man suspicious, distrustful, angry and more rebellious.

The steps leading up to the second floor bathroom and bedrooms were lined with photos of happier occasions – the graduations, weddings and anniversaries for all to see. Faces smiling for the camera, displaying memories one wants to cherish. Good events, good times with family and friends. But, today would be very different and would start a series of events that would alter the direction of young Rayco and his family for a long time.

"We heard someone fall. We thought that it was my baby sister, Paris. My grandma told me to go up and check on her. I replied that my mama was up there. Her friend Marcus was up there and came down and mumbled, 'your mother' as he ran out. Then, we heard a second loud noise. Two falls now and little Paris started to cry. That's when I went upstairs.

For the young mother, life in the Rust Belt city took on a more ominous display. Like the city that had started to downsize with more and more jobs being outsourced, young Connie's life started to get out-of-control. Like the city itself, she started on a decline with catastrophic results.

Pittsburgh is a rough city, strong like the steel and coal areas surrounding it. It's a city that prided itself as a city of neighborhoods surrounding the famed three rivers that made it a strategic point for trade since its founding as Ft. Duquesne. A gritty, no holds-barred attitude is evident in its residents from the hardworking factory workers to the fanatical fans that shut the city down whenever its prided Steelers have a chance at the Superbowl playoffs. Indeed, its fans are among the most fanatic in the country whether the Steelers are in town or on the road. When the Steelers are playing, Pittsburgh becomes a ghost town. No one on the street, no cabs cruising and no take outs while the sainted Steelers are playing. And the year that Rayco was born also saw the Steelers, the oldest and championed franchise in the AFC to go on and win Superbowl IX in January, 1975, in New Orleans with the help of the African-American Italian running back and local hometown hero, Franco Harris.

It is also the city that, like many Northeastern metropolises, has gone through a revitalization. It was beginning the slow climb back and it was most evident in the 1980's. In 1983, 1985 and 1989, Pittsburgh was ranked as one of the top five "Most Livable Cities in America" by 'Places Rated Almanac'. A city of contrasts, it boasts of 8 great schools of higher learning, such as Carnegie Mellon, University of Pittsburgh and Duquesne University. 13th largest city in the nation, with a lot of pride in being the city that introduced the world to the likes of the Big Mac, the first nighttime World Series Game in 1971, the first TV station in 1954, the nation's first gas station in 1913, the first banana split in nearby Latrobe and the first motion picture theater in 1905. A city made up of its ethnic enclaves of Irish, Italian, German, African American and an assortment of Eastern Europeans from the Ukraine, Poland, Lithuania, Russia and Hungary and newer residents from Latin America, Africa and Asia. Like a crazy quilt of many colors, its neighborhoods abounded with the churches, synagogues, temples and schools that made up the city.

Young Rayco Saunders was a product of the city and influenced by it.

"As a kid, nothing would be done once the Steelers played. We talked about it in school, church and in the yard and in the home. Decals displaying the familiar black and gold colors were in store windows, bedrooms, on tee shirts, cars, school and even respected on the graffiti walls that aligned the yards of abandoned buildings," Rayco recalled.

Like the city that needed an extra ego boost, the Steelers were the high gods that were worshiped by all, regardless of class, race and income. It kept at times a tense, polarized city united and it could break a heart with its defeat. People took defeat personally and who knows how many dates were broken, marriages compromised, dinners delayed, friendships ended all for the sake of the Steelers. That pride was evident to any visitor to the city for the first time. At the confluence of the Allegheny, Monongahela and Ohio Rivers, stood the new stadium. A stadium that even the ancient Romans would have marveled at. Prominently in the heart of the city, it dominated the junction of the three rivers and, no doubt, would be the subject of discussion for the tour guides, taxis, corporate executives and the everyday tripper coming in from the nearby Pennsylvania countryside to spend a day in the city. What a marvel of mankind and a tribute to the city of fanatical fans!

But, Pittsburgh, like any other big town, had its share of problems that the great, new stadium couldn't heal. Putting up new buildings, stadiums, renovating neighborhoods still didn't solve the day-to-day meager existence of its most vulnerable. Like most cities, the good and bad intertwined and the results could be devastating. The big banks downtown seemed a world away to much of the inner city population. The projects were slowly being pushed out by the younger and educated class as they revitalized neighborhoods, making the city a segregated enclave for those who could pay the higher rents.

Its drugs, crime, gritty in-your-face attitude was one thing. Many of its citizens struggled day to day to eke out a living, looking for jobs that had been long sent overseas and trying to reclaim neighborhoods that now saw young people idle and up to no good. Soon, the drug and crime problems that plagued the nation's urban cities and the crack epidemic of the 80's came to the Steel City. Regardless of the Steelers' success or the building boom downtown, the city was still a place for many to withdraw from and enter into the dark shadows of escaping one's own life. These events had terrible consequences for those trapped into its web. This was especially so for the young mother that had so much promise. The young mother that had given birth to the healthy and beautiful young boy at Mercy a decade earlier.

Yet, events in one's personal life would overshadow any event the Steelers or any of the other sports venues that made Pittsburgh known nationwide. Fans didn't want to hear of the problems within earshot of the old stadium. They knew that their love of the sport would eventually be replaced with the new, shining architectural gleam that would be testament to the revitalization downtown. That place to escape from the trauma of one's life. The tailgate parties, the local pubs and restaurants would make a fortune while the struggling city's poorest would fall prey to the temptations to escape. To hustle and make a fast buck. A need to escape. The need to escape, the need to be in control of situations that had now taken over one's body and soul. No one seemed to care. No one. It was a city that wanted to show its pride and have everyone forget the real city a few blocks away with its blighted graffiti-laced buildings, the parks that sold every drug that would make one's mind wander and forget the pain, the neglected storefront assortment of boarded-up former neighborhoods and a police force suspect from its youngest to oldest residents.

The Pirates' Baseball team or the Penguins had their share of fame but no one could come near the Steelers' fans. So the news was always about the Steelers, the concern was with them and to hell with the job, family, sex, and oneself. They would be placed on the back burner. The Steelers were the gods of Pittsburgh and everything and everyone shut down to pay homage. A new stadium in the works would be great. The much-needed housing, apartment, schools would wait. It was the Steelers that mattered most. Bets were won and lost, love lives compromised, barroom fights among otherwise good friends were common, arguments over who was the best running back or quarterback made for a drama that the city at once relished and embraced. For one afternoon, the city's divided neighborhoods were united. Black and white, rich and poor, educated and ignorant, the Steelers knew how to unite Pittsburgh more than any mayor or politician. The rough town somehow showed the rest of America what true grit and sports were all about. Yet, for Rayco and his family the city was about to have a very devastating effect.

"She started smoking, bringing in friends whose only interest was in getting high. They couldn't care less about her or her well-being," recalls her sister.

Connie still had her youth and beauty and that was the problem. She was vulnerable and it eventually caught up with her.

"She would step out into the street and get noticed at once. She knew how to carry herself and get noticed and get noticed she did." Indeed, the young mother had many suitors after her. "Not all of them wanting to serve her best interest. Interested in a good time and idling about.

"I didn't like some of the fellows and the friends she hung out with. I could see the trouble coming," she further explained. It also showed. The boyfriends without jobs and intent on getting high were the source of the trouble.

For the 11 year old Rayco, walking into the bathroom and finding his mom motionless, the needle still in her arm, was devastating. He froze, not knowing what to think or say.

"I froze, knowing what I was witnessing. I ran downstairs and called my grandmother. Within a few minutes, the ambulance came. "Even though I was a kid, I could see it was bad.

"My grandmother and I knew it was bad and not much could be done." Indeed, by the time the ambulance had come, it was apparent that there was no hope of saving the young Connie Saunders.

"Too late!!!! I know they tried, but nothing they said or anyone said would shake me out of this nightmare." Years later, the pain is still etched on his face. Tragedies of any sort affect people in different ways. The unexplained death of anyone in tragic circumstances never really leaves. People speak about it as if it were yesterday. For Rayco, it was the start of a series of events that led him on a path of near self-destruction until he came to terms with himself. It was a struggle and a challenge that would test the young man to the limit. What's worse is that the challenges nearly went unnoticed until events in his life seemed totally out of control.

CHAPTER 4

Faced with the worst tragedy that could befall an 11 year old, the death of Connie Saunders transformed the young man. "It changed him," his aunt recalled. "His initial mistrust of people grew worse." What resulted was a more reclusive and angry young man. A bad attitude based on that initial mistrust took over. That mistrust would cause a number of challenges to the young man. They would begin with school.

"Rayco started getting into fights not long after Connie passed. Too many fights. Fights over nothing – looking the wrong way, anger at misinterpreted remarks and a deep and painful hurt that no one seemed to address. Suspension after suspension led to him being transferred from school to school," recalled his grandmother. One incident led to another and before long, he was sent to Pressley Ridge School.

Pressley Ridge was for the city of Pittsburgh, a refuge for its most troubled youth. When you went to Pressley, it meant that you were trouble.

Going to Pressley was like going to the Big House for youngsters. It had a reputation that everyone knew.

Serving the Pittsburgh community since 1832, Pressley Ridge prides itself as a "place in society where young, troubled youth can become healthy and find joy in life." A nice aim that not often got accomplished.

From the road leading up the hill that encompasses the complex, one is greeted with a gated front that might otherwise question the mission as being a place of solace and achievement. From the road, it looks more like a monastery or a spa, surrounded by nicely manicured lawns and an assortment of maples and oaks that soar to the heavens. But looks are deceiving and Pressley was no spa, no monastery or country club.

Since its inception, it has assisted the neediest and most troubled of Pittsburgh's young and rendered services in the field of an education that is community-based while providing residential foster care. A quick examination of its objectives shows Pressley to provide: "unconditional care, empower youth and serve individual needs."

Rayco was sent to Pressley after a series of schools he attended found the young man in need. Needs that were not met by his elementary and middle schools. His aunt recalls: "Things had changed so much after his mom passed. He was more introverted and kept to himself more and more. He challenged everyone and felt that people couldn't be trusted. He hated to be touched." This change was most notable in school, of course, and a cause for concern.

While at Knoxville Middle, he got into fights and was transferred to Allegheny Middle, where some changes were evident. As with most young men, he started growing into a very lean, athletic frame that got the notice of the soccer coach. His athletic prowess started to assert itself. He became a good soccer player and excelled on the field. Before long, the now tall, solid young man stood nearly 6' and had tremendous energy. Some of his teachers saw in the young man a potential athlete that needed guidance. Yet, his past was still very much a part of him and the loss of his mom never left. Before long, an incident at home sent him to Western Pennsylvania Psychiatric Hospital.

Police were summoned when Rayco began screaming and pleading "don't touch me, stop sitting on me," to a friend of the family who was trying to restrain him over what someone said. No one really knows the nature of the incident, but he was getting out of control. The police took him to the psychiatric hospital where he remained for a two month stay. From there, it was determined that the best treatment would be at Pressley.

Pressley proved to be a challenge for the young man. It had a reputation as a refuge for the most troubled and for Rayco it was an unwelcome place and a reminder of his already troubled young past. Yet, despite its reputation, it did give him the attention he so desperately needed. It also provided the social network that led him to realize that he not only had athletic ability but tested well academically. Within a few months, he was settling down and ready to enroll in high school. A good high school. Of the ten high schools that served the city, Rayco lucked out. That school was Schenley High School.

Located in the heart of the cultural and educational center of Pittsburgh, Schenley High School prided itself in its academic programs for the computer based age. Nearby were the pride of the city's academic universities that brought people to the Steel City from all over the world. Thus, the University of Pittsburgh, the prestigious Carnegie Mellon Institute, Carlow University and Chatham College were nearby to Schenley. The school also had notable alumni, including: Larry Brown of the Washington Redskins; Bruno Sanmartino, pro-wrestling's "living legend"; the eccentric and world-famous artist Andy Warhol; the great jazz musician and composer, George Benson and Derrick Bell, Harvard Law's first African American professor. So, the young man, fresh of out of Pressley, enrolled in the school and soon found a niche in its high tech computer program. Rayco also joined the football squad and it appeared that finally his life, despite the recent tragic past, was now in front of him. He proved he could be a team player and follow directions. He was becoming a man in every sense of the word – tall, handsome with fine cheek bones that complemented a physique that got noticed by the girls. At 5'11", his looks, height and deep voice made him popular with the females and he was starting to feel good about himself.

Yet, his past was again coming to haunt him. As it was in the past, it started with a school fight.

He was suspended as a result of a fight that resulted from a fight because someone broke into his gym locker and stole his school bus pass, and was sent to Oliver High by the tenth grade in 1989.

Oliver High, unlike Schenley, was known as a neighborhood high school that had an assortment of students from throughout the city. Rayco arrived at Oliver and found the climate and temperament different. Very different from Schenley. Students were bold enough to challenge him found that they had better think twice.

Yet, his past was again coming to haunt him. As it was in the past, it started with a school fight.

He was suspended as a result of a fight that resulted from a fight that occurred on Thanksgiving, and he was sent to Allderdice High school.

"Allderdice in 1989 was like a fortress," he recalls. The security staff was quick to accuse anyone who dressed well or was carrying a pager of dealing with drugs."

Rayco prided himself in his attire and was always dressed well.

"Like everyone else, I wanted to dress well and did. I wore Levi jeans, Guess jeans, Ralph Lauren shirts and a variety of warm-up suits – Chicago Bulls, LA Lakers, etc. Shoes depended upon the season – Nike Air Max (had every color at $100 each). In addition, Adidas, Reebok, Timberland boots. I made sure I made a fashion statement."

He recalls one morning when an incident with the security staff proved to be his undoing at the sprawling campus.

"I had several bills and some guy asked me to change an $100 bill. When I walked into the school, the security team accused me of being a drug dealer because earlier that morning I tried to get the $100 bill changed so I could eat lunch I had the big bill plus a pager. I never knew that I couldn't use a pager." Indeed, in city schools throughout the nation, pagers were used in the late 1980's to communicate and deal with drugs and anyone carrying such an item was immediately suspect. It would be true of the new student to this new school.

"I was also dressed "fresh to death". It was a new school. I wanted to make a good impression and I always prided myself in my gear. They see an Afrikan kid, born and raised in the United States, and automatically they think the worst." What happened next, was a series of events that led to a suspension.

"After I made a phone call to this girl that I was friends with, they took the pager. I was new to the school. I didn't know I couldn't bring it into the building. I explained that I used it to communicate with my elderly grandmother. They, of course, would not believe me. One of the deans really pissed me off when he said: 'You're dressed too well. You got a large bill. You must be dealing, as you were transferred here.'"

"I might be brown skinned, but I'm not stupid."

"'Fuck this school and all of you!' I said and walked out.

" I felt violated just because of my gear!"

Yet, the trouble didn't stop there. Later that year, he was involved in a major altercation.

At that age, we often had spats. Some of them were trivial, some not.

"I went to 'The Hill,' to watch a basketball game. It was the Connie Hawkins basketball tournament and lots of people hung out there. It's held every year at Kinard Field.

A hot summer day. A basketball court. Seemingly innocent. A neighborhood game with the usual amount of bravado and sweat and yet for Rayco, it was that afternoon in 1990 that would haunt him as well.

"I saw the group that jumped and stabbed me a month earlier. I was with my cousin Jamie and him and his crew confronted the group. I was down for whatever but, my other cousin Porkie, told me to stay with him because I lived in the same hood as these guys, and had to go home. A fight broke out and shots were fired."

An afternoon on a Pittsburgh basketball court now was a homicide scene. The police were looking for suspects and the area was cordoned off for prints and forensic tests.

"I had fled. I found out that the police were looking for me, so I layed low for a minute. "I went to my cousin's home in Swissvale."

Located just nine miles east of the downtown that caused so much tension in his young life, Swissvale proved to be a panacea. Away from the city and its alluring albeit dangerous streets, the small suburb named for Jane Swisshelm, an early abolitionist and feminist, proved to be just the right place for the energetic and growing young man. With its Westinghouse plant nearby, it had a niche that attracted some of the people from the gritty streets and allowed one to at once relax with a less hectic pace and the temptations of the inner city. For Rayco, this time at his cousin's proved to be an educational, psychological and therapeutic remedy that would have otherwise resulted in more difficulty.

"Staying there was boring, but it got me to think hard and reset my priorities. I realized that I needed to change.

"After I heard on the radio that the police were looking for me, I knew that it was dead serious. I was hustling, so I made as much money as I could in the time that I allotted myself. I visited a couple females, paid the service bill on my Cadillac which was in the shop and then I turned myself in.

"When I turned myself in, the police who interviewed me told me that they knew I didn't commit the murder. They told me to tell them who the shooter was or shooters were, and I could go home with my brother's father, Paul. I told them that I could not tell them this because I didn't go down where the shooting took place. The police insisted that I tell them or else I would be charged with the homicide. After Paul tried in vain to convince me to give the police what they wanted, I was arraigned on first degree murder charges."

By the time of his 16th birthday in 1990, Rayco had already been through a lifetime of traumatic episodes that would have tested the resolve of any person. He was about to enter adulthood and it would take him down a road that also would test the very fiber of his being with some life-changing consequences. Changes that would eventually involve a bout with the law, parenthood and an introduction to boxing.

CHAPTER 5

15. Normally, an age that is full of promise and awe. An age when most teenagers have a bit of trouble finding their niche. Countless books are written about coming of age, such as "Catcher in the Rye." Wanting to grow up but yet still very much a part of the nest. Indeed, their families still cling to them as children; their peers are testing their very fibre through school sports, grades, girls and yet, they come of age. That great taste of freedom. Just around the corner. Fifteen year olds start to see the world and have a great deal of excitement of what will come. Responsibility, heightened sexuality and a future of promise. A coming of age that is at once both frightening and yet so eagerly sought. That is, for most 15 year olds.

Rayco recalls vividly as a youngster hanging out with older and wiser people than himself. It quickly became an introduction that would change his young life altogether. The troubled young man, still mistrustful and introspective in nature, was about to see his world change.

"When I was 14 and 15, I was cool. I avoided trouble. I wasn't aggressive until events unfolded later.

"When I was 14, I met Melvin. Although I was several years younger than him, we quickly bonded and he found in me a person he could trust. Trust was the biggest asset I had. Trust was what made you either have friends or no one. Melvin liked me and knew I was the real deal and we got along. And Melvin became a role model and big brother all rolled into one."

Within a short span, at age 14, Rayco started hustling drugs that had been introduced into the Northview hood since 1986 when the crack epidemic hit the streets and neighborhoods of Pittsburgh.

"Once I earned Melvin's trust, I knew I was on my way. He liked the fact that at 14, I had no fear – not of other dudes, police, family or anyone.

"Melvin became a mentor and started teaching me how to hustle. I liked his style, his low-key attitude. I was starting to notice the young ladies and they were responding to me.

"I was having girl problems. Some of these women were starting to get demanding and Melvin shared some knowledge with me."

"He was a bit shorter than me but he towered. He said, check this out my man." I knew a lesson in growing up would follow and I was ready to heed his warnings.

"I remember his advice about the girls: 'Women are just like men, they do the same things. They just are a little more sneaky!' He went on and added something that stays with me even today: 'If you, for one moment, underestimate a woman and think that you've got the upper hand because you're a man... she got you beat every time!'" That advice resonated well with Rayco and he adds: "To this day, I deal with all women with that assessment in my mind."

Like most young students, Rayco emulated his new mentor and made sure that Melvin took notice.

"Melvin taught me, never carry drugs on me. Never! He showed me how to casually stash the drugs in areas where I could keep watch over them, yet far enough away not to be blamed if the police showed up." Rayco was a student eager to learn and learn well he did.

"I owe a lot to Melvin. I can honestly say that in the years that followed, his 'schooling' paid off – I never got convicted of any drug offenses!"

Rayco mentioned that he was arrested and charged twice with drug offenses. "One was a false charge for heroin, that was actually dog medicine – later confirmed by the crime lab. The other was for marijuana that was close to a spot where I was stopped by the police, because a week earlier I got into a confrontation with police informant, Shawn 'Grimm' Davis."

Northview, annexed in 1931 to the city of Pittsburgh, is a residential area. In 1962, a $14 million expansion of low income housing resulted in the building of 999 projects. This grand expansion isolated the projects from the surrounding residential areas and was, from its construction, a place that old residents avoided and thus became a segregated area based largely upon race and income. This impressive construction resulted in the building of 516 row houses, 7 three story buildings and two 10 story buildings.

"I had phony ID's. They were easy for me to get. I was 5'11" and looked and dressed older. I had clothes that I could buy with the money I made hustling."

The crack epidemic had come to Pittsburgh by the early 1990's. Bigger cities with more resources, such as New York, Chicago and Philadelphia were addressing the same problem with a big spike in homicide related to the drug trade. Neighborhoods became fortresses with frightened residents drawing the shades and staying indoors. It didn't matter if you lived in a row house, a project, an apartment with terraces; no one was immune to the ravages of the new epidemic. Stray bullets killed even the innocent – a principal in a Brooklyn project checking on an errant student and killed by the cross-fire; children shot playing or riding their bicycles; grandmothers gunned down mistakenly as they entered a drug shootout on the way to Sunday service. The epidemic at once attracted the gangs and made life hell in the nation's cities while creating a subculture of crime, respect, death and money to be made. Forget the police and the system. The drug lords ruled the streets and the occasional innocent deaths were just a part of the deal.

This is what came to Pittsburgh and no place was it worst than in Northview and in the crack haven's Penfort Street.

Known as the 'crack street' to residents, police and city officials, Penfort became symptomatic of what Pittsburgh and the nation were enduring.

"The tension was in the air all the time. If someone we didn't recognize was walking down the block, we shut up, thinking it must be a plain clothes cop. We knew who the teachers were, the mail men and the garbage men. It was the stranger that always kept us posted. We used the beepers in those days and we alerted others who were about to make sales to be on guard. We would send a simple message: 50. Everyone knew that it meant to chill; the police or suspected cops were coming in."

Luring restless, young, vulnerable men into its web, its mantra became one of complete control. Quick money, easy money was the name of the game and the appetite of the addicted became their source of wealth. Guns ruled the streets and the helpless residents were subjected to the rules of the street. The gangs. All sorts of gangs ruled the inner city neighborhoods. Gangs that 'tagged' their logos on the walls of bodegas, 24-hour grocery mom and pop candy shops, billboards adjacent to bus stops and the walls of the projects and even schools and houses of worship. A culture gone amuck. A society totally beholden to the lure of the quick fix. Its evil web swallowing the youth, causing death and overloading the jails from the county to the state to the federal level.

With the easy accessibility of illegal guns, young men had their armaments and weren't afraid to use them with deadly results.

The Pittsburgh Tribune Review reported: "The police can't even stop open air drug sales." Unafraid and defiant, many of these young men strutted their stuff with an arrogance and misguided respect from others who saw their flashy clothes, 'bling,' fancy cars and women who were often in their company as role models.

"We packed more heat than the cops – AK 47's, glocks, mac 10's, tech 9's and any kind of handgun. We suited up with a bullet proof vest and mask and made the streets our own," Rayco recalls. Indeed, throughout the inner cities, resources were drained trying to stop the lure and greed and escape from the streets.

"I had people working the streets for me. "Having been brought up in both St. Clair's projects and Northview, I knew where every alley was. I also knew how to hide and get myself out of trouble. By the time I was 15, I had a 1977 Sedan De Ville. I paid for the car in cash. I was 15 and making thousands of dollars a day on the street! It was one of three cars that I got in that year."

The Pittsburgh Police Department didn't get the respect from the residents who were trying to fix the neighborhood too.

The unfortunate truth was that in city after city, the police were outgunned, outsmarted and unable to connect. The mistrust, some of which was based on real fear, neglect, abuse, intimidation and entrapment formed a secret bond that the residents of Pittsburgh as well as many other communities resorted to. As a result, many of the notorious LA gangs sent their minions to the smaller towns and established a channel to feed the appetite that the drugs induced.

For the now 15 year old Rayco it meant that he belonged to something and was respected what he showed off in public. Dealing drugs gave him a sense of power that he had never imagined and at once allowed him to explore.

"Money, power and respect. Three things I guess I craved for." In reality, there was no dominant male figure in his life – no father, no grandfather, no uncle that he bonded with. His journey in life was about to make a dangerous turn and lead him down a path of self-destruction. No doubt this was in part a reaction to the events in his young life – the trauma of his mom's death, the neglect by his teachers and the disdain he had for any authority. He was a risk taker when risk-taking was at its zenith on the mean streets of Pittsburgh. It was about to catch up with the young stud from the hood.

CHAPTER 6

Life was catching up with the young man from Pittsburgh. Fearless at 15, he nevertheless was about to enter into a web that would entangle him. There was no way out. This situation was in his face and refused to go away.

Rayco was sent to Shuman. A detention center located adjacent to Highland Park and the banks of the Allegheny. It was to become home to the young teenager for a year and a half.

Opened in 1974, Shuman became a stable environment not only for Rayco but also the other 3,500 troubled youngsters from age 10-17 in Allegheny County. Abused, neglected and lonely youths as well as those, like Rayco, that had an encounter with the criminal justice system, found a safe haven within its walls. Its mission was to: 'create an environment that fosters social, emotional, intellectual and physical development for all those who enter its doors.' With services ranging from education, recreation, health and pastoral care, it was, for many the first time they had a private room. Indeed, Shuman's reputation, at its onset, was to create a place where dignity is paramount and with its reputation for individual needs, it fit the bill for many. It also had an impact upon young Rayco Saunders.

"Shuman was like a school that you couldn't leave. They had a lot of staff that treated us well. It had a nice school, nice basketball gym, nice weight room, nice cafeteria, good food, pool, ping-pong. It was nice considering the circumstances.

"I spent 15 months locked-up there. I had my share of fun, too. Shuman Center was co-ed. I used to go to the females' unit to get my hair braided. They had a co-ed unit. Unit K, the honor unit. This unit was totally for suckaz. You pretty much had to be an ass kisser to stay in this unit. Guys like me didn't last long there, so I had to take advantage of my short stay. I almost got sexed, but not quite."

The educational program became, for Rayco, a place to test his academic skills. It was also a place that allowed him to explore. For Shuman was still a place for people to meet. And like most schools, it was an environ to socialize and get someone's attention. His good looks and appeal soon caught the eyes of several females. One female stood out.

"School was probably the best activity in Shuman, at least for the smart guys it was. We did our school work as we were supposed to, but we plotted and planned; some of us on how to have sex with the girls, some of us on how to breakout, some of us on how to kick somebody's ass. Me, I plotted on how to get sexed. Then one day me and this girl, I think her name was Chrissy, agreed to do the do (have sex). She was Anglo-Saxon, about 16-17, pretty, and had a nice body. One of the teachers didn't come to school, so her class was empty and dark. Now there was a male teacher, I think his name was Chris, who went around to all the classes and took roll call. The school went in a circle, so I knew where he would start. If a person was missing from class the first thing he would do is check all the other classes first. Well since me and her were missing from the same class, I think he instantly suspected something was up. And it was... ME!"

He now was ready for the conquest! No one could stop him.

"This is how I pulled it off. The bell rang for class change. We were going in that direction to get to our next class, so we slipped in the class unnoticed. Some other girl in our class screened for us. We were in the bathroom with our pants down before the next bell rang to signify the start of the new period. And just like it goes down in movies where you see two horny people anxious to do what they've so been missing, she turned around and bent over the sink. Man, that had to be one of the happier days of my life. The sex was over in about two minutes. Three minutes she was out the door (class change is only 5 minutes long). It was a good thing, too, because Chris was on his way. When she left, Chris was directly on the other side of the circle. I was still in the bathroom cleaning up. All of a sudden, the door flew open and a voice said 'Ah ha!' I responded by saying, 'Damn man, I'm trying to use the bathroom.' Since I was in there by myself, he just said that I shouldn't be in there. I went back to class with a smile on my face."

"Getting over," Rayco strutted back to his classroom. He had won the day and, like most episodes, he triumphed.

Yet, there were problems at Shuman. It was, after all, a place of confinement and forced stay to rehabilitate. Sometimes the pressure of forced stay would manifest itself in occasional outbursts. Other times, it took on more serious tones with ominous consequences. Rayco knew the deal and also began to know what staff was real and caring. But, breakouts or attempts at breakouts became the source of interest and awe. Rayco was witness to at least two.

"I've seen two breakouts. One that involved throwing pool balls through a window in the cafeteria and another where two guys climbed through the shower area walls. A staff member was involved in one, but I won't elaborate any further. I still have friendships that I developed with a few of the guys that worked there at that time. Til this day, I still kick it with Stan Drummond, Al Hanner and B. White. These are a few of the guys, just to name a few, that really looked out for us. They understood us. Bernard White is like an older brother to me currently. We kick it how brothers kick it to the date. I got sent to Shuman days before my 16th birthday. I spent my entire 11th grade school year there and part of my 12th."

He also cultivated the friendship of several other staff members. He was popular and got to know one particular staff member. Rumors flew, but Rayco kept his cool. That female, Terri, still brings a smile to his face when he thinks of her.

"There were also some female personnel that looked out for me, too. One of them was my probation officer, Terri. Terri was a cool individual. She was a young female, about 22 and attractive. Right in my league! I was already experienced with women her age. It didn't take me long to get close to her. P.O.s are supposed to see us maybe once a week to keep us updated on our case or just to see how our behavior was unfolding. Terri came to see me every day! We would talk for hours. Sometimes, she brought me food from the outside. There were a lot of very jealous staff members, too. Our relationship was so cool that I got asked on a regular basis, 'What's going on between Terri and you.' My buddies knew what the deal was though. I always let them know that it was strictly platonic. All but one believed me. Poindexter! Poindexter used to walk past the visiting area when I was on my visit with Terri and give me this look that suggested, 'Rayco, I know better. You and she are closer than you say y'all are.' He was good people, though. He looked out for us, too. After my visit, 'Point' used to come to me and beg me to tell him it was more. We had a lot of laughs after those visits."

"Terri was definitely an attractive female and I was definitely attracted to her. I think she was attracted to me also. If I would have met her under different circumstances, I would have tried to take it past the platonic! We are still cool to this day. We speak on the phone or email every so often."

These positive effects on the staff resonated well with Rayco. It soon showed on his overall academic performance. He applied himself and became a model student.

"When I took my placement test, I tested 13+ on every subject but comprehension. And that's only because I see things different than others. My IQ tested 138."

Yet, Shuman was but a way station to the big house. After his 15 months, he was transferred to New Castle. That's what had to transpire.

New Castle was a totally different environment from Shuman. Unlike the circular-shaped Shuman, New Castle, a maximum juvenile penitentiary, was a lesson in hard-core prison life. It looked, acted and smelled like the real deal it was. It was a mini-subculture that had its own set of players on a stage for a captive audience. A theater of intrigue, corruption, exploitation and a winner-take-all attitude. It was indeed the real deal!

Upon entering the fortress, one was greeted with barbed wire. That barbed wire! Barbed wire coiled with jagged edges that gave way to a medieval-looking castle with thick walls that looked like it was misplaced from the Scottish highlands. But it was not an idyllic countryside manor. To the contrary, its walls stood out and challenged anyone brazen enough to enter and see for themselves what awaited them. The other side of those thick, gray and faded walls. Those wretched individuals assigned to the interior soon found out this was no castle or a place to spend a night. Once you entered, you were now the player subjected to the rules, regulations and lifestyle of those in charge. For those foolish souls who challenged these rules, a seismic shock wave awaited them.

"I was soon transferred to New Castle Max, because I was becoming hard to deal with. New Castle Max was an interesting experience. It was like a miniature penitentiary. Guys having sex with guys, stabbings, gang wars, etc. Staff members there were known KKK members. They had tattoos on their bodies, with various designs saying 'White Power'!"

Rayco started to assess the staff and inmates alike. He would know who to trust and who to avoid. It didn't take him long. His ingrained suspicion of others took hold and made him a survivor in this foreboding environment. Like a good detective, he was able to ascertain who was real. As with any encounter, he remembers vividly the good and the bad. Rayco observed much and took with him some lasting memories. One staff member clearly stands out.

"There was one staff I'll always remember. His name was "Catch 'em"! That's what he went by. He reminds you of an Anglo-Saxon, 50 year-old, Red Fox. He had tattoos everywhere. Three that stood out were, the spiderweb on the elbow, (I know what that stands for), the dotted line going around his neck with the words "cut here" under it, and last but not least, the "White Power", that ran down both forearms. It gets worse. I think he was in prison for bank robbery or something before that job. I never had any problems from these guys though, and I seen guys get beat down."

Quite a contrast to Shuman. Ever observant of others, Rayco distinctly remembers a staff member who would soon be anathema to him. He represented everything he disdained from his manner to his actions and his abuse of power.

"Ironically, the director was of African decent. Collins was almost literally the color black. However, he was the poster child of both a sell-out and a sucka! This dude did everything in his power to make young males of color uncomfortable in life, while playing to them like he really cared. I'll explain: I studied for months, preparing for my GED. I also took the pre-test and I scored very high. Collins knew this because I had to go talk to him once a week so he could make sure everything was alright. He didn't want any problems like the couple I had in Shuman. Anyway, the morning that I am supposed to take the GED test, I was informed by a female staff member that Collins said that I could not take the test. He never gave a reason. I had trial in a few weeks and Collins avoided me for the remainder of my time there. After I was found not guilty, I drove to New Castle to get my belongings, and who do I bump into in the parking lot? Sell-out, Sucka-ass, Collins. He didn't say one word. He was scared to death! His demeanor reminded me of a house slave upset when a field slave was set free! He absolutely hates his color!"

Rayco left the area, free. He was still determined to get his due – he wanted to finish the GED. "Since I was freed in April 1992 (my graduating year), I immediately went to see where I could take the GED test. At the time, my grandmama and I didn't know that I still could have graduated from a high school. The upside was, I did very well on the test. The downside was, I had to wait til my 18th birthday to receive my diploma. I'm proud of it, too. I went out and got that!"

CHAPTER 7

Back home, he decided to take classes at the Boyd School of Business. With his GED, he knew he qualified to enter the business program at the downtown facility. His first encounter was not what he expected.

"I applied and was accepted into the Boyd School of Business. I was told that 'we don't allow our male students to wear their hair below their ear lobes or male students to wear earrings.'"

I pointed out to the interviewer that I saw a young Caucasian male with earrings and was told, 'he is not my student!' A few months later I received a letter from another member of the school. I didn't even respond to it.

This first impression left him cold. He decided to go back to the neighborhood and began expanding his trade. Back on the Pittsburgh streets he knew all too well. This time, things would be different. He was older, wiser and always, in control.

The experience at New Castle hardened him both physically and mentally. He began to show himself off. His businesslike attitude became more lucrative and he was in control.

"1992, I added heroin to my list of drugs for sale. You could say that I was a young conglomerate. I also bought another Cadillac. My brother's father let something happen to my first caddy while I was in the juvenile facility. It was a 1979 Cadillac De Elegance. In 1995 after this Cadillac was shot up three times, confiscated and sold by the police, I got it back and put about $7,000 into it. I got it painted with a custom mixed pearl paint. The color was Hawaiian Orchid. It had white pimp stripe and a white leather roof. It had $2000 deep dish, 100 spoke Dayton's with low profile, 1 & ½ inch white wall tires. My sound system was incredible. I had two, 700 hundred watt, 15" B52 sub-woofers enclosed in two separate band pass Plexiglas boxes, a 14-band EQ with crossovers, a monstrous legacy 2 ohm amp and 14 high- and mid-range speakers with several small amps. Almost everyone that knows me or knew me from that time, remembers that car. I still get asked, 'Do you still have that purple Caddy?' At that point I was moving pounds of marijuana through Fed Ex."

The stand-out car plus the ever-growing trade made Rayco a standout to everyone. He had his own contact in Houston and things were going well. Never one to lose the entrepreneurial spirit, he was also a most reliable, supportive and in-charge kind of guy. He gained respect and soon was able to expand his trade.

"At first, it was coming straight through Pittsburgh International via George Bush International. A girl from Texas used to bring it straight through the airport. She used to bring two big suitcases full of marijuana. I used to call her "Hitler's perfect woman." She was tall, pretty, blond hair, and had deep blue eyes. She always had a nice tan, too. She looked like a Dallas Cowboy cheerleader. I used to pick her up and take her to a hotel on 279 South. I think it was called Kings Hotel. One time after the bags took a little too long to come out the baggage claim, we decided that it was time to find another way. FedEx!

An elaborate system of deception and yet a legitimate haul of contraband product coming through FedEx. But, as with most enterprises, egos got in the way. Greed set in and the nefarious trade had to go through some changes. Trust became an issue when dealing with so much contraband and soon it manifested itself with results that warranted immediate action.

"Me and a few of my partnaz had a program set up where we would have the drugs overnight-ed from Texas, to an address in Pittsburgh. We would overnight thousands of dollars to the connect, who was in Texas. The connect (person we brought the drugs from) had a person working at the FedEx drop off station in Texas, that would let "her" know when it was cool to drop off the package. (There were security measures that had to be avoided.) Here in Pittsburgh, we would sit in strategic positions to make sure the police weren't on to us. We had cell phones to notify one another and also the house if something didn't look right. Once the mail was delivered, we would pick it up from the person and pay them a few hundred for their services. There was a certain amount of trust between us and the connect, until packages started failing to arrive. I knew right off that the connect was behind it, but my partna was against me on my thoughts. It took us to lose $90,000 in one year before he said that I was right. We stopped dealing with her in 1996."

Rayco needed to step in and take control over the transfer. Packages weren't coming in when they were scheduled. Time and again there were delays. Something was afoul.

"We went to Texas ourselves to find another connect. Finding another connect was easy. Getting the product back proved harder than we thought. So I reached out to a few of my old connects here in Pittsburgh. I maintained a good relationship with all my connects because I always came right with the money, I never got out on no one, and everyone knows that I will die before I turn snitch. I was looked at as someone that could definitely be trusted. Unfortunately, I was sent to prison for 4 years in 1997, for a crime that never happened."

"I made my last drug deal from the Allegheny County Jail in January 1997, for $6,000. I had 250 grams of crack-cocaine stashed, and I had a buyer for it. So I had my young partna Rave, do the deal for me. I coordinated the transaction over the phone. I assured both sides that everything was cool, and it went well. Throughout my many years in the drug game, I retired a couple times only to be pulled back in because of lack of financial income. I put in just as many applications as anyone else trying to get their first job. I was called & interviewed for one job out of the many, but wasn't hired. McDonald's didn't even call me back. So I did what I knew I was good at. Selling drugs is one of the hardest things I ever did. You have to deal with so much. I don't acknowledge the word or definition of the word stress, but if I did, I would use it to describe selling drugs ...VERY STRESSFUL! People that are not a part of it think that drug dealing is easy... well let me tell you. It is just as hard as running any legitimate business in the United States. When you reach a certain level in the drug game, you take on a lot of the same responsibilities as legitimate CEO's, Presidents, Vice Presidents, Chairmen, etc. It is not easy, not even for a legitimate low level street dealer."

CHAPTER 8

The crack epidemic that had swept the nation had a firm hold on Pittsburgh as well. By 1994, arrests were up and the growing drug problem was exacerbated by the number of homicides on the city streets. Guns, obtained easily on the black market, spiked the crime rate throughout America. Pittsburgh was no exception. The lure of the trade, the fast cash and the growing number of addicts easily hooked by the 'pipe' meant a profitable albeit deadly lucrative business for anyone who gambled. For Rayco, the ultimate gambler and risk taker, this was his moment.

January 1994, saw the first big snowfall of the season. This was not just another few inches of snow, causing a momentary interruption in one's activities. This was one for the books. Once it started falling, no one would be in its way. With a mind of its own, it was determined to test the resolve of the city's public officials from the mayor to the sanitation crew that already were on high alert and told to do overtime. It hit the city of Pittsburgh with a vengeance and would be a storm that would be talked about around the water-coolers and the office towers downtown for days to come.

It was a white-out, the flakes coming down with more intensity every minute. It wasn't long before the streets were awash in a blanket of heavy, wet, white snow that pushed up against the buildings. Added to the mix was the wind that felt like pellets hitting against the face as the snow defied anyone who ventured out that night. It was a time to be home, cuddled up with some hot chocolate, the sounds of Luther Vandross on a CD to let one escape the inevitable disruption that surely would be the hot topic on the news. Yet, it was for some just another day to hustle, get paid and let the chips fall. In the world of drug dealing, even mother nature, determined as ever, met her match on the mean streets. No

climatic extreme would stop the rounds to make the fast buck, get a trans-
action over and later, join the multitudes of fellow citizens in the comfort
of one's surrounding. All that was put on hold while the business of the
streets was met.

So, that same evening, while much of Pittsburgh was safely watching
the ever-increasing inches accumulate and make a mess of things, Rayco
Saunders ventured out into the dangerous, dark night in his 1979 Cutlass
Supreme. His goal was to get to Penfort Street, the epicenter of the crack
trade in the Northview section of town.

"I was driving up Penfort St. and something didn't feel right. So I put
my car in first gear for extra traction if needed, in case I had to get away
from something extra fast!" That feeling of invincibility recurred and it
hit Rayco hard. He knew with the onset of crack that money was easy, but
like the storm now encircling the city, was much more dangerous. Ever a
cautious person who had the instinctive mistrust of anyone too near, he
felt that something was about to occur. His instincts were correct and he
didn't have to wait long. Not long at all.

"I saw two people to the right of my car, suddenly running away and
ducking. All of a sudden, I could hear guns shots being fired at my car
from the left!" What seemed like an eternity was over in a flash. The car
had been shot at but Rayco had somehow come clean. He had the fore-
sight to escape unscathed and uninjured. Lady luck or good instincts
saved the day.

"I went home, determined to find out who was shooting at me." He
found out who the shooter was and decided to get back.

Despite the ever-increasing, accumulating snow, Rayco, dressed as a
warrior, 'suited up' with a bullet-proof vest and ski mask and headed out
the door. He had a pistol grip, sawed-off shotgun and a 'thirty eight' snub
nose.

"I went back to the set, looking for the person that I knew did the
shooting. It was snowing and cold." Yet, he at once recognized three individuals.

"I crept up on them. One of the dudes was cool with me and used to
hustle for me. But if you were cool with me and you knew that me and
someone had a problem, and you still chose to hang with them, it was

your fault for whatever happened to you! I wasn't looking for faces once my target was spotted!" The snowfall had yet to stop and created a blanket of white on the city's streets and sidewalk.

"I started creeping up on them, very slow. I knew I had to move slow and quiet. The snow was that good snowball snow, and every step I took, it made a noise, so with my pistol-grip pump in my right hand, I crawled on my stomach. When I got close to them, I heard one of them say, 'what you got on the weed?' Another said, 'I got five on it.' At this time, I see this woman that I know, walking with her young daughter, coming towards us. The guys start to walk away now! I stand up, pump in hand! I'm between the two groups! I look at the woman and daughter, and say a silent sorry. Turn towards the three... BLOOM! The three scatter in three different directions, hollering and screaming! Even if you don't get hit by a 12 gauge shotgun, if you are close enough the sound that it makes when it is fired will make you react as if you were hit! I don't know who ran where, but I saw one of them run through the building that leads to the back of the projects, so I ran back the way I came to cut him off! When I got back there, I didn't see no one. So I continued to my car, which I parked about ½ a mile away. When I started to cross the street on the way to my car, I saw two of the guys walking in the middle of the street holding onto the woman, crying and complaining about the pain. I knew the police would be there soon, so I kept moving towards my car."

Rayco had shot all three and the images of them on that cold, crisp January night are still with him today.

"I rolled out as quickly as I could, not knowing the fate of the three."

To his relief, all three had survived and refused or couldn't give a description to the Pittsburgh Police Department. Detectives, looking for forensic evidence had a tough time, as the snow had buried much of the evidence. For Rayco, it was a night that stayed with him and made him reassess his priorities.

"I got charged with the shootings about 6 months later while I was in jail on another shooting which occurred in St. Clair's Village. They didn't have enough evidence, so they had to let me go." Rayco's disdain for the police department fit right in with his mistrust of authority.

"I've seen innocent people, young and old from school age kids to grandmothers treated bad by the police for no reason."

In the complex, troubled world of the now 20 year old, could things get any worse? In a word, yes.

By July of the same year, Rayco moved to Beltzhoover and continued the hustle routine. He was always aware of the dangers associated with the drug trade and never stopped looking for the individual who had shot at him that cold, snowy January night.

It wasn't long before he felt the pain of losing another friend to the mean streets.

"A hood war was starting and I was in the middle of it. My partna, LS got killed by some guys that I grew up with from St. Clair, a.k.a The Dark Side!

"I was at my girl's, at that time. Her mother always listens to a police scanner and heard the call as it came over the radio. She came into the living room where me and my girl were with the news. I jumped when I heard that someone from the hood had been shot! I had my heat on me, but decided it would be better to leave it with my girl. When I got to the scene, one of my partnas walked up to me crying! He said, 'Rayc, they got LS!' There were cops everywhere! I quietly, but swiftly walked past everybody to where LS was lying. That's when I saw the ambulance doing CPR on him." Within a few minutes, police and first responders were on the scene. Rayco ran up to the EMS crew and saw the lifeless body of his friend being transported in the ambulance and, no doubt, to a pending autopsy at the morgue. He knew that it could have been him. Anger, hatred of certain guys from the rival neighborhood coupled with the loss of one of his closest confidants made Rayco seethe with vengeance.

"After I gathered all of the information that I could, I went back to my girl's crib and told her what had happened. All that kept running through my mind was that we were just together about a hour ago before the shooting. Me, LS and C's, were hanging all day. I had my heat and they kept trying to convince me to put it up. They persuaded me when they said that we would not be in the hood (the battle ground)! It was hard for me to not carry my hammer. I was in a personal war (I don't get into neighborhood or gang wars) with some of the guys from the same neighborhood that Beltzhoover was going to war with, because my cousin, who was from there and lived up there most of his life with my family that at that time still resided up there, was robbed at gun point!

The wild side was that I, who was from there too, was still hanging with or around these same guys when I got the call that my cousin was robbed by them. I immediately tried to defuse the situation. I got a call that the guys who did the robbery were on the basketball court. I put on half of my business attire, bulletproof vest, pistol grip pump, thirty eight snub nose, and my coat with the special pockets to hold and conceal everything. When I was seen approaching the court, one of the guys told the others, 'grab the heat!' I told them, 'I come in peace.' I spotted the guy that I wanted to talk to, but could see that he was afraid by the way he kept going in the opposite direction as me. After some long distance conversation between us, I convinced him that I came to talk. We spoke for a few minutes, but was constantly interrupted by one of his buddies that kept yelling, 'you don't have to talk to him!' So we decided to finish our conversation at another time. As I started to walk away, I had a few words with some of the other guys on the court. Then I was shot at twice. This didn't bother me. What did bother me was the fact that two of my aunts were close by watching everything and the bullets were fired in their direction. I told the guy that fired the shots, 'uma kill you... and it won't be by the cover of night... it'll be in broad daylight!' So now, with my already personal war going on, one of my partnas was dead."

"I already went through that neighborhood a few times because of my reasons before LS's death. One night I went to get the individual that fired the shots at me from the basketball court. I put on my full business attire: sweat wicking underpants, undershirt and socks, black jogging pants, black boots, bulletproof vest, black gloves and black ski mask. This day, I packed light for speed. I carried two 16 shot Barrette 9mm's, with two extra clips. I called one of my partnas to go with me, for back up. He carried an 'Anything Killer', AK 47, with two 35 round clips, taped together. Growing up in this neighborhood, I played in the woods almost everyday. So I knew every trail and short cut, like the regular streets. Plus, I had satellite images of the neighborhood that I printed from the computer. I knew my entrance point and my escape route or routes!"

"We were dropped off by a guy named Otis, who was instructed to wait for us in a certain location until we returned. When we entered the neighborhood, we could see about thirty guys congregated together. My partna wanted to hit'em all, but I just wanted to take out the shooters! As I said before, I wasn't into neighborhood or gang wars, I was there to settle something personal. I knew what individuals I wanted. So we waited."

"About four hours later and a few location changes, our target was spotted! He was driving a four door compact. The key for me, was to get us to a perfect ambush spot! This would be hard since I couldn't predict where the target would drive. Then! Fate took over! The target and another guy pulled side by side at a certain stop sign. Growing up here, I knew what this meant. They were going to race, and I knew the race course! I got excited! I told my partna to follow me. We hurried to the perfect ambush spot. When the cars turned onto the narrow street, the target was in the lead car. I was telling my partna where they were coming, when the first car turned the corner. I immediately broke conversation, walked into the middle of the street, raised both guns and fired! As I'm watching the bullets hit the windshield, I saw the target duck down, and the car started to slow down. As the car started to pass me, I started shooting into the driver side window! The second car turned the corner. When he saw what was going on he jammed on the brakes! I turned my guns to him and opened fired! As the bullets hit his car, sparks were jumping everywhere! While I was trying to hit him, my partna was behind me letting his AK 47 do what it do, to the first car! He was shooting everything though! After I emptied both guns and the second car got pass me, I had the pleasure of watching the AK 47 go to work! Both cars, after a brief slow coast, sped up. Me and my partna ran to the getaway ride. While running to the getaway ride, I noticed that one of the parked cars on the street, had holes all through it, like Swiss cheese! I asked my partna what happened? His response was, 'I tried to shoot over it, but I couldn't control the AK, holding it like I was, so I shot through it!"

The getaway driver, dropped us off about a half mile away, as instructed, then drove back to Beltzhoover. When I heard that the intended target nor his buddy, didn't even get a scratch, I asked GOD why guys like these were being protected? I later discovered that it wasn't these guys that GOD was protecting, it was me that was being protected! Several months later, Otis, the getaway driver, was arrested for homicide! He, like me didn't think someone could go through a storm of gunfire like that and not be hit, so he tried to make a deal and told the police everything! My only mistake to an almost flawless crime, almost came back to bite me. Amazingly but fortunately, no one was hit!"

"So now, LS is dead! Shot through the chest! And I've become part of a neighborhood war! While I'm driving, the last few words between me and LS, is playing through my mind: 'LS, you know them boys are coming down here tonight! Stay off the set!' 'Rayc, it's cool. I know they're coming. I got my strap!' 'Aight, keep your eyes open and be safe!'"

"I asked another one of my partnas to come with me. The rival hood knew we were coming, so I needed the extra fire power! When we got there, I used the same entrance point, as before. This time, someone was there! Not expecting anyone to be there, I moved without caution! When I jumped down from a small wall, I saw him! He saw me! He said, 'who dat?' I said, 'who are you?' He took off running the other way. I knew it wouldn't be long before they started swarming like bees, so I moved fast!

"Before I left Beltzhoover, I called a female friend in St.Clair, and told her to leave the back door unlocked because I was coming through. But since the guy ran in that direction, we went in another direction. When we got deeper into the hood, via the back trails, we were able to see groups of guys pointing in the direction where we were spotted. I made the decision to go deeper into the neighborhood, so we would be behind them! 'No one searches their own house for an intruder! They always assume that the intruder, once spotted, has vacated the premises!' We stayed!"

"When we came upon the back of the building of another girl that I knew, we stopped. Looking out onto the street, I noticed that a car full of guys kept circling the block. On the third pass, the car stopped at the building we were behind. Two guys got out and started walking towards the building. When they got closer, I stepped back into the darkness, thinking that they would go into the building. They didn't! They kept coming towards the back of the building. I peaked out once more to confirm. Affirmative! I warned my partna and pointed my gun head level. As soon as the first guy became visible... POP, POP! The first shot hit him in the neck! The second shot hit him in the back! He's shooting back! POP, POP, POP, POP, POP! The bullets are hitting the ground right in front of me! The dirt is jumping up and hitting me in my legs! The second guy is firing now from a slight distance! POP, POP, POP, POP, POP, POP, POP, POP! I refocus my aim on him! O' SHIT! My gun won't fire! It's jammed! I cock it. It un-jams. They're retreating. I tell my partna we gotta go! I knew the shit hit the fan, so instead of following the game plan, I went to the girl's house whose building we were behind. Bad Move! It was so much gunfire that everyone that had a window, was looking out of it! It wasn't long before the police had our location. I watched through the peep hole as this guy showed them where we were.

"I knew I was going to jail, so I called my girlfriend and told her it was a pleasure to know her, and that she should forget about me and live her life because I probably won't be out for a very long time. She cried.

"I thought I shot the guy in the head, so I had to make the conspiracy go away, which would give me good chance at a self defense case, so I told my partna to say, 'that I dropped him off and went to park the car. A few minutes later, he heard gun shots and I came in the house.' I would take care of the rest.

"We end up beating the charges because neither one of us gave a statement and the guy that I shot was a soldier, and refused to testify."

Just a few months later, in early 1995 life was to take a new turn for the soon-to-be 21 year old. A phone call from an ex-guard at Shuman changed his life that day. A simple call to invite him to the gym to shoot some hoops, bond with some positive people and maybe meet new ones. The ever curious Rayco decided to accept the offer from Al Hanner, his old mentor at Shuman and he showed up to play basketball. Instead of seeing a court size gym with two basketball nets on each end, his eyes wandered to the section where posters of the boxing world were displayed. "I saw the pictures of boxers on the wall: Michael Moore, Ali, Norton, Holyfield Tyson and some local guys." Rayco stared at the photos and soon noticed something. As he stood there, looking over these icons, he felt someone coming up to him. It was the boxing coach, Chuck Senft. Senft looked at the young man, sized him up immediately and asked: "Do you like boxing?" "Can you fight?" and most importantly, "Do you want to fight?" Rayco looked at him, ever suspicious of anyone, especially someone so brazen as to cast doubt on him.

Not giving him a chance to respond to an immediate rapid series of questions, he continued:

"Well if you think you got what it takes, just show up tomorrow and we'll see what you're made of." That day, that evening changed the life of Rayco Saunders.

Rayco Saunders decided he would show up and show up he did!

CHAPTER 9

Rayco entered the boxing world the way most up-and-coming pugilists do: he joined a boxing gym that was supervised by local coaches who had trained youngsters for the Golden Gloves. The Golden Gloves! Your meal ticket to success in the boxing world and it began for Rayco in the best boxing gym in Pittsburgh's Brookline area, the second largest neighborhood in the city. With its curved roads, tree-lined streets and private homes, it remains an idyllic setting in the city's South Hill section. It's also the neighborhood that helped catapult Rayco to the boxing world.

The Brookline Boxing Club or "Charlie's Angels" dates back to 1957 when its founder, Chuck Senft decided that the Monroe Park Recreation Center needed to extend its sports activities to boxing. It started, like most venues, in a small room. Little by little, he attracted more and more young men to consider boxing. The little space allocated soon became a Mecca for many upstart boxers. Word spread in the city and within a short span of a few years, the club became the place for wannabe boxers. For a long period of 47 years, the Brookline Club had become a premiere venue in the boxing world for Western Pennsylvania. Its success was the dedication, determination and drive of Chuck. During his long tenure as coach, Chuck Senft brought home an amazing and impressive 50 team championships in the Golden Gloves competitions. One person can make a difference in the lives of others. Giving encouragement, making them accountable and respectful of others whether it be on the field, in the classroom or the workplace. For Chuck Senft, his calling was to motivate his young talents who had the drive and skills to be a contender in the ring. Young men who needed to know that someone actually cared and would be there to push hard and make their dreams come true. To be somebody when others looked the other way. Winner or loser, much is owed to Chuck. He singlehandedly saved many a young man from the streets and gave them hope. Yes, one individual can make all the difference. For Rayco, that person was Chuck the day he stepped into the Brookline Boxing Club and became one of many of "Charlie's Angels". Since 2005, it is now called the Pittsburgh Boxing Club. Its goal is still the same as it was a half century ago: to give the young men of Pittsburgh a place to test their will in the ring. Indeed, for many young men, like Rayco, it was a whole new world.

"I started learning to box in January 1995. I had my first fight against a guy that used to fight for Chuck, for two years, but was at that time fighting for Hogan's gym. Records could probably tell his name. He was a hyper guy. During the other fights he was cheerleading the other fighters on very loud. Coach Chuck, pointed him out to me, and then told me that he normally does not show his guy who he's fighting because he doesn't want them to get scared. I explained to Chuck that I know NO FEAR! I was done with fear after I looked "life in prison" in the face at 17 years young!

"It was a hard fight. The guy came out very aggressive, but I grew up in an aggressive environment. I was more than equipped to handle him. I kicked his ass!

"After the first round, Chuck asked me was I tired. My answer was no. He asked me was anything wrong? I replied, my damn legs are burning. I've never felt anything like this burning that I was feeling.

"The fight went the standard 3-three minute rounds (the rounds have since been changed to 2 minutes now). I was the winner OF THE FIGHT! I went to the locker room to get dressed with two of my close friends. We were discussing the fight, but I wasn't feeling too good. I actually laid on the bench and couldn't move. I asked one of my friends to get me something to drink. He brought me back a Coke. I took a sip and all I could do was reach for the trash can that was to my left. I spit up everything that I ate for the last two weeks! I mean I think I spit up for five minutes straight. After that I felt fine.

"I went on to have a couple more fights and won all of them. Then came the championship. I was fighting a guy from the same gym as me. Sometimes it happens like that in these tournaments.

"At this time I had some street beefs with some of the 606 crips from St.Clair Village, going on that stemmed from my cousin being robbed at gunpoint, and me being shot at when I tried to get his jewelry back peacefully. Some guys from their neighborhood were fighting that night too. There was a lot of back and forth talk between them and me and my partnas. So as it got close to me fighting, the words became more threatening. I was told that I wasn't leaving there alive.

"Even though there were a lot of police there, I started thinking, maybe this is not so safe to be here. We were out numbered 2-1 certainly, maybe 3-1.

"I never went anywhere without my hammer (gun), and I had it this night. Being that we were in the hotel, with security all around, I think they thought we didn't have protection. Me and my partnas were ready to throw down though. One of my partnas was licensed to carry a firearm, so he was strapped. My other partna's gun was registered in his name, so he was strapped. I, of course, was always strapped! After I had enough of the threats, I asked my partnas were they ready. I told them that my plan was to go right through our enemies, shooting! Like a half back following a full back on a 4th and goal play, down by 5, with 1 second left on the clock! Being that they were blocking the closest exit, and I didn't want them to get outside before us. So I put my hand in my bag, grabbed my hammer, stood up and asked are y'all ready. When the other guys saw this they sensed what was about to happen and started getting out the way in a hurry! One of them said, do he gotta a gun. I answered, I always got my hammer! He went and told the police on me!!! I won't say his name. He was young then. A scared little boy trying to impress the older guys.

"Anyway, I went to the other side of the ball room to tell Chuck that I can't fight because it was going to be some problems out here. That's when one of my partnaz came to me and said, the police are searching us. I immediately dropped my bag in a pile of 50 other bags. I was reaching in my pocket to take the extra clip out, when a cop walked up on me and said what's in your pocket? I said nothing. Then patted it for him so he wouldn't search me. It worked! The cop then said, where's your bag? I said, what bag? The cop said, that bag you had? I said, what bag? The cop got the picture. Then he told us we had to leave. So I left the bag with the other fighters' bags. Chucked returned it to me the next day. That memory brings a smile to my face. Chuck said to me, I don't know what's in there, and I don't want to know.

"So, I lost the 1995 Golden Gloves Pittsburgh championship by no show. The guy I was supposed to fight couldn't beat me. We sparred many times before the tournament. I was too fast. Too strong and too skilled for him. But he's in the history books as the winner.

CHAPTER 10

"The Pittsburgh Golden Gloves was over in April, and Chuck's Gym, unfortunately shut down for the summer. They didn't participate in any of the other tournaments that I later found out existed. So I did what every other youth my age did... hung out and partied. 1995 was looking to be a good year. I just felt good about this year. I was making money. One of my of closest partna's was the co-owner of a night club called Ramie's, where we had an endless choice of women. Everything was good."

At 21, Rayco had the looks, body, swagger and reputation that made others both envious and fearful. Soon, Ramie's became the perfect venue for him.

"Ramie's was named after my partna's deceased brother. We had so much fun in this club. There were things that happened in the club after we shut down for the night that I can't tell in this book. However there are some things that I will speak on." Rayco goes on to explain the appeal of this special place.

"Ramie's was a nice bar with a kitchen, tables and chairs for eating, pool table, dart game and some poker games. At night, it turned into a full blown night club. Some of the women that came through there were very sexy." No doubt, it had the perfect recipe for a hungry young man intent on meeting women while showing off. It became the place for Rayco and his friends to meet women who wanted attention, sex and felt like they were special. Smooth-talking, handsome and muscular Rayco would find a special niche here. He could walk in and his presence was immediately noticed by the females. He soon became one of the favorites at Ramie's.

"Me and my partna use to make bets, sometimes on pool, but most of the time on women. We use to bet whether or not each other could pull a certain female that particular night. We use to take oaths on New Year's Eve that for the new year we couldn't have sex with someone that we already had sex with. We had to find a new female to have sex with, and until we found a new female, we couldn't have sex!"

A test of wills, a game of chance, an opportunity to compete to see who would get the prize. Like any test, an element of surprise always awaited. Yet the lure of the hunt overpowered Rayco and his friend. What resulted was a series of show-and-tell performances that enhanced the hunt. As with any hunt, the element of surprise was always lurking. Confident of the outcome, the hunter knew his prey and was intent on complete conquest.

"A lot of one night stands happened after a night at Ramie's. There were even times when I would leave from the club with a female, have sex with her, take her to her home the next day and wouldn't know her name the whole time! I developed a slick way of asking what's her name without actually asking her. Before she got out of my car, I would give her a pen and paper and tell her to write her number down. I learnt, all women will write their name down with their number so the guy doesn't forget her. Smart, I know#!" The hunter knew his prey.

Like his performance in the ring, Rayco's technique worked. He was soon known by many of the women in the club. But, like any game, there were risks. Soon, he developed a unique strategy that reinforced his basic instinct to survive. Was she a friend or a set up? Can I trust her? Does she know my past? The dangers of the hunt were there but, ever the entrepreneur, he was determined to conquer.

"There were also dangers in not knowing a female and taking her with you from the club. In the 1990's, there were a lot of guys being set up by women to be robbed by their current boyfriends, relatives or even your enemies. So I had certain rules that I used to stick to and still follow some to this day. These rules probably kept me from being tied up and put in a few car trunks like others that I know and knew."

The strategy worked. He never strayed from it. It kept him vigilant, focused and organized. Regardless of how 'foxy,' the female, Rayco wouldn't allow the passion of the moment to take over and followed his own rules with success. His rules were simple.

"When I left the club with a young lady or took her out for the first time, I never drove directly to my house. I always drove through every back road and alley I could find. I never took a direct known route to my house. Every female I knew thought that I lived in Beaver County on a farm or somewhere similar. If we went to a hotel, I made sure I went somewhere they were not familiar with. If we went to her house, gun in my hand, I searched every room in the house with her in front of me as a shield. I didn't make them being my shield obvious to them, but that's what they were."

He goes on to explain the necessity of these drastic procedures. What developed was the result of years on the streets and knowing never to let his guard down. Little things taken for granted were a major focus of attention – the open window with a curtain gently blowing in the summer wind, the illumination from the moon on the darkened kitchen, the noise made stepping on the creaky floorboard leading to the bedroom.

"If one of my partnas were driving, and one of us had a female or we both had women, we would make eye contact in the rearview mirror and it would be understood. Sometimes we would simply say, 'take the short cut'. Chic's got a kick out of that phrase because it would take so damn long to get to the crib!" Loyalty became a badge of honor and cooperation from his partners were essential. Rayco's trust in his closest friends or partners became an integral part of his being. Everyone wants to feel liked. Everyone wants to rely on someone in times of need. For Rayco and his friends, the coterie of close contact with his buddies was paramount to their survival. No one outside the circle of friends was to be trusted. How could they be? He had seen and experienced so much in his early years. Others would have long given up, succumbing to the temptations of illicit drugs and quick fix. But, this was the tough guy, always suspicious yet always loyal to a friend.

"I had a few partnas that were very close to me. If you were close to me, I considered you like a brother to me. I had a few partnas older than me and I had a few younger than me.

"Two of my younger partnas stood out at this particular time, because they were like my younger brothers. I taught them everything and shared most things with them, even women. As I speak about them now, they both stand out for very different reasons. Quay, (R.I.P) and J.C, were two little dudes that stood out to me when I moved to Beltzhoover. When I met Quay, he was more into woman than money. I taught him to understand that money was the first priority out here on these streets. Everybody wanted the women, the clothes, the cars, but lacked the understanding that it was the money that allowed you to obtain all of the above. Being that I grew up in Northview Heights, under guys like the Dunbars, the Bivins and the Beasleys, just to name a few, I understood this very clear. In the movie 'Scarface,' Al Pacino, a.k.a Tony, made a statement to his partna. This statement became very popular in rap songs, and still makes perfect sense to this day. Tony told his partna, 'First you get the money, then you get the power, then you get the respect/women.' It took a few serious conversations between us, but eventually he understood everything that I said to him. A few of my partnas my age tried to discourage me from getting involved with Quay because he allegedly owed out money. I asked him about the allegations and accepted his answer. We all had to be taught the game. Quay was a good learner, and eventually became successful at this crooked game. Unfortunately his success was short lived. In 1996, he was shot to death in the Oakland neighborhood of Pittsburgh. I received this news while I was in the Allegheny County Jail. This was the first time in years that I shed tears for a fallen soldier.

"J.C, a.k.a J-lock, a.k.a James Guscharles Jones, was a few years younger than me. Our families grew up together in St. Clair's Village. So we knew each other since we were children. When I moved to Beltzhoover, we immediately resumed our childhood friendship. J.C, was like the little brother that you had to baby sit. He couldn't do too many things independently. You had to walk him through a lot of things. He was the outcast in the neighborhood that did dumb stuff just to fit in and get noticed. He even shot his younger brother, Daniel, in the face and disfigured him permanently, He went to a juvenile camp for this."

Rayco soon became the mentor that the young JC needed. Realizing the power he had in others, he also knew that he could use his hold on others to create and micro-manage his business. What he saw in young J.C. was an outcast looking for attention and desperately wanting to 'fit in.' Rather than being another person to ridicule the dependent J.C., Rayco let him into his web and the result was a loyal, reliable and respected partner.

"I, as well as others, could tell that J.C wanted to be me. From being around me, he developed courage. He learnt how to approach girls. He in a sense started to grow up. Me and J.C hung a lot. I knew his family. He knew mine. We were close. I thought I knew him well, but I learnt that you can study the eyes of a person but you can't see the temptations behind them."

Into this web, a new person emerged. Unlike the type-cast males from the 'hood, this person – single mother, petite, young and attractive, became a catalyst in Rayco's growing enterprise. His encounter with her added to the mix, giving a safety niche needed from the ever-growing drug trade.

"One day this girl asked me could she buy some crack from me. She was a little younger than me, attractive, had a nice body and a nice walk. I asked J.C, what her story was. He told me that she doesn't get high, she resales them to double her money so she can do more for herself and her daughter. After her second time buying from me, I started thinking to myself that it would be nice to have someone on the team that fly's below the police radar, like a girl. Where she lived was ideal also. For she lived directly on one of Beltzhoover's drug spots. I asked J.C, what he thought about me putting her on (giving her drugs on credit). He told me that it wouldn't be a good idea, because she was stupid. I told him everyone can be taught. I had to be taught. He had to be taught. She can and will be taught. Soon after, I approached her and asked her what she wanted out of life, etc. From then on, it became a good relationship between me and her. She started becoming known as a person that had the best product. Drug addicts wouldn't buy from no one but her. It came to a point where she was bringing me $2000 to $3000 a night. This money along with other money I had coming from other parts of the city, I was doing pretty good. Some other smaller dealers had a hard time buying from her because of their pride, but after a while, they too were her clients. It wasn't long before most of the drug traffic came to this block in Beltzhoover. So I made sure that my product and only my product was being sold on this particular block. I let everyone know that if I caught anyone buying or selling product and it wasn't mine, I was taking the money and the drugs. For the most part, that rule was respected. One could never tell what happened when his or her eyes are closed. A few times when I would randomly pop-up, I would see her conversing with some of the competition. These individuals would leave as soon as I appeared, so there was never any confrontation. I almost got into a war once, because one of my competitors tried to get her to come to his team. It all came about because my connect wasn't on, so I tried to supplement until he came through. In the process of trying to obtain some drugs, I asked this guy to ask his supplier if he had what I was trying to get. This dude goes to my worker and tells her that she might as well get on his team because I am trying to get it from him. I was furious when she told me this. So out of respect for his supplier, I went to his supplier and told him what happened. I also told him that if I see his worker doing or trying to do business on my block, I'm taking his product. I didn't have any more issues from this dude."

Ever the loyal friend and confidant, Rayco began to respect this young lady. Soon, a bond developed. With her good looks and savvy business skills, Rayco learned to respect her and soon she found him desirable. Always strong yet suspect and vigilant, Rayco seldom allowed his passions to get in the way of business. He maintained his tough edge. Yet, with an attractive someone he could relate to on an equal plane, the dynamic changed altogether. He was about to break one of his cardinal rules. Life is about changes and changes are either accepted or rejected. Rayco was only human and the desire set-in and soon their relationship took a more intimate and personal turn.

"This girl became such an attraction that other guys that were respected in the hood, started coming to me asking can they take her out. The reasons they came to me were 1. Everyone thought that me and her were messing around, and 2. Out of respect for me. No one wanted a war if they didn't have to have one. Despite what the outsiders looking in thought about us being Gangsta's, we were both, Gangsta's and Gentlemen and conducted ourselves as such, depending on the situation. Now did I have a special type of relationship with this female... yes. That was a rule that I broke. Never mix business and pleasure. When I first met her, I had no intention on sexing her. But the more money she made, the more power she started to obtain. Power has magic qualities. It can bestow glamour and style on whoever has it. Because people are somewhat powerful, they are treated as if they are attractive, and when they are treated as attractive, they often become attractive. As I already said previously, she was already attractive. With money she was able to dress better, keep her hair done right. She was eating better which showed in the glow of her skin and the shape of her body. Yes, we slept together a few times. And the sex was good. I never told anyone they couldn't take her out though. Me and her had an understanding and that was nothing shall stand in the way of this money. Fun was fun. Business was business."

The "business" was about to face a major crisis as the Pittsburgh Police Department started a major crackdown in the neighborhoods that Rayco and others had controlled. Soon, the drug wars took an ugly turn with Rayco in the middle of it. What resulted were changes that no one could have imagined. The upstart boxer would soon find that this lucrative trade and fast life of cars, sex, money was about to challenge more than any opponent in the ring. It began with two Pittsburgh police officers.

CHAPTER 11

"Everyone on the team was eating (making money). This is about the time I met two Pittsburgh cops, Ed Fallert & Robert Stowman." A new phase of Rayco's life was about to unfold.

"We saw each other periodically as they patrolled Beltzhoover. For the most part we had a mutual respect for each other, so I thought. For the short time that I knew these cops we had numerous encounters, some fun, but most bad." Soon, their worlds would clash and Rayco became the center of their efforts.

"My first encounter with these two cops was when they put one of my former friends(J-Dank) into the back of the police wagon because he allegedly blew a kiss at them. I reasoned with them and convinced them not to take him to jail. Thus was the start of our relationship.

"One time me and a few guys were on the set, standing in front of the female's house that I just spoke of previously. It was around midnight, and we were talking quietly, when the Stowman and Fallert pulled up. They said they were responding to a loud noise call. I ask them to ask the dispatcher where the call came from. Fallert asked, and the dispatcher said the call came from a payphone located a mile away. All of us agreed that someone was playing games. I later figured out that James Jones, who was with us earlier, was the one who placed that call in hopes to get someone caught selling drugs."

Rayco knew the deal. He knew that others in the 'hood' were constantly competing for turf and would do anything – anything! Even acting as a decoy for the cops. Like any enterprise, the competition had to be eliminated. Rayco's savvy outlook, cool demeanor and lack of fear earned him respect from all corners, even the police patrolling his neighborhood.

"The knowledge that I showed these cops that I had of a part of their system, I think made them respect the fact that I had more knowledge than the average street hustler. We spoke to each other on a regular basis after this. The next encounter came one night when me and Quay were racing our cars. I had a 1984 Pontiac Trans Am. Quay had a 1987 Grand Prix. We started racing from Climax Ave. We turned on to Beltzhoover Ave, with Quay in the lead. We went past an alley between Orchard and Jucunda. As Quay past the alley I saw the police van activate it's lights. I went past before it could pull from it's parked spot. We were doing 80 mph, easy. Now Quay had an illegal firearm in his car. Since I knew this, I took the heat (cops attention) away from him. Quay went past Chalfont St, and turned right on to Michigan St. I turned right on to Chalfont St. From there, I turned left on to Bernard St. Quay shot past me going straight up Michigan St. I turned left onto Michigan St., the direction Quay just came from. I made a right turn back onto Beltzhoover Ave. Then a quick left into an alley called Eisenburg Way. I shot straight up the alley, made a few more turns, parked and got out. When I was back on the set, Stowman and Fallert, pulled up on one side and another police vehicle pulled up the other side. I knew why they were there, but I didn't flinch. Fallert asked me did I know anyone that drove a black Trans Am. I responded that could be anyone. Fallert described the car in detail, and I knew of another very similar Trans Am, who's owner lived in Beltzhoover. When I mentioned this, they described the driver who had on and wore a hat like me. I asked how they could see all that in a car going 80 mph at night. And further more, would a judge believe them. They said, that they could take the driver to jail, just to inconvenience him. I politely mentioned that it would also be an inconvenience for the cop that has to do the paper work and report to court for a very minor violation that would more than likely be dismissed in court. They agreed. And after they indirectly gave me compliments for my NASCAR like driving ability, they left."

Rayco, was in top form. He learned the old maxim to "keep your friends close and your enemies closer!" Ever the showman, be it in the ring, behind his fancy car or with an attractive female, he was in total control. His encounter with the cops that day was evident of his ability to thwart a legal complication for a friend while arguing a case as well as any defense attorney in arraignment court. He knew the deal. He was ready. It wouldn't take long for the next crisis.

"My next encounter came the very next day. I was behind Quay, in my car on Climax Ave. Stowman and Fallert, were traveling in the opposite direction and made a u-turn when they saw us. Quay immediately made a right turn onto Haberman St. I followed. Quay went down to Warrington Ave. and made a left. I turn left onto Industry, a street before Warrington Ave. I had my hammer on me, so once I hit Industry St., I put the pedal to the floor. I couldn't take the chance of getting searched. There were two stop signs between where I was currently, and my house. I disregarded both.

"I pulled up in front of my house and immediately exited my car. As I was about to go in to the house, Stowman and Fallert pulled up. Stowman said to me, 'Don't you think that you were going a little to fast under the conditions?'

I responded, "What conditions? It's not raining or snowing."

Stowman said, "There are kids out."

I replied, "I will slow down."

Fallert said to me, "Come look at this picture and tell me if you know this kid."

I replied, "That's all right. I'll pass."

Fallert said to me, "Just come take a quick look."

I replied, "Even if I look at the picture, I'm not going to tell you if I see him." I could tell that Fallert was upset. He didn't hide his feelings well.

Rayco wasn't about to cooperate. A drug war was underway and tensions on all sides were high, from the dealers to users to police. Yet, despite all the dangers, things were settling down. With his business acumen intact, Rayco could rule the roost and no one was going to get in the way. As with any business, he approached his job the way he had been taught – always know the consequences of your actions and be able to take the heat.

"Now around this time, business was good. There was still a war going on between Beltzhoover and St.Clair's village, but for the most part it was kind of a cease fire going on. I was in a neighborhood bar called

RED's. RED's is a bar located on Warrington Ave, in Beltzhoover. That's where just about everyone from Beltzhoover that was of age hung out. RED's had a dart game, jukebox and for parties, a dance floor upstairs. A lot of things went on in this bar.

"I remember one time I was in the bar and it was packed to capacity. Well it was this girl in there and she was at the bar with her boyfriend. As a child growing up in St.Clair's village, I had a crush on her. Just about every dude that knew her had a crush on her. Anyway, she goes to the bathroom. Now the bathrooms in RED's sit back in their own enclosure, but the men's and women's rooms are side by side. If you are at the bar, like her boyfriend was, you can't see whether someone is going into the guys or the girls room. When I saw her go into the restroom, I positioned myself right by the restrooms, with my eye on the boyfriend. When she opened the ladies room door to come out, I went in and closed the door behind me. She was surprised and nervous at the same time. Without saying a word, I started kissing on her neck. She responded by putting her hands on the back of my head and moaning slightly. Then being that she had on this sexy little skirt with this belly shirt on, I went down to one knee and started kissing on her stomach. She started moaning louder. Then in a slow soft sexy voice she said: 'Rayco stop, I've been in here too long. He's going to know something is up.' When I didn't stop, she begged me to stop verbally in the softest sexiest voice, without physically trying to stop me. Because I didn't want to get her in trouble, I stopped. I left the ladies room and went straight into the men's room.

"But back up to speed, I'm in RED's and these dudes walk in, Fat Donny, Lovey and Big Bird. The first person I saw was Big Bird. I couldn't figure out who he was immediately but my internal alarms went off immediately. So I slide behind this wall out of his view. I searched my memory banks quickly, and about three seconds later I knew who he was. The guy that I shot in the neck & back, was his homie! In the next five seconds in my mind, I ran through two scenarios. I pulled my gun out checked my bullets and decided that I didn't have enough to get into a major shoot out with three of them. If RED's had a back door, I didn't know where it was. I made the decision to walk right past them and out the front door.

"I put my head down, said to Crystal, 'Ville boys are here,' and left quickly. When I got outside, I ran into one of my partna's, Dirty Jewels,

(R.I.P). He's asking me what these guys are doing down here. I'm asking him the same question. The conclusion was, St.Clair boys are not allowed down here, not right now. At that moment I had two of my big guns at the house. I had my SKS with a thirty round clip that shot 7.62 x 39's and my favorite, a pistol grip 12 gauge pump, loaded with hollow point rifle slugs and 00 buck shot, alternating. Me and Jewels are on our way to my car, which was parked in the back of RED's, discussing what we are about to do to these dudes. While walking between the houses, which was pitch black, to get to my car, I saw the light on the other end distort slightly. My hand was already on my hammer, and as I pulled it out I seen four shots fired from the direction that we were walking in. I managed to squeeze of a couple of shots, but it was too late. I was hit in the left side of my chest and knocked to the ground. Dirty Jewels was hit in the leg. He still managed to run and get help. Once my vision came back and my ears stopped ringing, I tried to walk, but noticed that I couldn't. I looked around and realized that I was on the ground. When I picked myself up, I noticed that my back was hurting... bad. I thought that I hit it when I fell... until I felt the blood running down my chest and stomach. I said to myself, this pussy shot me in my heart. I knew that I had to get to the hospital fast, so I put pressure on the hole and started walking towards my car. After about five steps, I figured that it would not be wise to try to drive myself to the hospital, so I turned around and went back towards the bar. I could hear Jewels yelling: 'They got Rayc'. When I got back to the street, people were running to me. One of my partnas, Tuc, turned the corner in his car. Gun still in my hand, I flagged him down. When he stopped, he had a car full of guys, the music was loud and they was smoking weed. He didn't have a clue what was going on. Jewels made everybody get out the car. I didn't say too much. I knew I had to save my strength. When we got in the car, this girl that I was cool with, Tammy, came with us. Tuc asked me what hospital did I want to go to. I felt myself fading, so I said Southside, which was the closest hospital. Tuc was flying. I made everyone in the car laugh when I said, 'slow down man. Don't kill us before we get there.' While we were driving to the hospital, I gave the gun to Tammy. Tuc asked me did I have any work (cocaine) on me. I gave that to Tammy too. It would have been terrible to wake up hand-cuffed to the hospital bed. When we got to the hospital, Jewels is arguing with one of the guys that brings out a wheelchair for him first before they bring the stretcher for me. I told him to go, I'm alright. When the stretcher came I got out the car and almost fainted. They rushed me to the ER, but they didn't have a trauma unit. So they were going to life flight me to another hospital. My body closed up the hole in my chest, and even though I only had one functioning lung, my vital signs were good.

"They kept trying to get me to lay on my back, but my back was killing me. I told the Doc to get the bullet out of my back. They wanted to do x-rays first. I told them to hell with x-rays, get the damn bullet out of my back. The Doc obliged. They shot me with some numbing stuff and cut my back open. The Doc had a little trouble getting the bullet out, but when he did get it out, I felt 100% better. I started to fall asleep, and the Doc's started to get worried. They kept waking me up, saying stay wake. I kept repeating 'I can't.' Jewel's kept telling me to stay wake too. He kept saying 'Rayc, fight it.' The police kept trying to get me to stay wake long enough just to get a report. Even though I was down and out, I still didn't give them any names. Good thing too, because the person that I thought shot me was not the one who did it. As I was being wheeled away on the stretcher, I was speaking to the person that shot me, telling him who I thought shot me!"

With his life hanging in the balance, Rayco's survival instincts kicked in. Something else happened. He knew it was time to quit this life. It came to him as he faced death in the face and what resulted was a total change in the man that had 'run' the streets and had power and prestige coming at such a cost.

Was it worth it?

"Through all this trauma, there was a time of true peace. I guess this is what they mean when a person sees the light. After the bullet was removed from my back, and I was isolated from family and friends, a measure of calmness all of a sudden came over me. I felt at peace for the first time in a long time. I was tired of the way I was living. I was tired of hustling. I was tired of paying bills. I was tired of responsibilities. I was tired of life.

"At this moment I had a talk with the Almighty. I said 'God, if it's time for me to go, I'm ready. If my son will be alright without me, take me home. If my son needs me to be here to make sure that he'll be alright, then let me stay.'

"When I got to Allegheny Hospital, they were rushing me to the operating room. I kept trying to get the Doc's attention because I did not want them to cut me open. I called out 'Doc', about three times. When he answered me, I said 'Doc, don't cut me.' He granted my request.

"I woke up in the intensive care unit. If you ever seen the movie 'Hard to Kill', that's just what I looked like with tubes and wires on me. The Doc came in, asked me did I know where I was. I got the name of the hospital wrong. I didn't know I was transferred. He said that I needed to get x-rays immediately because I didn't get cut via my request. The x-ray revealed that the bullet broke two ribs, touched my heart, went through my lung and got stuck in my back. I was already given a chest tube operation. That was to save my lung."

Rayco was indeed lucky. It was times of such trauma that he got to know who was there for him and who he could depend upon. The blanched walls of the intensive care unit, the tubes in his arms and the constant din of the machines recording his vitals were a wake-up call. The peculiar odors of the room giving it an antiseptic bathroom smell made this strange environment all the more foreboding. But it gave him time and time to think and reevaluate as the healing took over.

"The healing process was the most painful part. While the chest tube was in me, my left arm was paralyzed. The worst part about the chest tube was I had to get a second one. The doctor that they sent in to remove the first didn't know what he was doing and as a result, my lung collapsed again. That had to be the most painful thing that I have ever went through in my life. To make matters worst, I had to fight with the attending nurse because I wouldn't let them shoot me with morphine anymore. The nurse actually told me that it will help heal me. My reply to that was, 'I didn't come as a junky and I won't leave as a junky neither.' So they switched me to a lesser dope, percocet. I won't lie, I needed something. The pain was too great. I promised myself everyday that I would kill the person that done this to me."

Revenge, reflection, remorse are all feelings that are endemic to victims. Like it or not, Rayco was a person in need. The nurses who wanted to ease his healing process realized the tenacity of this young man.

Tough to the core, even with excruciating pain. Refusing the morphine was one thing. Wanting to get up and get at the persons who were responsible for putting him in this state was another. As time passed, he was able to put his mind at ease and he started to reevaluate his life. So near to death, what direction would his life now take? What would he do?

"While I was in the hospital, I thought a lot. I had thousands of dollars hidden in a box at my grandmother's house. I felt that through all the hustling and struggles that I was going through, I haven't enjoyed myself yet. Now I almost died! So I picked up the phone and called one of my closest partners. I told him to take my car to the shop. I instructed him to tell the shop to start stripping it down. I'll tell them what I want done to it when I come home. He did. I got a lot of love while I was in the hospital too. My family and friends showed me a lot of support. When I was discharged from the hospital, I never got the prescription for percocet filled. I chose to suck it up and take it like a soldier. Besides, I didn't like the way those drugs made me feel." Still tough to the core and no compromise. Always in control. That's Rayco!

"My first day out of the hospital, I was being driven home by one of my partners, when we saw JC and this girl. My partner stopped the car and the girl walked over to us and asked me how I was doing and feeling. JC came a few seconds later and did the same. We spoke briefly about the streets, then I went home.

"After a few days, I went to the club. Guys in there thought they seen a ghost! I was on the dance floor dancing the night away. Rumor had it that I died, so I had to make a statement.

"A few days later, this girl called me. We talked on the phone then she came to my house. She saw my bandages and asked me was there anything that she could do to make me feel better. I thought of a few things. We ended up making a sex tape. It was good too. Something she said to me though didn't register until years later after I found out who shot me. She said making the video would be great if I didn't have the bandages on me. I'm thinking she's talking about the bandages messing up the picture. She was speaking about the time frame and the events that occurred before I got shot.

"After I got my strength back, the doctor cleared me to work out again. My first day back on the weights, I almost had an emotional breakdown. A weight (135lb) that I normally do thirty warm-up reps, twice with, got stuck on my chest after about the 10th repetition. After I managed to get the bar off of my chest, I wanted to cry, holler, bust out all the gym windows, punch the walls, etc. I was emotionally hurt. I didn't give up though. Instead, I gave myself 30 days to get myself back to normal. It worked."

The Rayco that was determined to survive wanted it all back. He had set the bar high and wouldn't look back. His whole life up to now had been challenges that would have broken anyone. But he was himself again. He was the Rayco that everyone knew. The Rayco that was steadfast, focused and ready. The bar was set and no one would stand in his way. Determined, cocky, sometimes arrogant and yet coming from a life-altering encounter made him even stronger. Mentally, emotionally and soon physically, he would be tougher in all areas and would prove to himself that he had the stamina to persevere and not back down. It was vintage Rayco ready again – stand aside!

"Things for me were starting to get back to normal. I was back on the set, overseeing my operation. The women were loving me more. I was excited about my Cadillac, that was being custom painted, due to be done on my birthday. With the exception of me having periodic pains from my gun shot, and the mental, emotional agony of trying to figure out who actually did this to me, things were good.

"A few weeks after my car got out of the custom shop, my former little partna, JC, a.k.a. J-locc, a.k.a. James Guscharles Jones, came to see me. He told me that he could get me some cocaine cheaper than what I currently pay. He also told me that he could get me some more guns. Me being the business man that I was, and already knowing the what, I asked the other four "W's": who, why, when, and where; in that order.

"When he told me from who, I said: 'Hell no!' I immediately thought that it was a joke or they were trying to set me up, but I stayed cool. I asked why. He went on to explain how cool these cops were, and how we could move the drugs and not have to worry about the cops messing with us. It sounded good, so I asked when was this supposed to happen? He told me as soon as I said yes. I asked him where was all this supposed to go down? He told me that one of the cops lived close to Beltzhoover and that we would meet at his house. To gain my confidence, he showed me a 9 millimeter semi-automatic hand gun that he allegedly just got from one of them."

Rayco, ever suspicious and on guard, let his better instincts take over. It just seemed too good and he had been through hell already and had the scars to show for it.

"Something about the whole situation didn't sit right with me, so I asked him what was the catch. I told him that it was more to it than what he was telling me. I would figure out what that was a few months later.

"I turned down his proposal, for two reasons. One was I didn't trust these cops. I saw this type of stuff in the movies but I never even heard of it on the streets. The other reason was, my connection was great. The product was great. The price was right. And the trust & respect was already established."

Rayco's intuition proved insightful. He knew from the streets to be on guard always. His recent brush with death had only reinforced any 'too good' scenarios.

"The very next day, JC came to see me with another proposal. He said that these two cops wanted paid every week to allow me to sell drugs. Basing my decision on the fact that they couldn't keep the other cops or other police organizations off me, I dismissed this with a 'whatever'. The police raided my house that next day, two days after JC's first visit. On this raid, my family was notified that the police were in the house. When my family arrived, the police were in the house watching some of my personal home movies that me and some of my lady friends made. They were also going through the collection of pictures that I had of some of the same female friends too. When I got to the house, all thirteen tapes as well as all fifty plus photographs were gone. The house was wrecked. Stuff from flour to dog food was scattered all over the floors. None of the missing items were reported on any of the police reports or ever came up in court. When I asked Stowman & Fallert, about my video tapes and pictures, they responded they didn't know what I was talking about."

All suspicions were now verified. While he may not have had the most ideal lifestyle, the raid on the home proved that the police were corrupt and would stop at nothing. With the thefts of the video tapes and their denials, Rayco knew that he was a prime target. It didn't take long for events to unfold.

"Although I was charged with heroin & gun charges, I didn't have any drugs in the house. The police found some blue balloons that contained dog de-worm medicine in them, and falsely charged me with possessing heroin. I was also charged with multiple gun charges, but knew that it is perfectly legal to posses as many firearms as a person desires in his/her home in the United States, as long as they are not a convicted felon. One of the guns, a SKS, semi automatic assault rifle with a 30 round magazine was registered to me. I never saw or heard anything about this gun again. I also had several false charges of assault placed on me as a result of my uneventful arrest one week later."

That arrest came while in the comfort of his home.

"I was resting when I heard my female pitbull, Jaws, running through the house. I immediately became alert to breaking glass coming from a back room in the house. I quickly jumped up and started getting dressed as quickly as possible. Beings that I spoke to my lawyer about the police raid a week earlier, I had one gun in the house, but it was in my stash spot. I'm glad that it wasn't out too because it was the police with an arrest warrant. Once I was almost dressed, I yelled out, 'Who the fuck is that?' 'This is the police', came back. At this moment, Stowman & Fallert came through the door, guns drawn. They brought a third cop, Yacht, with them. They're yelling: 'Get on the ground!' I'm yelling, 'Let me get the dog'. The dog is in attack mode. I'm yelling at her to chill, meaning stay still. Everyone is yelling. Then it happened! Jaws grabbed Stowman by the leg and started that vicious, pitbull shake. Yelling turned to screams! All guns were redirected towards Jaws and Stowman. Stowman turned into a straight sissy at this moment! I could have fled, but I knew they would have killed my dog. So I, like the good citizen, walked over and gave Jaws the command (put it down) to let sissy azz Stowman go. She complied and I put her in the basement. Fallert immediately ran over and put one hand cuff on me. I requested that he let me get my ID and money from the bar. He complied, then cuffed the other hand. After Stowman squeezed his poop back in his behind, he got real tough again. He says to me, 'Tell us where the street sweeper(12 gauge riot pump shotgun) is or we're going to tear the house up.' I told him to tear it up. He knocked some miscellaneous stuff off of a shelf. I made a remark about how he bitched-up just a few minutes ago, and at this moment he tried to sucker punch me in my face. I was boxing for Chuck then and my training kicked in. I moved my head ever so slightly to my right and the punch hit me on the left shoulder. The other two cops immediately got between me and Stowman. I said, 'Take these handcuffs off and I'll whip your ass!' He told Fallert to take them off. I told Fallert to take them off. Fallert didn't take them off. He played peacekeeper as he always did back then, that's why I used to have a lot of respect for him then."

Ever the tough guy, Rayco, despite the insurmountable odds, didn't flinch. He knew which cops were real and which ones were out to get him. A continuous, non-ending drama that got worse with each moment. He noticed the third cop, Yacht looking at him. He could see that he wasn't 100% into the continuing act.

"While Stowman & Fallert searched my house, the other cop, Yacht, pleaded his case that he was not the one fucking with me. He said that he didn't want any trouble, such as bullets coming at him while he is driving through the neighborhood. I gave him my word that he was cool."

Rayco didn't need additional no-win situations. He knew that Yacht would respect him, despite all the craziness. Yacht's pleas would not go unanswered. Once again, Rayco would keep his word and Yacht would not be a target with Rayco.

"I respect a man that knows when he is in a no-win situation, and is not afraid to acknowledge it. One of the most vulnerable positions a cop can be in is when he/she is in a vehicle. They have no where to run or hide. They cannot fight back effectively from inside the vehicle, especially if they are ambushed#! It's almost impossible to identify the person responsible, especially at night. Yacht knew this. He knew I knew this.

"I went to jail, was given a $25,000 straight bond, and was out the same day. When I returned home I immediately checked to see if my money was still in my cash stash spot, it wasn't#! $40,000 in cash gone! I didn't have to check my other stash spot to see if my street sweeper was still there, because I wasn't charged with possessing it, so I knew it was still there.

"Fallert & Stowman knew that I couldn't make an issue about the money. I never had a job before. I couldn't come up with a legitimate reason for having this amount of money. If the three letter boys (FBI, DEA, ATF) weren't on to me yet, this was a good way to get them on me. So I took it as a loss."

The money, of course, never came up after that episode. The police merely had it as additional cash which was never entered into the inventory of goods taken. No investigation, no questions. The police got the cash and nothing would be done.

"My next conversational encounter with Stowman & Fallert, was when I approached them one night they were parked at a place called the mini park, after JC, came to me and told me that Stowman & Fallert were asking him about me. He said that they were asking about my street sweeper and a few other things. When I confronted them, Stowman, was furious. He told me that the person volunteered this information about me and this street sweeper to them. When I asked him who it was, Stowman said, 'You bring that cocksucker to me and I will tell you in front of his face that he told me you had a street sweeper#! As I continued to try to get a name, they had to respond to some police duties.

"Now while this conversation was going on, I later learned that JC, who I was with just before I approached the two cops, was contemplating to shoot at the two cops while we were talking. The other person, Crystal, that we were with stopped him from doing so. Later after everything came out, I came to the conclusion that JC was going to actually try to shoot me, to keep me from getting the information that he was the one snitching, then say it was an accident!"

Rayco never let his guard down with the police and now had to be extra vigilant when it came to someone who had gained his trust and now became an informant. Yet, he wouldn't let JC know what his intuition clearly spelled out.

"As months passed by, in between, JC was catching cases (getting arrested). He was getting caught with guns & drugs, frequently. He would call me from the Allegheny County Jail, and I would go bail him out, like a true friend was supposed to do. I even introduced him to my lawyer, Marty Scorotow.

"One time he called me at 2:50 am. I was in bed resting deeply. I answered the phone and it was a collect call. When I accepted it, JC asked me to come get him. I responded by saying that they stop taking money at 3 am, and that I would be there first thing in the morning. He begged me to try this night. He wouldn't take no for an answer. I gave him my word that I would try. I jumped in my TA (Trans Am) at 2:55 am. I had to get to downtown Pittsburgh from Beltzhoover (approximately 5 miles), park, and make it to the night court window by 3:00 am. When I got to the window to pay the bond, the clerk turned to the window and said, 'you just made it.'"

Loyalty was always important to Rayco. Despite the suspicions with JC, he wanted to keep him close to the vest. His lawyer started to give him sound advice. He started taking the advice. It started with the use of his cell phone. The old maxim of not trusting your closest associates resonated well.

"I paid JC's bond at least on three different occasions. However, I never paid any attention to what was going on with his cases. To this day, to my knowledge, I can't recall a day he ever went to court for any of the charges. I had no way knowing when the cases were disposed of because I always put the bond in his name. Our lawyer started saying things to me, but he would never be specific. I would use my cell phone in front of him, and he would say, 'don't say anything on that phone that you don't want to come back.' He also told me that if I use pay phones, make sure that I rotate them and not to use the same pay phone consistently. He never told me why he was saying these things to me. I just figured that he was looking out for me. I never expected that one of my closest partners, that he worked for also, was working with and for the police.

"One day a light in my head was turned on by Stowman & Fallert, unbeknownst to them though. We were in court. I was there for some gun charges. A couple of weeks earlier, my cousin Jeremiah was shot on my front porch. Stowman & Fallert, through my attorney, Martin Scorotow, told me if I tell them who shot my cousin, they would drop all of my charges. I responded, through my attorney, that I can't tell them what I don't know. Stowman & Fallert countered with, 'If I tell them who shot my cousin they will drop all of my charges and they won't raid my house anymore.' Although that was a nice deal, I needed more. I countered with, 'Tell me who the informant is that is snitching on me, I'll tell you who shot my cousin.' Stowman had enough. He yelled out: 'Hell no!' I threw up my hands. Stowman yelled out some profanities. I went to court and beat the charges."

With proof from the cops that an informant was close to him, he became more and more careful. Always looking for something out-of-the ordinary – a parked car with occupants, people walking by, phone calls with no one on the other end. Rayco knew he was a target and his guard was up!

"When my cousin got shot, I was in Cleveland attending a Tupac concert. I got a call from this girl with this incredible news. I called my house and the police answered my phone. They told me that my cousin was all right, and everything was good. What they didn't tell was that they found and took my twin chrome 38 snub nose revolvers that JC, got from some cops and sold to me. I never heard a word about those guns, neither."

Rayco started to be on the lookout for the two officers who were clearly stalking him and out to get him. Forget the 4th Amendment. Whenever a car is pulled over, unless the object is "in plain view," a search is not to be executed. Yet for Rayco, with his history known to all law enforcement officials, the rights were set aside and he became a marked man. What was about to transpire would be proof to Rayco that his suspicions were correct from the start. The incident started with yet another police car, siren blazing – a signal to stop and be questioned.

"I knew I had to really watch myself when I was pulled over by Stowman and some other cops. Fallert was not present this day. Stowman pulled me over on Arlington Ave. He and about six other cops surrounded my car and made me get out. I was searched. Stowman took out his gun, put it to my head and start telling me what he could do to me. Then he cocked it, took the round out, put it close to my face and said, 'You see this. Take real close look at it. This will be the last time that you see it like this. You never know where it might come from or when it might hit you!' I looked him dead in his eyes and said, 'exactly!' Stowman and the rest of his boys knew that everything that was just said to me, I just said it back with my eyes.

"The war between Beltzhoover and St. Clair Village, had pretty much come to a halt when one day I ran into one of my childhood friends, Marco, a.k.a. Sca-dark. He was from and still lived in St. Clair. Regardless of the feud between the two neighborhoods, we remained cool.

"Marco was like my brother from another mother. We were like twins. He was just light brown. While growing up, we use to hang a lot. We use fight each other a lot. Then we would hang again. We always had that real recognize real, bond. When I saw him, he had just got out of lock up. We greeted each other as friends due. We spoke about the things that went on while he was away. His last words before we parted were, 'I got the power in the Ville, you got the power in the Zhoove, let's make it peaceful.' And we did."

Despite his going with the police, the truce between the rival hoods took hold. It was a respite from the constant tension and shootings, the constant wail of the police and ambulances. Peace, however, elusive in such an environment, started to descend upon the gritty streets.

To Rayco and others, it was clear that the police needed an incident or a resumption of the war between rival gangs to make their collar and make their mark. The quiet streets were for some, just too eerie and action was needed. The police got antsy and soon events took a different turn.

"Months went past without incident between the two neighborhoods. It felt a little good that things were quiet. This didn't sit well with certain cops. Despite what the police say about fighting crime, the facts are, without crime there are no criminals! No criminals.... no cops, no district attorneys, no judges, no jails, no jail guards, no parole/probation officers, no jail counselors, etc! You get the picture. If it weren't for crime, there would be a whole lot of jobless, homeless, hungry individuals. Contrary to what the masses think, there are a lot of forces rooting for crime." To someone like Rayco, he knew it was just a matter of time before an incident would ensue.

"It took me to take a trip back to my old neighborhood to break this good feeling. Me and my cousin Jeremiah, went to see my Aunt Helen, who still lived in Northview Heights. I was driving my partner's car. I didn't want to drive any of my cars, for the same reason of what happened that night. When we pulled up and got out of the car, a voice from a crowd of guys said 'Who is that?' I didn't respond. The voice asked again.

This time I responded with, 'You know who it is.' The voice said to the crowd, 'Y'all know who that is right'. Me and Jeremiah just went into my aunt's house laughing. I had my hammer, so I was protected. However, just to make sure that we were safe, I called one of my partners and requested some back-up. While the back-up was on its way, I was speaking with my aunt and her boyfriend. Instinct told me to look out the window. When I did, I saw four guys surrounding the car with their guns out. A second later, they started shooting the car! I immediately pulled my gun from it's holster, opened the house door, ran outside, aimed and fired! The four dudes stated running, while at the same time returning fire. I aimed and fired some more until I ran out of bullets."

Rayco knew what would happen next. Like a good soldier, his instincts took over, saving his life. The sound of shots fired, the smell of gunpowder and the instant urge to get out of the way, take cover and look out for others. He had to act fast and act fast, he did! Knowing that the shots would mean the police would be there, he took some drastic steps.

"I hid the gun because I knew the police were coming. When they did get there, they patted me down like I knew they would. While they were taking the report and inspecting the car, I went and retrieved my gun and put it back on my hip. It was best to leave while the police were there, and I wasn't leaving without my hammer. One of the cops recognized me, and asked me my name. I said Ray. He said Rayco Saunders. Then he looked at my cousin and said his name, too. He left it at that."

Heading towards his car, he could see that the vehicle sustained a lot of gunshots. He gave the car a once-over and noticed the extent of the damages. Looking around, he saw one police officer approaching him.

"The car had a few holes in it. The driver side window was shot out. But it was still driveable. And one of the cool cops gave me a card with some numbers on it in case I got pulled over on the way home. We got home without incident though."

Life was good, but things were about to take a dramatic turn. It happened in just a few days.

"One day, I was driving around Beltzhoover, and when I hit Curtin

Ave and Sylvania, the police were up there in full force. I stopped to see what was going on. The police shot and killed TP's pitbull. As TP is telling me what happened, one of the cops says something really disrespectful to us. I responded by saying, 'Y'all always fucking with somebody for no reason.' The cop told me to drive away. When I didn't move, the cop went for his gun. I called him a pussy for doing that and told him, 'I'm not scared of your gun. You are not the only people with guns.' The cop replied, 'Get out the car then.' I responded, 'For what? Y'all have me out numbered.' The cop said, 'You're the pussy now.' Then slowly, he tried to get in front of my car. So I pulled off and said 'Fuck you bitch,' over my shoulder."

"Later that evening I went and picked up a female friend, Rosalind. She lived in Baldwin. This is where Johnny Gammage, the cousin of former Pittsburgh Steeler football player Ray Seals, was killed by the police, after a traffic stop. Everyone of color knew when driving to and/or from Baldwin, you absolutely did not carry anything illegal. We went back to my house in Beltzhoover, kicked it for a few hours. Then I took her back to her house. On my way home, I stopped at a store called Cogo's, in Mt Washington. The police are always in this store, as they were this night. They didn't bother me, and I didn't bother them. I bought a microwave pizza and some vanilla ice cream. As I was driving down Haberman, I came to a street called Warrington Ave. To the right is the trolley/bus station. A cop car was sitting in the entrance, as they always do at night. I went across Warrington and proceeded up Haberman. A police van went past me on Climax St, headed towards Gearing Ave, at a high rate of speed. Immediately after they passed me, they slammed on their brakes, but didn't come to a complete stop. I made the left onto Climax St. When I got to the stop sign at Climax and Curtin, I saw the van, and it was closing fast. I figured it was Stowman & Fallert. This was their shift at this particular time. Feeling relaxed and nonconfrontational, I just kept on cruising about 20mph. I turned right onto Curtin Ave. Made another right onto Freeland. The police van flew past me, but hit the brakes. I made another right onto Estella. Then another right back onto Climax. It was hilarious watching dumb & dumber, chase something that wasn't running. When I got back to Curtin & Climax, I stayed on Climax, and went to Beltzhoover Ave. I made the right onto

Beltzhoover Ave. The van finally caught up to me and made the right turn also. Shortly after, the van activated it's blue & red lights. I pulled over immediately, still laughing. When the police got out of the van, Stowman wasn't present. It was Cane & Fallert. Cane was a brown skinned cop that wore green or hazel contact lenses. There were Dumb & Dumber and he was Dumbest!

"I rolled my window down about 6 inches so I could speak, but stay warm at the same time. This didn't matter because Fallert opened my door immediately, then said, 'Get the fuck out of the car.' I was both surprised and angry.

I responded, "Do you have a warrant? If not, I'm not getting out of my car."

At this time, Cane came up behind Fallert. Fallert repeated himself, 'Get the fuck out of the car.'

I said, 'I'm not getting out of my car.' Then I looked to my right because the marked cars were close to my car, but the unmarked police car pulled over on Freeland and was barely visible from where I was. I found this very suspicious. In that same second Fallert hit me across my chest with his nightstick. I guess he expected me to do what the average person does, "get scared". Instead, I looked him in his face and said, 'What the fuck is you doing?' He got scared and hit me again, harder this time. When I didn't respond how they wanted me to, he reached for his gun. I knew it was time to go then. I leant over anticipating the gun fire, and started my car. Fallert yelled out something then smashed my windshield with his nightstick. As I pulled off, Fallert started shooting at me. He only fired two shots, but the first shot was close. I smelt the gun powder.

"I drove all the way up Beltzhoover Ave, with my head down and the car in 1st gear. When I start going down Beltzhoover Ave, on the other side, I raised my head up and shifted the car into its proper gear. The police were in hot pursuit. I made a right turn onto Michigan. Michigan is a cobble stone, straight away, but it dips up and down like an amusement park roller coaster ride. Once I turned onto Michigan, I put that Trans Am power to work! I said out loud, 'You can't fuck with the TA.' I worked that 4 speed automatic like it was a six speed manual. 1st gear to

2nd then 3rd. 4th was not needed. I kept it in the torque gears only. When I climbed to Michigan and Estella, the car went airborne. While I'm airborne, I down shifted the car to 1st gear. This would give me more control when the car landed on the ground. When I hit the ground, I bounced around for a second, but quickly gained control. 2nd gear, 3rd gear, police are getting farther and farther away. Now I'm climbing Michigan again, this time headed towards Gearing. Airborne again, but this time the landing space is a lot shorter and it's coming up fast. I down shifted to 1st and hoped to GOD that I landed in time to turn, stop, anything! When I landed, the car would not slow down. Then I realized that I was sliding on salt and snow. There were only two ways to go, right or left. Straight ahead was a fence that bordered a drop from street level that was not good for a vehicle. I did everything I learnt over the years from the best car thief drivers I knew. I pumped the brakes, downed shifted the transmission, engaged the parking brake. I did everything. The car hit the fence and stopped. I jumped out and started to run, but forgot my keys, so I turned around. As I was grabbing my keys out of the ignition, a cop car came flying over Gearing. I grabbed my keys and took off. The cop was not as fortunate as me. He went right through the fence and into the ditch.

"I jumped a few fences and while doing so, dropped my keys. I ran onto someone's back porch and hid under some boards and doors. I could hear the dogs, helicopters and police on foot, looking for me. I waited almost until daylight to move. I only had on a leather Perry Ellis jacket, jeans, t-shirt, sneakers, no socks and no underwear. I was cold stiff. I managed to get my cell phone out of my inside jacket pocket. I called my partner Koss. I whispered to him to ride around to see if any police are out. He told me it was cool. I met him over his cousin Elisha's house. The damage from being hit with the nightstick was starting to take effect. I was cold. It was just not a good day. I told them what happened and they weren't surprised, being that their cousin Stoney Bey had just been shot dead by the police, being shot a total of 16 times, 14 of those in his back."

Fast car chases are endemic to action flicks. They've become part of the American movie audience. Yet, this was the real deal. No stunt men need apply! Rayco's ability to outmaneuvre the cops was legend. Even the police had respect for keen knowledge not only of the streets and back alleys but also the places were he knew he could outpace the police. Pittsburgh's own version of NASCAR! Yet, for Rayco it was no action flick, no game of chance. It was a life and death situation. To this day, he credits his bravado, his skill at the wheel and his appreciation to go the distance. It was a dire situation that demanded immediate and drastic action and the scenario, unscripted and unrehearsed, proved decisive for the illusive Rayco.

"I called my lawyer Marty, at 8:30am, that morning and told him that the police tried to kill me last night. Marty said, 'Rayco, you have eleven charges against you sitting here on my desk.' Then he started to read them to me; Attempted homicide, Aggravated Assault, Violation of the Uniform Firearms Act, etc.

"I asked how could this be when I didn't even have a gun! Framed! I was being framed!"

CHAPTER 12

Framed! Where was Rayco going to go? Was there anyone who wouldn't turn him in or 'rat' on him? Life's events were about to start unraveling. Yet, ever the warrior, he decided he had to act and act quickly!

What was Rayco to do now? Where was he to turn? Who could he trust? He had to make quick decisions. Decisions! What to do and where to go? Events were unfolding and he had to come to terms with them. He decided on a strategy. He would outsmart the police. It wouldn't be easy, but life hadn't been easy for the 21 year old and he wasn't about to let go. He was the warrior. He was ready and like most people prepared for battle, his strategy was put into place.

"I was camped out over at one of my partna's cribs in Beltzhoover. I was on the phone daily with my lawyer trying to figure out the best way to play the situation. I was informed that the police had a shoot-to-kill out on me. That's when the police have the go ahead to shoot first and ask questions later. People that knew about this shoot-to-kill, thought that it was a result of me shooting at the police. I knew the truth behind this order though. They were trying to silence me! Now they had the official go ahead! What they didn't have was the ability to recognize that I wasn't the average 21 year old. I had lawyer buddies, probation officer buddies and cop buddies. I knew their every move. That's why they were always one step too late."

The pugilist-turned-warrior, turned survivor. Did the police know what to expect? He had outsmarted them time and again. And for a while, even when the odds were stacked against him, the warrior instinct took hold. He was a survivor. Shot, stabbed, let down by informants, he was not going to capitulate. Never! There wasn't much comfort in such a bind, but Rayco felt he had to reach out to a sympathetic ear. Before long, events started to unfold.

"While I'm contemplating what I should do in a gangsta state of mind, I did reach out in my gentleman state of mind to some people and one particular organization that I will speak about. This organization, the National Association for the Advancement of Colored People or NAACP, was contacted by me. I wanted to file an official complaint and being that I knew I was capable of making bail, also turn myself in through them. I explained the entire situation, including the fact that I was considered armed and very dangerous, and probably would be shot on sight. The people that I spoke to at this organization told me, 'it is our policy that we can not take your report, complaint or statement over the phone. You must come in person.' At first I spoke to a female. After she saw that I was not going to give up my position on the matter, she transferred me to the boss at that time, Harvey Adams. I once again explained that if I was seen by the cops, I probably would be killed this time. He reiterated what the female just told me. At this time, I concluded that the NAACP don't give a shit about guys like myself that survived an assassination attempt and lived to tell about it. There was not enough publicity in it for them. Now had I been killed, the NAACP would have been the first people at my family's door trying to do a senseless march/protest that was neither going to bring me back to life nor change the fact that Pittsburgh, Pennsylvania has some of the most atrocious, biased, crooked, degenerate, egomaniacal, faceless, Godless, (I could go from A-Z) cops in this nation! This is not to say that the entire police force is like this. There are those that live and die, 'protecting and serving!' I honor and respect them."

Frustration with the premiere civil rights organization. An organization that always sought justice from its inception as part of Dr. WEB DuBois' Niagara Movement in 1909 to defend and advocate for change from Jim Crow laws in the South to the Civil Rights Movement of the 1960's. An organization dedicated to justice and fair play despite the virulent racism in every facet of America. But, even the prestigious NAACP didn't deliver for him. Yet Rayco felt that they dropped the ball and they saw no opportunity to assist someone whose rights were clearly violated. Ever the strategist, he had other plans. He knew he had to act and act, he did.

"Once I saw that the NAACP was not going to help me, I stepped outside of the box and contacted some people of law enforcement. One of these people was a woman named Kathy. She was the probation officer of my cousin. Through her, I spoke to a detective who was not part of zone 3's "Good Ole' Boy" network! We arranged for me to meet them in a very public, populated area on the south side of Pittsburgh. Kathy came to the house that I was staying at and picked me up. We went to the meeting spot which was about a 10 – 15 minute ride. When we got there I stepped out of the vehicle and out of no where this plain-clothes cop appeared. He moved towards me a little too aggressive, but I kept my composure because instantly, I realized who he was and I knew that he was more scared than anything else.

"I 'LET' him put the handcuffs on me and escort me to the police car. Once we were in the police station, the detectives went into standard procedure mode. They interviewed me, not to get to the truth, but to get any information that could help their comrades."

Rayco knew the deal. But, he was going to cooperate. Smart and knowing what was to come, he let the procedural matters take hold. Patient and circumspect, he checked their every move. He was a master at body language and could detect what was next.

"After I told them what happened (only because I committed no crime), the older of the two detectives knew that I was telling the truth. He made this statement: 'See, the problem with these young cops is that they think that they can do whatever they feel without any repercussions.' He knew that it was very improbable for a spontaneous shooting to take place, and there not be 'ANY' evidence to show that a shooting occurred."

Yet, the procedures had to take hold and soon Rayco was escorted out and en route to a holding cell. Still patient and very calm, he let the ensuing judicial matters pursue their now familiar course.

"I was transported to the New Allegheny County Jail. I stayed there until my preliminary hearing (about 10 days) , thinking that the charges would be dismissed because there was not any evidence to even suggest that a shooting happened. I was wrong in my assessment. The judge on the case, "Coles", dismissed the attempted homicide and said about the gun, 'Since there is no evidence of this gun, I'm tempted to throw it out, but I think it will be cleared up in big court.' From the start of this hearing to the end, I was furious. I kept my eyes on Ed Fallert. I didn't even blink! Now I was going to trial for something that never happened! I was beyond furious. I was 1 atom away from turning into my alter ego, "WAR", right there in the court room! It took every ounce of me not to lose my mind nor shed some tears. So with revenge on my mind, I made bail."

Clearly, the decision to go to trial was one that didn't sit well with Saunders. He knew that the judge wanted no part of this case and deferred it to criminal court. For Rayco, despite making bail, the strategist set in again and he was ready for a fight. Not a fight in the ring before loyal fans. No, this would be a fight to not only exonerate himself but also point out the injustices, the plots, the revenge on the part of the Pittsburgh Police Department! He was ready, he was eager and he wanted justice!

"When I got out, I maintained a low profile. The police didn't know that I was out, and that was a good thing. But as they say, 'all good things come to an end.' Well, thanks to snitch lock, a.k.a. JC, the police found out that I was home through one of their many conversations. One day JC said to me, 'I seen Stowman & Fallert today, and they were talking shit saying, 'Rayco will be down the County for a while. He has like a million dollar bond.' I said, 'Rayco's out!' JC then says to me, 'Fallert, eyes wide, stumbled back a couple of steps and says, 'You wouldn't know where he was staying by any chance?'

Now at this time, I didn't pay any attention to this statement. But later it all became clear to me."

JC was one not to be trusted and a major factor in the nearly successful assassination attempt on his life, Rayco set out to make changes. As the warrior instinct set in again and again, he prepared for the inevitable. He had to be.

"Life went on. I switched my residence, tightened up my hustle and plotted some 'get back'! Being that I knew someone was giving the police information about me, I started to focus my hustle more away from my hood. I wasn't sure about certain guys around me, so the partnas that I had in other neighborhoods became more important. Slowly but shortly, I stop dealing with certain guys in Beltzhoover. I even stop dealing with the girl that I was suppling because she dealt with certain guys that I didn't want to know that I had work. She also questioned my integrity one day, because of something JC said to her. That was the beginning of the end for her. That was also the day that I really started to put some distance between me and JC."

It was becoming increasingly clear to Rayco to watch his step, be mindful of what he said and to whom he said it. Ever suspicious of "friends," he started learning to be more discreet in his conversations and observe the eyes, the overall demeanor of the person to whom he was speaking. The master boxer was also the master observer and he could sense the nervousness in a person who was not being candid. The look in the eyes, the movement of the hands, the tone of the voice. It was all there for him to surmise. It was evident that he was a target, even among some of the people he had entrusted and done so much for in his life. He hurt, yet he knew he had to be a visionary and not look back but put his entire focus on himself for survival. Like always, the fighter was ready. It wouldn't be easy. Especially abandoning the ones who he had bonded with, entrusted and learned to love.

"Distancing myself from JC was hard because I had love for this little dude like he was my younger brother. Then there were moments when he would show that he was a loyal soldier to me. Like one time I had some words with the mother of my first son. I told her that I was on my way to her house. JC came with me. She lived in St. Clair Village. When we got out of my car, JC had his gun in his hand, cocked and ready, making sure that no one got the drop on us. Now keep in mind that Beltzhoover was in a war with St. Clair. From the time we entered St. Clair, til the time that we left, JC had me covered. Then the most mind-swaying deed of all, that he done, although I didn't find out about until he was locked up again and needed bail, was he gave $500 towards my bond when I was arrested for the made-up police shooting."

Actions like this made it difficult to imagine the disloyalty and yes, betrayal of a person who was so close.

"It was actions like those, that kept me close to JC. Now at this time JC had his own hustle. I don't know who his supplier was, but it wasn't me. Whoever he was getting it from, they were looking out for him. JC had weight now, meaning, he was able to distribute. Today I know who he was getting his drugs from. At that moment, I didn't."

Embedded in his mind were a few episodes that troubled Rayco and made him wonder what JC was really all about. A particular disturbing event stood out.

"One day I went to his house. The door was wide open (unusual). I called out, 'J'. No answer. I called out again and was answered. I went in and what I seen made my visit very short! This dude had at least 9oz's of crack cocaine, bagged up in quarter ounces, scattered across the kitchen table, with a digital scale sitting there also. I said, 'man are you fuck'n crazy? You got the fuck'n door wide open with all of this shit on the table like it's legal! I'll be outside!' He smiled and said that he was going to be 5 seconds. I didn't care. I was out of there."

"My first day of trial was very interesting. Here I was charged with attempted homicide, aggravated assault, violation of the uniform firearms act and other charges. The district attorney, Patrick Kenneth Nightingale, offered me a 3 to 6 month plea bargain! I turned it down. I understand now, why they offered me this plea. 'If the prosecution in Allegheny County feels that the defendant might not be guilty, instead of dismissing the charges, they will move to deal with the situation in the least painful way, and that is to offer the defendant a plea and sentence too good to be refused. If the defendant takes the plea, then the acceptance of guilt is on his own head, and the prosecutor and the police are off the hook!' I learnt this from Patrick Nightingale the same day I sat in his office and he told me that he couldn't help me get back into court to right this wrong because he could be disbarred! This sit-down between me and him happened years later, after my release from prison and after he became a criminal defense attorney. It is also my understanding that's the ultimate test for a prosecutor; they only really know they're good when they convict a defendant who's innocent!"

The criminal justice system needed changes. Rayco wasn't about to fall for this jockeying of his future. He was steadfast and believed he would be vindicated for all the corruption and mismanagement that occurred in the system. Again, the warrior instinct took hold and he was out for justice.

"Needless to say, despite there being 'No evidence' I was found guilty by a jury of my 'peers' (a joke!), which consisted of eleven Caucasian men and women and only one brown-skinned woman. I was sent to prison, solely on credibility. The police at that time had more credibility than me. At my sentencing hearing, Patrick Nightingale recommended to the court that I be given 14 to 49 years in prison. Judge Durkin almost jumped off of the bench and punched him in his face! She gave him a harsh verbal reprimand. She knew that this case was some bullshit. But she didn't overstep him totally. When I tried to challenge the weight of the evidence, Pa.R.Cr.P 607 (A)(1) or the sufficiency of the evidence, Pa.R.Cr.P 606 (A)(5), Durkin wouldn't let me, but instead told me and my lawyer, Martin Scorotow, 'Your lawyer should have filed a post conviction motion.' I'm saying in my head, 'this is exactly what I was trying to do!'

"Judge Durkin knew that I was being fucked with no Vaseline. But instead of doing what was right, she tried to lessen the hurt, and sentenced me to 1 to 2 years in prison, with 8 years of probation. Now remember that I was convicted of shooting at the police. Doesn't add up right?!

"My other 2 years came from a guilty plea that I took for a gun that I was caught with 3 months after the made-up police shooting, on my son, little Rayco's 3rd birthday. I had just took one of my younger brothers, Raymont, home to Homestead, from the party that I had for my son. On my way to the night club, I stopped to get gas. While I'm waiting for my car to fill up, I saw a cop car go pass the gas station. About 10 seconds later another cop car goes past in the opposite direction. I checked my oil as recommended with every gas fill up. When I shut my hood, I saw that the cop cars were parked on each side of the gas station. I knew they waiting for me. I was in my Cadillac! They never saw me before in this neighborhood. Were they doing their job? Doubt it! Jealous... probably! Envious... probably! Hating the fact that I'm a young African born and raised in United States, with a car that they wish they could have... Definitely!

"As I was pulling out of the gas station, the lead car pulled off from his spot. His assumption in what direction I was going was wrong. I turned toward him, not away. We drove past each other at about 25 mph. As I stated earlier, I was headed to the night club, so it was about 12:00

am. I was on 8th Ave, I turned left onto the high level bridge. I saw them turning around to follow me. I could have put the pedal to the floor and let that 425 motor make me a distant memory, but I was legit and I had no reason to run."

Another incident was about to unfold.

"The cops caught up with me on the bridge and pulled me over. When the cop came up to my car, he looked at my stickers on my window and said, 'Oh they are 7's. I thought they were 1's.' Whatever! It's June. Why would I be driving around in this nice azz car with January stickers on it. Ok sir, have a nice evening. Doubt it! It turned out that my insurance expired the day before. My mailing address was at my brother's from where I just left. Being that I was less than 5 miles away, I asked the cop can I take it to the house and park it. I would have had the insurance issue fixed the next day. He denied this request and said that my car was going to be towed. This is how some cops find a legit way to search your car. Before the car is towed, they have to do an inventory search. This is to document all the items in your vehicle at the time it is towed, in the event that you allege that something is missing when you retrieve your vehicle from the tow pound.

"When he did his so-called inventory search, he found my gun. It was a legal gun. I just wasn't licensed to carry. After the failed suppression hearing, I received 2 years for a legal gun. That's like giving someone 2 years for driving a car without a license. This sentence ran consecutive with my other. As a result, I was sentenced to 4 years in prison."

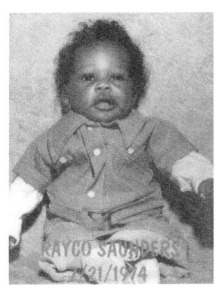

Rayco
7-21-1974

Raymond, Mom, Rayco
12-11-1977

Ray 2 Yrs, Rayco 5 Yrs
1980

Rayco 12 Years, Paris 1 Year
1986

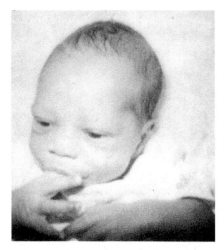

Rayco Jr 9 days old
1993

Daddy, Jelani 1 month old
2005

Jelani – 3 months
2005

After NABC Title Fight
2004

Caddy – Reconditioned – Lil Rayco
1996

Caddy Pre-reconditioned
1995

Trans Am after police chase
9-89

Trans Am
1996

Trans Am - Involved in police chase
1989

House Raid
1995

House Raided
1995

House Raid
1995

Raided House
1995

Rave, Rayc, Dripp
1996

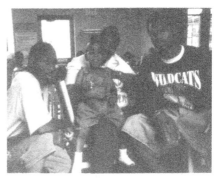

1st Day with son after prison
2001

Lil Rayco 3rd Birthday
1996

Wachi & Rayc in Denver
2002

1st hours out of prison
2001

Just out of prison
2001

Apollo – New York
2001

Golden Glove National
2002

SATURDAY, FEBRUARY 14, 2004

3 men arrested in plot
to kill boxer over woman

BOXER, FROM PAGE A-1

police, Korey had waited outside Saunders' Beltzhoover home with an assault-style rifle. But he didn't carry out the killing because Saunders never left the house, the affidavit said.

Police said the conspiracy was spawned by jealousy over a woman. Keilan Walls, who was charged with hiring Korey to kill Saunders, was angry about a relationship he thought his girlfriend was having with the boxer, police said.

"She liked Rayco, and the guy got jealous," said Saunders' promoter, James Cvetic, a retired Allegheny County detective. "That's how he decided he had to handle his anger and hurt."

Korey, 15, of Baldwin Borough, faces charges of attempted homicide, criminal conspiracy, theft and a firearms violation.

Walls, 27, of Arlington, faces charges of criminal solicitation to commit homicide and criminal conspiracy.

Police identified the third suspect as Shawn Davis, 23, of Beltzhoover, who lives close to Saunders. He was charged with conspiracy to plan to commit homicide and a firearms violation.

On Feb. 3, Pittsburgh homicide detectives got their first inkling of the conspiracy from a confidential informant who was with Korey during the aborted attempt to kill Saunders, according to the affidavit supporting Davis' arrest.

On Jan. 24, the informant and Korey drove to Davis' house on Climax Street. Korey returned to the car with a .223-caliber rifle. Then Korey directed the informant to drive to Saunders' house, where he planned to kill the boxer.

After Saunders failed to come out, Korey and the informant returned to Davis' home. The informant said Korey gave back the rifle in return for two bricks of heroin, according to the affidavit.

Later that day, undercover narcotics detectives arrested Korey in a car in Mount Washington. He had 100 stamp bags of heroin on him, and a 9 mm handgun was found at his feet, an affidavit said. Police lodged drug and gun charges against him.

Ten days later, homicide detectives Steve Hitchings and Dale Canofari learned of Korey's alleged involvement in the plot. They and detectives Harold Botin and George Satler put the case together.

Cvetic and Saunders first learned of the scheme last week from the homicide detectives. Cvetic said he was shocked, but described Saunders as stoic.

"He sat there and asked the detectives what was going on," Cvetic recalled. "He didn't have any idea why."

Saunders declined to be interviewed for this story. A cruiserweight who stands 6-foot-1 and 195 pounds, Saunders fights under the nickname "War." He has a 9-2-1 record and was a Golden Gloves state champion several years ago, Cvetic said.

Saunders has his own troubled history, having been arrested six times between 1994 and 1996. In 1997, he was sentenced to prison for shooting at a Pittsburgh police officer.

Since then, Cvetic said, Saunders has kept out of trouble and tries to give back to the community by mentoring up-and-coming boxers.

Korey, as well, has had run-ins with the law. Much to the consternation of police and prosecutors, he has beaten two homicide charges.

In November 2000, Common Pleas Judge Robert E. Colville found Korey and a co-defendant not guilty in the July 1999 contract slaying of a drug dealer, William J. Kuhn III, 24, of the West End.

Deputy Pittsburgh Police Chief William Mullen said he was "puzzled and dismayed" by Colville's decision. During the trial, police contended that Korey had confessed. On the witness stand, Korey said he had made up the story.

In January 1996, a jury acquitted Korey of the February 1988 killing of Joseph Brucker, 17, of Whitehall.

In addition to the current charges against Korey by city police, he is being held on a federal detainer by the U.S. Marshals Service. Last week, a federal grand jury indicted Korey on charges of violating federal firearms laws.

According to the indictment, Korey used and carried a gun while trafficking in drugs in July 1999. He also was charged with possessing an unregistered silencer, two counts of possessing stolen handguns and possessing a firearm while addicted to, or using, illegal drugs.

Davis, who was arrested Thursday and arraigned yesterday, was held in lieu of $160,000 straight bond. He has pleaded guilty in recent years to drug possession and receiving stolen property. He also pleaded no contest to statutory rape and corruption of minors.

Walls has had seven cases in Common Pleas Court, mostly involving arrests for simple assault, disorderly conduct and underage drinking. Last year, he pleaded guilty to firearms violations and criminal conspiracy.

Jonathan D. Silver can be reached at jsilver@post-gazette.com or 412-263-1962.

Jason Korey

Keilan Walls

Shawn Davis

NABC Title Fight
2004

Rayco and Grandmama

CHAPTER 13

With a four year sentence imposed upon him, Rayco Saunders was eventually transferred to the largest state prison in the Commonwealth of Pennsylvania, Graterford State Correctional Institution. Located 31 miles west of Philadelphia, its location was far from the streets of Pittsburgh, some 300 miles to the west. The prison, built in 1929, housed 3,000 inmates when Rayco entered the walled fortress in 1997, complete with nine manned towers. As was the case in most maximum prisons in the 90's, it was overcrowded and a powerkeg waiting to explode.

For Rayco, it was another obstacle in his young, troubled life. There was no easy way out on this one. He knew the deal. He had to come to terms with this situation and adjust to his new environment. An environment that, like it or not, would control him and render him another inmate with a number in the maximum prison. He was hardened by the streets, the boxing ring and the events in his life. He would deal with this situation and be better for it.

Transferred with other inmates in a bus to the facility, he was given the standard items: prison uniform, unlaced shoes and assigned to a cell. The constant din of the steel clanking behind him, the armed guards with night sticks and the dim rays of light emanating through the windows was testament to this new environment. The unpainted and cracking walls would now be his home, like it or not. The peculiars odors reminded him of the many gyms where he had fought. The old venues replete with a dressing room that was always in need of a good disinfectant. That same odor was now reappearing and would welcome him to his new environ. Yet, he was ready. He was Rayco Saunders and no one would step in his way!

Standing tall and walking proudly, Rayco sent a message to anyone within sight, be they correctional officers, other staff and other inmates. He would be one that wouldn't take any nonsense from anyone. He was already hardened by his past and this aspect of his life, however unfair and unjust, had to be dealt with in his way. He would soon find out what was in store.

The first stop on this unwelcome journey was a stint at Western Pennsylvania Penitentiary in the 'burgh' itself. Western Penn had the distinction, since its opening in 1882, as the oldest and one of the most arcane correctional facilities in the state. Overcrowded with periodic flooding, it stood as a stark reminder of the old prisons seen on classic movie channels. With its high walls whose cracks allowed water to seep in during any sizable rainfall resulting in a musty odor apparent to any unfortunate newcomer that was about to call the place home. Over the years the facility outgrew itself, becoming overcrowded with high operating costs that demanded constant monitoring due to the flooding. Finally, in 2005, it became a haven for alcohol and drug abuse patients. But, for now, it was for Rayco and the 1500 others, a temporary hiatus to the big house. Yet, it was a place not foreign to him, as he vividly remembers accompanying his mom to visit a friend.

"So now I'm entering the gates of Western Penitentiary, in Pittsburgh, PA. Growing up, I heard many stories about this place. I can even remember, when I was a child, my mother bringing me here while she visited someone. As a man, and having the experience of seeing many women have their children around different men who are not the fathers, I'm ashamed for her. Whoever this man was, he wasn't only not my father, but he was also locked up. Some role model to have your child around, huh!? The good thing about the visit was the guy was in the hole (solitary confinement), so we were separated by a very thick wall with a small glass window that they could see each other through.

"On my first day, I just went with the flow of things. I know NO FEAR, so I wasn't scared at all. I heard all of the stories and saw the movies about what happens to new guys behind prison walls. I also knew that those things only happen to guys that are afraid to die and afraid to kill, which I am not. Some of the guys that were transferred with me were very worried. Some even formed alliances with each other."

Rayco, ever the warrior, was ready. Ready for any unforeseeable venture that would ensue. Unafraid and prepared for the worst, he survived the streets and he was not about to let the thick, musty old walls control him. Never!

"We were placed in the clinic for quarantine. We had to get the mandatory test for diseases. This was also where they housed some of the snitches. The clinic was separated from general population. Once the other guys saw this, they were a little relieved. For the first three days we were locked in our cells. No movement at all. Then after this period, we got to move around. We were allowed to eat with the general population now. Some of the other guys were back to being nervous. Everyone could tell that we were the new guys, because we had on blue uniforms. The regulars had on browns."

Rayco recalls what happened next at mess hall.

"My first day walking to the chow hall was like a multiple neighborhood reunion. I saw guys that I haven't seen in years. All of these guys were older than me. A lot of these guys I came to know either growing up in the same hoods as them or meeting them in various walks of life. Most of these guys were happy to see me, but disappointed that they had to see me like that... locked up! A few guys even told me that they never thought that they would see me down there, because of the way that I carried myself. In movies you see a guy that is respected in the streets get locked up and his respect precedes him in prison. I found out that this was also true in reality. Nearly everyone that I knew from the streets, made sure that I didn't need anything. They made sure that commissary (food, chips, candy, lotion, soap, books, etc) was brought to me. I even got a walkman radio to use during my stay. I had 4 years to do, but man if there was a right way to start it, this was close to it."

The subculture of prison life was setting in. The old faces from the street, the knowledge that the warrior himself was among them. Like devoted fans, Rayco's reputation had followed him into the joint and he was the street hero, the dynamo who wouldn't lie down who had stood up to the cops and triumphed. He also savored the moment when his girl would visit him.

"Even though we were in the clinic, we were allowed certain privileges that the general population was. I immediately took advantage of the multi-hour 'contact' visit! At the Allegheny County Jail, I was only able to visit with my woman through a 2-inch thick glass window for 1 hour, two times a week. Now I got the chance to kiss her lips again! Touch her hands again! Smell her perfume again! This experience of being locked up can be credited for my love of women now. As a result of me being locked away for 4 years, going to sleep to men, waking up to men, being around men everyday, I love everything about a woman!"

Rayco was among the fortunate ones that had visitors. Many of the men had no family ties or had lost their link to both family and friends. For them, the loneliness of the routine added to the tense atmosphere. Hungry for letters, visits or someone who just knew they were alive, their situation became rife for academic studies in human behavior. They were the rejects and in this strange subculture, they were alone. Very alone. Rayco, however, had the respect coupled with the visits from girlfriends and family that made his adjustment far less foreboding. But this was still jail and the degradation didn't escape Rayco. He was, after all, convicted and subject to the same rules as anyone, like it or not.

Before and after the visits, a process ensued that clearly left its indelible mark on the boxer and redoubtable Rayco Saunders.

"These visits were incredible compared to the county jail visits. We were allowed 4 a month. Since we were being transferred soon, I used all of my visits consecutively. Just like with everything else, with the good came the bad. Before you got to have your visit, you had to be stripped searched. This was the most degrading thing that I've ever went through as a man. I have been stripped searched before, in juvey camp and the county jail, but not like this. When we took off every piece of clothing on our bodies (usually two or three guys at a time) we were made to turn around, bend over straight legged and with a hand on each butt cheek, pull our butt open and hold this position until the guard said ok. This same process was repeated after the visit was over."

It was a process that Rayco needed to come to terms with and he let his feelings out.

"I can understand why this is necessary after a visit, but before a visit is too much. If you need to get something out of the prison that bad, more power to you! I would never be able to do this job! I am not looking in no ones ass! There was actually a guard working there one day with my same feelings. After you do it a couple of times it becomes routine. Well, on one of my visits, the guard on strip search duty stopped us as we were about to do this humiliating dance in front of him. He said, 'I don't want to see that. When I go home to my wife tonight and she says honey how was work today, I don't want my response to be, 'It was fine. I just looked up a bunch of guys assess all day!'" So we were spared, at least going to the visit.

A moment of candor from a correctional officer vindicated Rayco's disgust at the system that undermined the fabric of all. No dignity, no rights, no shame. What a place! Yet this wasn't the worst part. Feelings set in and separation from one's partner hit at the heart of the matter.

"Though the strip search was bad, it wasn't the worst part. The worst part was having to say good bye and volunteeringly going back to your cell. This was very hard to deal with, especially for a man that has committed no crime."

The degrading dance in which everyone who had a visitor partici-pated. Rayco knew he had to follow the rules and yet, deep inside, he had a burning passion to right the wrong that was inflicted on him. Every movement, every command, every strip search, every kiss goodbye was a reminder of the new confines for a man who had been imprisoned on trumped-up charges. It wasn't fair. Yet, the dance continued and he had to play his role in it. But Rayco knew that he had made enemies on the outside as well. He started to perform his own ritualistic dance to no special rhythm. A dance unique to him and him alone. No partners needed. A dance of survival.

"After performing the degrading dance, I would make the long trip back to my cell. During my short stay at Western Penitentiary, this is the only time that I felt on edge and a little out of my element. After you left the building where you had your visit, you had to go outside and walk through the yard, where hundreds of general population prisoners congre-gated. Why on edge? After a 6 hour visit in February, that started at 12 pm, it's dark outside! So here I am, walking through a prison yard at night with no protection. Yes, I had friends, but I also had enemies. One of the reasons that I reached that point in my life, is because I never underestimated a situation, and I wasn't going to start then. So I walked fast and kept my chin tucked in my chest with my coat collar pulled up high, with all of my senses on alert. I never ran into any problems, but it was better safe than sorry."

His own private dance with no partner. Yes, his dance of survival. Looking around with the collar high and head resting on his chest, his every move was like a hunter who at times is the hunted. Each step is carefully orchestrated and his every cautious move a mere step to get to his destination in one piece. A dance of survival repeated time and again. Like most who practice, the dance became routine and the steps became easier to execute yet the threat of it being interrupted never wavered.

"We weren't allowed to have recreation with the general population, so if they were in the yard lifting weights, we were locked inside. One day a call comes over the PA system, requesting the 'blood clean up' team in the auditorium. Later, we heard that someone was stabbed up, beat up and might not make it. I wasn't in no hurry to see this kind of stuff."

Rayco had seen enough in his tough days on the streets of Pittsburgh. He didn't need to gawk and be witness to a violent episode that he had taken steps to avoid. His brief stay at Western was drawing to a close and he wanted no part of it. His next stop would be much further than his hometown.

CHAPTER 14

Camp Hill became the next leg of Rayco's journey. Located across the Susquehanna River from the capital of Harrisburg in the central part of the state, it was mockingly referred to by both inmates and locals alike as 'Camp Hell.' As a referral center or classification center, it was known as a way station on the road to a permanent facility. For thousands of incarcerated men, it was the place that gave them their assignment for years to come. 'Camp Hell' lived up to its name, despite the beauty of the central rolling hills that had nearby witnessed the greatest confrontation in North America in 1863 at the three day battle of Gettysburg. For the men at the 'Camp,' the battle continued and it raged without interruption and fanfare. Gettysburg raged every day with a different name. A never-ending battle that like the famous one that preceded it, tested the very fibre of a man.

Dark, confining with specialized areas, Camp Hill was not to be taken lightly. It had areas for boot camp for the youth it felt could be saved as well as designated areas for troubled men–RHU or Restrictive Housing Unit or SMU or Specific Management Unit. Inmates throughout the commonwealth of Pennsylvania were assigned to quarters and the enclosed, small units.

Camp 'Hell' became the place where Rayco came to witness the degradation that started at Western come full throttle. Restrictive, confining cells were one thing. Inmate treatment was quite the other. He had heard the stories about this place. To be there and witness the 'activities' was quite another story.

As with every prison, there were rules. Rules that seemed, even to the most hardened and stoic and inflexible, a test of the will. Rayco recalled his stay here with the wrath that, no doubt, others had experienced. It was indeed a test of wills to stay intact at Camp Hell. Every day was indeed a Gettysburg.

"After about 30 days, I was transferred to Camp Hill Penitentiary. Camp Hill is in Harrisburg, PA. It is known as the classification prison. You go here to get classified to your main prison. We were treated like pure shit in this prison. As soon as you stepped off the bus, you were either allowed to go through or you were sent to the barber chair to receive a 3 minute butcher job if your hair was too long, courtesy of the Department of Corrections. You were given two minutes to take a shower every other day, regardless of your recreational activities. If you went over the time, the water was shut off on you, regardless of how much soap was on you. If you were using the bathroom while your cellmate was in the cell with you and you had a sheet up to divide the room so you could have minimum privacy, you were made to take it down. If you refused to do anything, you were not permitted to eat the next meal. This prison was here strictly to break a person down."

Like the most vicious of tortures, Camp Hill knew no bounds. Rayco remembers the stories from the other inmates. The most vivid was a riot that had erupted prior to his arrival. The tension was in the air between the staff and inmates. He could feel it. He could see it in the eyes of both staff and inmates alike. The acrid odor of the place gave off a unique yet distinct odor. It was always there, a constant reminder that to the senses that this place was unlike any other. And like most traumatic situations, some came out heroes while others were scorned and mocked. In this case, it was the guards that were signaled out.

"There was a general population in this prison. They said that the guys classified to Camp Hill were treated better than we were. The guys that were there during the riot, used to point all of the guards out to us that were also there during the riot. They told us stories of guards being raped and beat up. These guards that were there for the riot were either super assholes or super pussies! The guards that understood that it could happen again were respectful to the prisoners."

Rayco absorbed these stories, anecdotes and decided that he would just shut down and blend. He knew his time at the facility was a short one. He knew he would be soon assigned to a maximum facility and he decided to make his stay unnoticed.

"My time at Camp Hill was uneventful. I got locked in my cell all day, one time, for staying on the phone past my time. It's very hard to talk with a person or persons for 15 minutes when you haven't seen or spoken to them in a good while. I'm a man before anything else (prisoner, criminal, convict, etc) and will be respected as such. The guard told me to get off the phone and I turned my back to him (excuse my back), as if I didn't hear him."

With over 200 miles separating him from his family, the phone was the linkage to the outside world. It was the one time he could find out what goings-on were occurring back home. He knew that visits here would be difficult given the distance. Yet, he did manage to touch base with a favorite of his, a music hip-hop star. It was one saving grace for him. A person who meant something in his days in Pittsburgh.

"The height of my stay at Camp Hill was when I met one of my favorite Hip Hop stars there, who, unfortunately was locked up for bank robbery. I used to listen to this guy's music all the time and watch his videos constantly... Steady B! Steady B was from Philly. He was one of my favorite rappers. I remember when he did a concert in Pittsburgh. It was sad to see him, see us like this! We talked a couple times. Took trips down memory lane. He was honored, but at the same time hurt, that I knew most of his songs.

"His partna in rap and crime, Cool C, was locked up some where. I wasn't sure where. These two dudes were on top of the world to me and guys that grew up with me. Now, years later, they were convicted bank robbers. Steady B told me that even though he made a lot of records, the money wasn't what people thought. It was conversations like this that helped me make decisions when it came to signing boxing related contracts. I do most of the work! I will get most of my money!"

You learn from others for better or worse. To listen to people who had made it yet faulted was a wake up call. The boxer in him knew deep down that he had a future and he envisioned himself back in the ring one day. Listening to these rap icons made him realize that he would ultimately dictate any contractual agreement before stepping in the ring. He started to think long and hard about where his skills in the ring would take him. Ever the warrior, he knew for the moment any dreams would be put on hold, yet the dream was still there and gave him the impetus and motivation never to look back or be bitter and vengeful. He was maturing and maturing fast.

"While locked up in Camp Hill, I was still going through the legal process of trying to get my case overturned. My lawyers all but gave up on me. When I took the plea deal for the 'legal' gun that I was caught with, the sentence was supposed to before 0-6 months. That's what the sentencing guide lines called for. The judge sentenced me above and beyond that. He gave me 1-2 years. I immediately made a request to withdraw my plea. I received a letter from my attorney Martin Scorotow, informing me that the motion was denied. I was also informed that his motion to withdraw as my counsel was granted. I had no prior knowledge that he was withdrawing as my counsel."

This unwelcome news was not what Rayco wanted to hear. He got a quick lesson in the criminal justice system at his expense. Was this legal? No representation? Whom was he to turn to at this critical juncture?

"When I checked the dates of each motion, I discovered that Martin filed the motion to withdraw as my counsel, the same time that he filed the motion to withdraw my guilty plea. So in a sense, I was left unrepresented in my motion to withdraw my guilty plea. This, along with the fact that I was not given a chance to present my reasons for my withdrawal, was a violation of PA Rules of Criminal Procedures. The judge granted his motion to withdraw as counsel, and denied my motion to withdraw my plea."

There was only one thing left for Rayco. He would become his own advocate. He would appeal and learn the law. He would begin the process by going to the law library, learn the process of appeal and begin writing it himself. No easy task, but this was again the warrior Rayco never backing down and giving up. From his street education and his tough persona would emerge again a person who would immerse himself in the minutiae of legal proceedings and challenge others who would take him to task. It would soon be put to the test. Rayco refused to be just another inmate that was put into the overloaded system, sentenced and forgotten. He wouldn't allow this degradation to occur. Events quickly resonated with catastrophic results.

"I was also working on my appeal from my cop shooting that never happened. I was appointed an attorney for my appeal process. Being that becoming a lawyer was once a childhood dream of mine and also the fact that I let Marty do all of the work and I lost a case without any physical evidence, I decided to be proactive in my appeal process. When I was contacted by the court appointed lawyer, Ira Houck, I already had my appeal issues ready. As we agreed, I sent Ira all of the issues that I wanted appealed, including but not limited to: insufficient evidence to convict, trial judge erred in allowing prejudicial prior crimes and bad acts that I wasn't convicted of to be heard by the jury, including testimony about me possessing banned assault weapons, bullet proof vest, numerous hand guns, heroin (that was actually dog de-wormer)."

All the time spent in outlining his case from the egregious errors on the part of the judge, the admission of his past to a jury and the misrepresentation of possessing controlled substance, had no bearing on his appeal. He was about to get a taste of justice that is all too common. Injustice within the system!

"When I received a copy of the brief of the appeal issues, none of my issues were appealed. When I contacted him to ask why, he said that HE went with the issues that HE thought were the best. I knew then that the fix was in. He was court appointed, meaning that he was getting paid by the court. I might've been better off going with a public defender who does just what his/her title suggests, 'DEFEND THE PUBLIC', only because even a blind man could see the railroad tracks that I was being dragged across."

Within a few days, as if as an omen of evil, he was called into the office.

"One day I was called to classification. It's a meeting between you the prisoner and maybe three prison staff. You don't have a say. It's just a formality to let you know what prison you are going to. I was sent to the worst one, SCI Graterford! Home to hundred's of deathrow prisoners and even more lifers! I was told that I was being sent here because I was convicted of 'fleeing and eluding'. Although this was a misdemeanor, the prison staff viewed it as the same as an escape! I did what I do to everything else that comes my way that is unjust, I sucked it up and continued to roll with the punches."

Graterford! Known as the 'prison within a prison,' it housed the toughest and most serious offenders in the state of Pennsylvania. While Camp Hill was difficult, Graterford was the 'big house.' It was 'The Fort.' With its massive walls and towers, it made an imposing sight for anyone within a mile radius. It's RHU (Restricted Housing Unit) was one that allowed only one hour outside the confines of the assigned cell. With over 300 staff, it was the main prison and far from Rayco's home. His journey from Camp Hill began with the routing bus ride. Soon those infamous walls came into sight. Looking about the bus, he could see some of the guys nervously glancing at each other while others just kept their heads too low to show any fear. Rayco knew the deal here too. And he was prepared. He had done his homework and was he was ready. The warrior was ready for any battle, however ominous.

"Riding on the blue prison bus on the way to Graterford, a.k.a. The Fort, in shackles, chains and handcuffs, I tried to think positive. Through my trips to the two prisons that I was already at, I was given a few names to look up once I got there. Hope for the best, prepare for the worst! A quick look around and you could see the fear on some of the other guys faces. I found these moments amusing. Though I didn't share their feelings, I understood."

The infamous walls were a sight to behold! So tall, so big. The entry gate looked like a movie set for a battle scene with warriors from the Middle Ages. Those walls! Yet, this was no Hollywood set. The real deal set in. That was the day that Rayco arrived at the fortress that would be home to him and the other 3,000 men. He suspected he would have to continue a variation of his dance of survival and he was not disappointed. He remembers his first impressions of the place to this day.

"When we arrived, the most noticeable thing was the massive wall that surrounded the prison. A huge gate opened to let us in, then shut behind us. That's when it set in that this was home for the next three and a half years. We were escorted off of the bus, just like in the movies, under the watch full eyes of wanna be tough guards with 12 gauge shot guns, loaded and ready to go. Once inside of the prison, we were forced to go through the humility dance again. We were given the standard general population gear, brown top and bottom, brown boots, sheets, blanket, soap, shampoo, toothpaste and shaving cream. We were asked the basic questions about emergency contacts, etc. But two things stood out to me. The first was the question of, "in case of death, who do you want us to send the body to?" Now, at that moment I didn't know how to take that question. For some reason, I got thoughts of my family getting a big ass wood coffin in the mail. Crazy, I know. The second thing was, I was given a form to sign that said, "I agree that if at the time of my release I am considered to be unsafe to myself or others, I can be locked up indefinitely!" I read this form three times! I signed it because I didn't want any trouble and also because one of the guards said it was just a formality that everyone had to sign."

What an entry! A delegated form in the event of your death and an additional form further restricting freedom once released. What does one make of such rules?

Life in the 'fort' was about to unfold. E-block awaited him. The most notorious and the most restrictive. Like the movies showing the long tiers in a straight line, E block lived up to its sordid reputation.

"I along with a few others was sent to E-block. E-block was a level 5 security block. This block is where most of the lifers are housed. When I entered the block it was like having tunnel vision. The block was so long that it seamed endless! I could not see where the block came to an end! The guard lead me and the others deeper into this thing! It felt like I was being swallowed alive by a concrete & steel monster, that had hundreds of steel teeth (the cell doors). When we got to the center of the block, finally, the guard control center for the block was there. The guard gave us temporary cell numbers. Me and this guy from Harrisburg was celled together. He was a little short guy, about my age, but he was scared to death!"

He had reason to be. The prison was a microcosm of society. All walks of life. All different types rolled up into the package that the walls engulfed. As they were soon to discover, Graterford housed the variety of types from the timid to the strong. It was also the place that kept you always looking out and watching your back.

"We were assigned to this temporary cell until all of our paper work was completed. Locked in again! This time, we were locked in for 48 or maybe 72 hours. When we arrived to the block it must have been count time because there wasn't any movement by prisoners. At a certain time, general population was let out. Hundreds of guys, big, little, short, tall, fat, skinny, muscular, were in there. Me and my cell mate are looking through our cell door window, trying to get a feel for the daily operations, the do and the don'ts, all that we can learn before we get out there. Most importantly, we were trying to see if we recognized any familiar faces that we knew from our hometowns, although we knew even this wasn't guaranteed to turn out being a good thing. Some guys that entered penitentiaries like Graterford, were no longer MEN anymore. Also, guys in the penitentiary were into so many things, such as, drugs and gambling that they might have been in some type of debt, that put them in a bad situation, and you didn't want to become a part of that situation. So you had to be very careful in who you associated yourself with."

As with every new environment, attitude and perception took over. Sometimes the appearance left one's eyes bewildered. Sometimes the eyes were challenged altogether. Rayco's 'celly' soon discovered the new environs and the perceptions didn't translate into reality.

"One day my celly was looking out the cell door window, when he says to me, 'Yo, look at the nurse! She got long hair! Look at her titties!' Being that I haven't seen a real woman in a while, I got up to take a look. At once, I noticed the long hair. Then I noticed the titties. Me and my celly had a brief conversation while we were looking out of the window. After I got over the initial sight, I started to notice certain things that didn't sit right. Now granted, we were about 100 feet away and looking down to the lower floor."

Reality was indeed distorted. Rayco set out to take a closer look and his suspicions were realized.

"The first thing that hit me was the T-shirt. Usually, the nurses would have on some type of clothing that wasn't too similar to the clothing that the prisoners wore. This made me look closer. The next thing I noticed was the similar brown pants. Now my heart beat is speeding up! What would seal the deal for me was the shoes. Even though prisoners were allowed to wear shoes that civilians wore, I just had a feeling that the person's shoes would confirm my suspicion... brown penitentiary boots! I said to my celly, 'That's a man!' My celly said, 'What? No it ain't, she got titties!' I said, 'Yeah, and he got on the same clothes and boots that we do too!'"

Rayco went on to explain to his naive cohort that the masquerade was indeed not what it appeared to be. At once, he noticed his cellmate starting to feel the discomfort and fear that many times hits you right up front when facing the real facts. He couldn't contain himself and Rayco now had to step in and save the day. He had to explain what it was all about. Rayco saw that fear in him. The fear that perhaps this is what fate awaited him. A new dance evolved. This dance, however defensive in nature, was a reaction to the events that had transpired. A nervous dance set off by fear and anxiety.

"My celly started bugging out! He starting pacing back and forth saying things like, 'where do they got me at? Why did they put me here? I don't deserve to be here!' He was scared! At that moment, reality set in for him. I don't think it was the sight of the guy/girl that scared him. I think it was the thought that, that could be him because he wasn't built, mentally or physically to keep it from happening to him."

And as fate would have it, both Rayco and his brief cellmate would part ways. Yet, he gave him a lesson to be alert and be prepared at all times.

"In a day or two we were moved to our new cells. He was transferred to Graterford's new side and I was moved all the way to the back of the tare, on the top floor. I think it was cell 391. My new cell mate was a guy my age, from Philly. He was one of Graterford's known hoop stars. He was also Muslim, as most of the guys that I met from Philly were. He was a cool dude. He gave me the heads up on who to associate with and who not too. He pointed out who was selling the prison version fast food sandwiches. He also let me know who had the drugs (anything you wanted) and liquor, in case I wanted to get high. I let him know that I didn't do drugs or drink, but I was interested in a good home made chicken or tuna sandwich."

The Philly guy had 'juice' and could help Rayco. He decided to test him and see if he would deliver. It didn't take long. He soon got to know who was the person to see to get things. He bonded and before long learned of the nuances that go along to survive. A few surprises were in store – even for Rayco Saunders.

"When I first got there, I didn't have a TV or radio, but my celly had a TV. I heard that people had cable TV in their cells but this was my first time I actually got to watch it. HBO, Cinemax, ESPN, ESPN2, you name it, some people had it. What really tripped me out was there was actually a cable man! And he did his little on-the-side hook-ups for packs of cigarettes. Paying this way was the best way, because cable in Graterford was just like everything else being sold in an area that is predominantly brown... it was way over priced! Basic cable on the streets is $13.00, Graterford – $22.00, SCI Mahanoy – $10.00. Cigarettes were cheaper in prison than they were on the streets (about $1.75). Two packs a week... way easier then $22.00!"

Rayco was out to get some perks too.

"My celly had a 13 inch black and white. At that moment it felt like we were watching a 46 inch High Definition TV. I ordered a 13 inch RCA color TV, with remote control. We weren't allowed to have the remote's though, because of the possibility of a prisoner manipulating it to control a door or doors that were remotely controlled. However, I knew guys that had their remotes. If I didn't learn anything else, I learnt that in prison, nothing was unattainable!

"When my TV arrived, I was very happy, for two reasons. One was there is nothing like having your own. I could watch what I wanted, when I wanted. The second was probably the reason that I was the happiest that my TV came. Ever since I was found guilty, I started having real bad dreams. Some would call them nightmares. Whatever the case, I didn't sleep too well for about my first year of incarceration! Being that I had trouble sleeping, the addition of my TV was a good thing. I thought about writing my dreams down, but after I signed that involuntary indefinite incarceration form, I thought better."

A TV was a godsend, a panacea and a relief for Rayco. He used it to relax and let the tensions out. The dreams, the bad ones that kept him up and angry, started to leave and before long, he adjusted to this new life as best as possible. Yes, the TV was a good distraction and a mechanism to forget his now angry past and the injustice of being here.

"Before I was blessed to watch TV or listen to the radio, every night I'd lay there thinking about my life, my son, my family. These happy but sad thoughts would be replaced by thoughts of Ed Fallert, hitting me with his night stick, smashing my windshield, shooting at me, putting his hand on the Bible, taking an oath to tell the truth, then telling lies before GOD, in a court of law, under oath! This used to make me so angry, I wanted to cry and scream, but I did neither. Although, I felt that I was crying, no tears would come out. I had so much hatred and anger that I think my tears ran down the inside of my face."

A catharsis was inevitable and it took the TV to save him from his demons. He knew outside that the cops that had framed him were on the Pittsburgh streets. He went over and over in his mind that these men who were supposed to uphold the law had fingered him. He was no angel, to be sure, but he knew his confinement would only be worsened if he allowed his anger to take over and make him bitter. He was still the warrior, the boxer, the man who never backed down. He wasn't about to now. He may have even come close to breaking, but it was not in his DNA and the fighter took over. A new dance would evolve and it would make him the champion of the floor. He knew the TV was an escape and he was grateful for it.

"Internally I was going crazy, but the support from my family and friends kept me more sane than insane. I started changing though, and I knew it. I felt it. I started to miss those close to me less and less. I was having strange dreams, dreams of people being gruesomely murdered, mutilated, dreams that I didn't understand at all! I would wake up at night covered in sweat. Now I could turn on my TV to take my mind away."

Part of him started to think about a future. A future with skills of the street or a future that enabled him to earn a decent living if not in the boxing ring than in some lucrative venue that he could contribute. Rayco was coming of age and he was determined to change. While the TV helped, he knew he needed something else to escape the insanity of this nightmare. There had to be.

"I was always into academics, so I went and got all the information on what I could get into such as schooling, trades, etc. Graterford had some college courses, barber school, computer classes, GED classes and some basic school classes. I was interested in the college courses and barber school.

"I sent for the information for college. When I received it, I discovered that college was no longer paid for by the tax payer! You the prisoner, has to pay your own tuition. The information instructs you on how to try to get grants or loans, if you are financially handicapped. Too much red tape for me! So, I applied for barber school. My application was sent back to me because of these reasons: 1. You must have at least 18 months to your minimum sentence or you can not enter! (example – if you have 5-10 yrs, you only can have 3 ½ yrs completed to get in barber school). 2. There is a 1 yr waiting list. (so now that 3 ½ yrs has been dropped to 2 ½ yrs, because after you wait a year on the list, you still have to have 18 months before your minimum sentence.) 3. You have to be a level 3 or lower to even get on the list. (when a person is new to Graterford, you were classified a level 4. It takes a year of no misconducts to get your level dropped) This entrance criteria applies to every educational course except, GED and basic school, such as general math. So let's look at this: by the time you get to Graterford, you already have about 1 year of your sentence completed. It takes 1 year of state incarceration to get your level dropped to a 3, which you have to do just to sign up. There is a 1 year waiting list. Then after you're on the waiting list for a year, you have to have 18 months or more before your minimum parole date. 1+1+1 ½ = 3 ½ yrs. I was sentenced to 2 – 4 yrs. I was denied all of these courses by sentence."

What requirements! It was mad and yet he wanted to do something constructive.

"I felt that this was very unfair. A short timer like myself should be one of the first persons eligible for classes like this, since I will return to society soon. This would have gave me a skill and a certificate to get a enjoyable job once I got out. Counter productive to the powers that be though! I'll explain later."

He learned that prisoners could file a petition or grievance to plead an injustice in the system. This was his start. He would use his confinement to educate himself and further his case. He knew he was set up on the streets of Pittsburgh by dirty cops and untrusting cohorts. No need to seek revenge. He would give himself latitude and take his time methodically to learn the system and become a 'jail-house lawyer.' He was ready and it begin with a grievance complaint.

"I filed a grievance. A grievance in the prison system is just like a grievance in any other system. If carried on long enough, it could go all the way to a court of law. My grievance was that Me, as a short timer, was being denied the much wanted and needed opportunity to learn a skill that I could use and be successful at once I returned to society. My grievance was denied and returned to me with the comment, 'Get your level dropped!' So, as I came to understand the system. I figured out that the classes and courses weren't put there for people with short time, that could take advantage of them and use what they learnt when they got out to be successful in life. They were put there to give the outside world the illusion of rehabilitation. The thing is, a person sentenced to enough time to meet the criteria to be able to take these courses would probably forget what they learnt by the time they did get out or what they learnt would be so outdated by the time they got out, it would no longer be applicable. So this means that a person returns to society with the same intellect that he had when he went to prison. This also brings me to the word 'Rehabilitation!' Most people in prison can't be rehabilitated because they've never been habilitated! Habilitate means: "to make capable, qualify." Most prisoners can't be "requalified" because they've never been "qualified" for anything before going to prison!"

The time spent in prison over four years was again a seminal moment in his life. While the world outside the prison walls functioned, he knew the system would do little to advance his own skills. The system acted as a safety valve for those on the outside who didn't have to concern themselves with the prison population. Yet, he was determined that, despite the unjust incarceration, the hurt and pain of the verdict and sentencing, he had to face reality. He was a hardened, disciplined person both on the streets of his Pittsburgh neighborhood and in the boxing ring. As a convicted felon, he knew he had to make changes in his life. Never one to back down from a challenge, he now looked upon this moment and decided that he would make the system work for him. Once outside these stone walls, he would be stronger not only physically but also mentally. A visionary and an advocate for reform. But, those walls and the cells were there – always a reminder of his present state. The walls! Like the warriors of old Athens and Rome, he would not allow the 'fort' to erode his character and demean his whole being. Rather, he would utilize this period and come away not as a jaded and bitter inmate but rather an optimist ready to prove to himself and the world that he had what it takes to succeed. An education. That education would begin in the prison. He was ready – was he ever ready! It would start with an analysis of the prison system.

CHAPTER 15

Rayco wanted to learn all he could about the system that was now a major component of his life. His instinctive curiosity and thirst for knowledge led him to investigate the many facets that make up the Pennsylvania prison system. He began this thirst with the dollar and cents amount that costs the taxpayers plenty.

"I took into consideration a lot more things that I started to see, pertaining to the system. I started to see the whole picture. Word has it that the Department Of Corrections receives about $36,000 a year of tax payer money, per prisoner! If this is the case, then why would a person or entity want to lessen this income? The more prisoners, the more money. The goal of a prison is the same as a hotel... keep the beds full! They are not interested in the betterment of the individual. It's all about money! If a prisoner gets himself together, becomes successful and never comes back, that's $36,000 x 5 or 10 or 50 down the drain, per prisoner! Who, outside of the Almighty, wants that? If the government gave this money to these same prisoners before they were prisoners, there wouldn't be any robberies, drug dealings, or crimes committed by people who are trying to survive. $36,000 a year could pay for housing, food, schooling, transportation and a little fun, comfortably. THIS thinking made me look for a bigger picture and I found it in the United States Constitution!"

Again, the thirst for knowledge kicked in and soon the ex-drug dealer turned boxer had now hardened himself to find facts.

"The 13th Amendment of the United States Constitution, states, 'Neither slavery nor involuntary servitude, EXCEPT as a punishment for crime wherefore the party shall have been duly convicted, shall exist within the U.S., or any place subject to their jurisdiction.' Prisons are producers of fruits, vegetables, milk, bedding, license plates and a lot of other things. The workers/prisoners get paid $0.19 – $0.50 cents a hour! LEGAL SWEAT SHOPS! Do you think an automobile manufacturer can imagine building a car for less than $25 a hour? The same people that condone the "exception clause" of the 13th Amendment, are the same people who have or who will lose their jobs to the prisoners/workers, in every manufacturing industry! Slavery abolished? Think again!"

Rayco decided it was time to acquire as much knowledge as possible and apply his quest in a positive forum within the walls. He had failed in his grievance. Now, it was time to stay focused, be a leader and a visionary. That would begin with classes.

"After I lost my grievance, I signed up for GED classes. I took these classes when I was 17, so I felt that they were the next best thing to keep my mind functioning at a decent level. I was also denied this class, because it was in my record that I received my GED in 1992. Now I'm starving for some type of academics. Incredibly, I was allowed to take general math! All through my school years, math was my best subject, so this class was most welcomed out of the unwelcome. I breezed through this class with my eyes shut. To further stimulate my mind, I went to the prison library regularly. I read academic books, such as: Basic Electronics Theory, Basic Math for Electric, Math the Easy Way, Prepare for College, learn foreign language, learning French, learning Spanish and many other educational books.

"Also, I was and am very into MY-story (mystery), as well as HIS-story (history)! Two of my favorite subjects to read are anything on or about Afrika and anything on or about religions of the world. I've read many books on these two subjects. I was raised as most typical Afrikans born and raised in United Stated, under the flag of Christianity. One key thing that was always missing from these teachings of Christianity was a face the color of mine, in any picture that I ever saw! When I read the Holy Bible, a lot of focus was on the Jews, Romans and Greeks. For these reasons, I wasn't satisfied. Then I ran into Islam."

Islam's powerful grip on many of the inmates attracted Rayco to explore a faith that many men found appealing. He was no stranger to the faith. He recalled his initial foray into the teaching as a young man in Pittsburgh.

"I was introduced to Islam as a teen when I was in Shuman Center. A staff member gave me a Holy Qur'an, that I still have this day. This was the first and only book that I've seen that opens from left to right. When I learnt to read & write Arabic, I learnt that it read from right to left, so it made perfect sense that the Holy Qu'ran, which is written in Arabic, would open opposite books written in English. Reading this book made me want to know more, so the staff member brought me more information. Through this information, I made contact with someone who sent me a newer Holy Qu'ran that was more simplified and explained, so it could be better understood, and stacks of information on the Five Pillars of Islam. I studied and learned."

Like most religions, he was quick to find out that Islam, like Christianity and Judaism had many faces, many interpretations and another learning exercise set in. Yet he was eager to further explore and try to find some meaningful purpose. His thirst for knowledge would not end.

"When I was transferred to New Castle Max from Shuman Center, I discovered that Islam was practiced slightly different there. This is when I started to find out about The Nation of Islam. Up to this point, I didn't know about the different sects... in any religion. Christianity has many sects. Read "A Glorious Institution: The Church In History". Islam has many sects. In Shuman, I learnt Sunni Islam. In New Castle, I learnt the teachings of Elijah Muhammad. When I got to Graterford, I learnt the teachings of Drew Ali, which is taught as Moorish American Islam. Even in Islam, there was something still missing."

Rayco still didn't find religion giving him answers, be it Christian or Muslim. Ever curious to find himself and instill what was becoming his own philosophy, he reached a conclusion. He wanted to discover a viable faith to adhere to, yet he was not satisfied. Where would he go to find some solace?

"I finally decided that religion was not for me. These particular religions originated from other places outside of Afrika. All of these religions have ties to other languages, cultures and communities outside of precolonial Afrika. I have great respect for all religions, but I am Afrikan! No one can tell me that what my people believed and practiced before the appearance of Christianity, Islam, Judaism, Buddhism, Hinduism or any other religion that is not mentioned, was wrong. My cousin, who is a

Sunni Muslim, told me that all of the Afrikans that died before the Prophet Muhammad was sent to teach, who didn't know Muhammad or didn't follow Muhammad, were going to hell. Christians have said the same thing in reference to Jesus. I don't know if any are right or wrong. I do know that all religions and sects say they are the way and all others are not the way. And by me searching for the truth, I have come to love the mystery (my-story) of Afrika and the history (his-story) of the world. I also figured out that only the Almighty knows the true way to paradise."

He would adopt his own version of religion and apply it to his confined world. This period of introspection allowed him to discover himself. He was the curious student and he cried out for more and more knowledge. Always the iconoclast, he never did and would not now let anyone or any philosophy stand in the way. He had applied the toughness of years on the street to his fighting days in the ring and he would be true to himself. He was the real deal and he came to terms with his inner self. He decided to further immerse himself in programs that would enhance his knowledge. He had no choice. He was locked up. He wouldn't give in and he was no quitter. Soon, an episode he had no control over reinforced that toughness to the core. It would come, as often prison events, with a request that one didn't turn down.

"So now I'm flowing with the program. My focus was to get off of the security block so I could make my time go even faster, by participating in different activities afforded to level 3 prisoners. One summer day, this almost became no longer a possibility. I'm sitting outside in the prison yard, alone in my own little area, thinking to myself, when this guy named Black, from Pittsburgh, walked by, touched my shoulder and said to me in an aggressive voice, 'Let me see you for a minute!', then proceeded to walk to the back of the yard where people go to settle their differences. Now earlier that day we had a little disagreement about something minor, but Black was the type of dude that because he was about 6'2", 225 pounds of rock hard, chiseled muscle, had to make sure that you understood his point, whether you understood it verbally or physically! Me being nothing less than a Grown azz Man, I lifted myself off the spot that I was sitting in and followed Black with no questions asked. The whole time I thinking to myself, 'what is wrong with this dude?' I thought everything from earlier was settled. Oh well, it's going to be what it's going to be. He knows that I'm a ride or die soldier like him. Black reached the weight lifting area before I did. There were about seven guys back there lifting weights. Black walks up to one of them and says, 'I got my partna with me now, what's up?' I said to myself, 'This Negro is crazy!' I had his back though. Although they had us out numbered, the guy tried to back out of a physical confrontation. Black wouldn't let him. I didn't know what was going on. I heard Black say, 'you and your boys were acting like y'all wanted to jump me when I was by myself. I got my back up. I want a fair fight.' I heard the guy say, 'I don't want to fight you.' Black just kept going. Then the guy said, 'me and you can do this when it's just me and you in a cell.' Black says, 'no, we gon do this now!' The dude says, 'ok!' They square up, fists up. Black attacks! Hard, thundering punches! 1, 2, 3, 4, 7, 10. I'm thinking to myself, Black is killin this dude! Then Black grabs him. The guy is from Philadelphia. They are more boxers than wrestlers, so his buddies break it up. I'm wondering why Black grabbed him. He was killin him with the hands. Now, other guys from Pittsburgh are back there with us. They square up again. Black attacks! 1,2,6,9, thundering punches! Black's arms are thick like tree stumps. He grabs the guy again. Again it gets broken up. This time the guy walks away from all of us. We're watching him, wondering where he's going, when he bends over and picks something up from the ground. He turns around and heads back towards us. As he comes closer, I see it. A long sharpened metal rod! He had it tucked up in his sleeve, but I seen the tip of it sticking out. I said, 'Black he got a whack!' The guy slide it out then. It was about 12 inches long! I immediately slide off to one of the weight benches and grabbed the weight bar off it. When I dumped the weights off of it, guys from the other side started arming themselves too! I head towards the guy with the whack. At this time, I notice that my squad is 50 feet away from the weight pile and I'm surrounded by the opposing squad. I keep my eyes on the guy with the whack. I also know that my time is running short because I heard other weight bars get cleared. The next moment, I get punched from behind! I drop the weight bar, and with the momentum of everything going on, I got out of there! I was so angry! I've never retreated from a battle in my life! I was upset at my squad because they retreated. Their issue was that they didn't have any whacks themselves. One rule of war is 'never take a position unless you are certain it can be defended against any onslaught.' Black disregarded this rule, and almost got all of us hurt and/or possibly dead."

A lesson of survival to live by. And to avoid. For Rayco, another wake up call and a test of wills. The survival instinct in him allowed him to further gain respect. But the incident stayed with him and the fighter instinct took hold, allowing him to walk away from a potentially fatal encounter intact and solid. As fate would have it, he met a person who had a profound affect on him. Someone with no agenda. A person to trust in a most untrusting venue. Another learning experience.

"An older guy who was the Imam of the Moorish American Muslims in Graterford saw what went on. He was from Pittsburgh, and also a good friend of my family. He spoke to the guys that pretty much won the battle that day and got the feud squashed. He told them, 'If y'all don't leave this alone, a whole lot of people are going to die. I might be one of them, but it's going to be a lot of unnecessary death!' The opposing squad agreed immediately to end the feud! This is one of the moments in my life where I learned to respect every man. Regardless of my first impression of them. This guy was about 5' 7". Weighed about 160 lbs. He wore thick glasses, and had these crazy plats in his hair. He was also serving an 80 year sentence. Prisoners and guards knew and respected him well. I always thought he was this nerd guy that didn't know how to lift weights. Little did I know that he was a stone cold killer!"

This small, unassuming peacemaker made all the difference and it helped Rayco deal with the stress and taught him a lesson. He was still angry from the encounter. Angrier yet at the person who had struck him. Should he save face and confront him, listen to the Imam or ignore the situation entirely? He soon found out.

"The situation got worked out. Guys from both sides agreed to let it go. I, however, wasn't feeling so forgiving towards the guy that punched me. A few of his friends apologized to me. They also told me how much respect they had for me because I showed that I had my partna's back. The guy that punched me knew how I felt about him. From that day on, he never allowed me to get near him. I never got close to him, but I'll never forgive him."

Despite the pleas of the Imam and others, the incident, now over, left Rayco in a flux. He couldn't trust anyone. He would become once again the warrior and self-survivor. He would be a collector. A private arsenal of weapons. Hidden from sight, he would use them only if in the most dire of predicaments. He would never go into battle, any battle unarmed and defenseless. Like a good soldier his prized possession became his small yet potent collection. The collector was a warrior and he knew where to stash his treasure.

"From that day on, I started collecting knives, or whacks! I had metal whacks, plexi-glass whacks and plastic whacks! I had a few hiding spots, but the best was in my cell door. The cell doors slide open and closed. They use to have windows that were replaced by a steel fence type of cover. Since there were no windows and the steel cover set on the outside of the door, there was a nice empty gap in the door. I hid one of my whacks here. I camouflaged it with old soap, cigarette butts and small trash. When the guards would come to search, they would slide the door and the weapon out of their sight of search."

Rayco recalls one close call during a surprise shake down.

"One time, the whole block was getting shook down (searched). They had dogs too! I had a plexiglass whack on the side of my bed. Me and my celly didn't know a search was taking place because we were into what was on TV. I heard a dog bark, and jumped up immediately. I went to the door and saw what was going on. I instantly retrieved my whack, and started to break it up and flush it down the toilet. This was one of the fortunate times they didn't turn off the water so people who had drugs couldn't flush them down the toilet."

He knew the consequences of finding contraband in one's cell. Isolation, 23 hour confinement and an infraction serious enough to jeopardize one's chance at freedom. Yet this was one incident that made him more vigilant. Other events, inevitable in such confining and restricted environs, were about to take hold. It would further his resolve and test his will.

"I've seen many things behind prison walls. I watched a man get stabbed up just before breakfast. One morning I'm coming out of my cell. I look across the tier and see four feet sticking outside of a door. They're in a laying position. This was strange. Then they start moving, in the door, out the door, kicking! The feet disappear inside the door. You hear a brief noise, then a guy runs from the cell, down the steps, down the tier. Another guy appears out the cell, covered in blood. He's cursing quietly, checking himself for stab wounds. I, like everyone else proceed to the cafeteria as if nothing happened. I watched a guard get the shit beat out of him by a guy from Pittsburgh that constantly asked me to show him some boxing techniques. The guard was a trouble maker. He pushed this guy for no reason when the guy was going into his cell. He asked the guard not to touch him, since it was unnecessary. The guard pushed him in his cell and tried to shut the cell door. The guy turns around and an all out brawl starts! The guard didn't back down, but he went down! When the guard hit the floor, that's when the other guards came and broke it up."

What Rayco witnessed was a protracted melee that seemed to go on for too long. Something wasn't right. The response from the other correctional staff seemed to take too long. Within a few days, he got to speak to a sergeant who related the truth.

"After things calmed down, a sergeant told a few of us that the reason the fight went on for so long is because, the other guards knew that this particular guard is a trouble maker. He said that him and the other guards watched the fight for a moment before they reacted."

Even among the staff, a subculture of loyalty and support was contingent upon how one felt towards the other. Personalities inevitably occur. Support was there, however delayed but a message was clearly sent to the errant guard not liked even by his colleagues.

When Rayco reflects on the time spent behind bars, one person sticks out. His former 'celly,' Big Moe.

"My best cell mate was Big Moe. He was about 50 and from Philly. He was doing something like 15-30 years for robbery. This was a cool dude. He had these really thick eye glasses that he himself made fun of. He could have been a comedian. When he came into the cell the first thing he did was read the cell rules that I had posted on the wall. They were things such as: 'If you do drugs, leave! If you don't practice proper hygiene, leave! If you like having sexual relations with other men, leave! If you are a sexual offender, leave!' Big Moe read the cell rules, turned around, introduced himself and shook my hand. He became a good friend to me. I treated him like my uncle. If he didn't have money on store day I would offer to buy him something. I convinced him to stop eating meat. I also convinced him to start working out. Word traveled around that I treated Big Moe well. This word reached the ears of his brother, who was also a prisoner in Graterford. He was a highly respected guy in Graterford. He was also in Graterford for robbery, but got more time while in Graterford for cutting some guys throat that tried to have sexual relations with him. Big Moe told me that his brother was a barber. One day when working in the barbershop this guy said to him, 'When you get done shaving my face, come to my cell so I can make love to you.' Big Moe's brother said, 'Ok.' While shaving the guys beard, he said, 'Make love to this!' and he slit his throat from ear to ear! The guy jumped out the chair, ran into every wall in the barber shop and then fell to the floor. Big Moe said his brother got 20 years added onto his sentence for that."

A good relationship evolved and it helped ease the tension and the drama known only to the people locked up. Big Moe was a person, like Rayco, loyal with a clear set of values and respect for one's turf. They learned to assist each other and learn from each other. Rayco was proud of the impact he made upon his celly. Respect is hard to come by and Rayco earned it by virtue of his demeanor, his pride and being consistently respectful.

"My level finally got dropped, and I was moved to D-block. It was the same as E-block with a little less restriction to move around. On this block, I ran into many other guys that I knew from Pittsburgh. Time seemed to go a little faster. There was always something to get into. We did a lot of joking around to take our minds off being locked up. I started this joke where if you were caught sleeping, someone would sneak into your cell and put as much stuff as they could into your bed with you, so when you woke up you would be pissed, but at the same time laugh because you got caught 'slippin' (off guard). If I caught you slippin, I would put shoes all around your head, all types of fruits, packaged foods, books, toilet paper, bottles of your cosmetics, if I could get your TV on your bed in a way that you didn't knock it over, I would put that on there too! This was fun, but also a learning experience if you got caught slippin, because it showed you that you need to be more aware of your surroundings. Someone coming into your cell while you were sleeping might not be your friend and may have different intentions than a joke. This was the penitentiary!"

Another lesson to be learned. Never let your guard down. Remembering the environment he was in and the dangers and level of tension and violence was a constant reminder that this was no ordinary place. Rayco soon found himself in another 'situation.'

"One day this guy approached me. He had a nice size to him. He was clean cut and had on a kufi, so I knew right away that he was a Muslim. He introduced himself as Jamil. This was Big Moe's brother. He told me he heard how I looked out for his brother on E-block. He told me if I needed anything or had any problems, to let him know. I became real cool with Jamil also. There was this animosity in Pennsylvania prisons between Pittsburgh prisoners and Philadelphia prisoners, that I didn't share, so I got along with anyone that had integrity."

Soon the athlete that was part of his DNA set in and he immersed himself in it.

"To speed up the time even more, I started playing organized prison sports. I played basketball for a couple of teams, but the coaches' friends always seemed to get the most playing time even if they weren't good. One game, I scored 26 points, and still didn't get much playing time the next game. When I heard that the boxing program was about to start, I couldn't wait. I was already a golden glove champion in Pittsburgh and couldn't wait to compare my skills with the guys from Philly."

The Pittsburgh pugilist was determined to show off his skills, learned so adeptly in the professional boxing ring. He was confident that he would excel and expected nothing else. He was about to get a wake-up call that would resonate with him and make him more determined.

"Since I got to Graterford, I kept hearing about members of the boxing team and how Bernard Hopkins comes there to spar in preparation for a fight, etc. I kept hearing about this guy named Keon, who was the champion for like 4 years straight. After about 1½ years in Graterford, I finally seen this guy. He was about 5'8", kind of pudgy for a boxer in my standards and very cocky! I saw him bragging one day, and said to myself, 'I can take him'. I got my chance! On my first day in the gym, they put me in the ring with Keon. I haven't been in the ring for about 2 years now. I wasn't even running. I was just weight training. So they strap me up. I didn't ask any questions. I wanted a piece of him anyway. Round one, we meet in the center of the ring. I thought I counted about 10 punches thrown between the both of us, two of them by me. I'm hunting as I do... 7 more punches... two of them by me. 4 more punches from him, then 2 by me, but Keon isn't there! He's on the side of me! 4 more punches! Wait a minute! He can't be this fast! The bell sounds the end of the first round. I get some water, but I'm tired as I was when I had my first fight. The difference though, is that Keon is way better than the guy I fought in my first fight. The bell sounds. Second round. Things are a lot slower, on my end anyway. Keon is so damn fast that it's frustrating me. This damn dude is on the side of me, behind me, is he that good or am I that bad? I kept on trying though. The bell sounds. That's it. I'm done! They didn't tell me to get out of the ring, I got out of the ring! From that day, I stepped my conditioning training up. I started running 4 miles a day, 5 days a week. The boxing team coach let it be known to all that you had to fight your way onto the team. The only guys that were automatically on the team were the current champions, Keon and the heavyweight John, I think his name was."

Like any good contender, Rayco wanted a rematch with Keon. A surprise wake-up call for sure and it molded him into a fighting machine, ever ready to prove once again that he would conquer any obstacle in his way.

"I didn't train harder to make the team, I trained harder to get Keon back. He and everyone else knew it, too. One sparring session took place between me and one of Graterford's legends. It was this sparring session, I was told, that made a Philly boxing trainer named, Hammer, want to work with me. I had the honor and pleasure to spar one of the members from the M.O.V.E Organization, Chucky Afrika!"

"Me and Chuck Afrika had a couple of good sparring sessions. He was about 10 years my senior, but he got down with the best of them. Getting to know this dude was a beautiful thing. I heard about the M.O.V.E. movement and what happened to them, but to actually speak to history was, as we say about something great, "THE SHIT!" I read books on how the city of Philadelphia dropped a bomb onto the housing unit that the members of the organization were inside of and ended up burning the whole city block to the ground. I seen pictures of the dead baby whose head was stepped on and crushed by the police. Now I got a chance to hear it from someone that was there. We also played chess together. I took heed to a lot from this guy."

Rayco had proved himself and was now an integral part of the boxing squad.

"When I made the boxing team, the guys from Philly showed me much love & respect. I actually opened the door for other Pittsburgh guys that wanted to box there. Unfortunately, Governor Tom Ridge, and the guy that was the head of the Department Of Corrections, put an end to the boxing programs around the state before I got a chance to fight in the competition that goes on every year between all the prisons. I never did get that rematch with Keon. When I approached him a couple of times on it, he gave me some excuse of why he couldn't spar. When the program came to an end, they also closed the boxing gym. This was a great outlet for some guys. This also gave some guys a chance to learn how to fight and defend themselves, which I truly believe is the answer to gun violence. But as I said earlier, prison is not for the betterment of the individual."

It was a let down not to further pursue his dream of showing the team and especially Keon that he had what it took. The discontinuation of the boxing program was a major let down for Rayco and the entire team. He now wanted to leave to another facility to shore up his time. He decided that a transfer would be best. He was also a dad and missed seeing his young son, Rayco Jr. Distance was a problem and the expense of travel from the western end of the state to the east incurred much sacrifice, both emotionally and financially. It also kept families living at the brink isolated and further stained in their relationships.

"Shortly after the boxing program shut down, I put in for a transfer. I was from Pittsburgh. My baby son, who's life I was a big part of, and my family was in Pittsburgh. Yet I was sent all the way across the state. Guys all over the state were experiencing this same fate. This didn't affect us prisoners, this affected our families that had to sacrifice a lot to see us! As always though, you would see the Father initiatives Program, sponsored by Tom Ridge. Bull Shit!!! If more MEN became fathers to their children, that would fuck up trillions of future dollars! So, they moved us as far as they could from our children and families. But in the public eye, they were promoting this "bringing fathers together with their children" lie!

The transfer to be nearer family and friends was denied. No explanation. He was a ward of the state and no reason was needed.

"My transfer to a prison closer to Pittsburgh was denied for no reason at all, even though I met all the criteria to be transferred. When I first inquired about a transfer, I was told to remain misconduct free for a year and to get my level dropped. I did all of the above, and was denied. After being denied a transfer despite meeting all of the criteria to be transferred, I really started to change for the worst. I'm in prison for something that never happened. I couldn't get into any schooling because 'I didn't have enough time'! There was no more boxing! Now my transfer was denied!"

With setback after setback, Rayco started to become his own worst enemy.

"I was transferred back to E-block, because I was sent to the hole for 15 days. I can't quite remember why I went to the hole, but this was some of my longest days. Solitary confinement was cold and quiet. It was located in one of the newer buildings that were added to Graterford. No radio. No TV. No phone. No commissary. Just you, the walls and a bed. When I got out of the hole, I went back to D-block, but was transferred back to E-block. To my surprise, I got a visit from one of my partnaz. He brought my son, little Rayco, to see me. That was a beautiful thing. I missed my little man a lot. The agony of the pre & post visit search, was worth it. I kissed and hugged him as long as I could before we sat down, because after the initial greeting, you can no longer embrace your child until the visit is over, thanks to some baby rapist dude, that was touching a child inappropriately in the visiting room. They should have cut his hands off... problem solved! But instead, every prisoner was punished by being restricted in the physical contact that one could have with his children, and by being made to wear one piece jump suits, that were too small, on the visit."

The visit helped restore a modicum of stability and before long the stress started to ease a bit. Then, he encountered his old friend and former cellmate, Big Moe.

"So now I'm back on E-block. Since I've been on another block, things have changed. I seen Big Moe again, but now he's thinner, but looking more healthy. He told me that he's been running, lifting what little weights he could and staying true to his diet of no meats. He also had a parole hearing coming up."

His affection for Big Moe notwithstanding, soon other events would again put a challenge to Rayco in this macabre web of prison subculture. It began with the drug trade, rampant in the prison and most noticeable in the most dangerous areas, such as E block.

"I noticed the drug users a little more than when I first got there. I was put in a cell with a prisoner that was a heroin user, although you couldn't tell from his appearance. He was a clean cut dude. He probably used any and every drug, but I saw him use heroin. This dude used to be bent over in front of the toilet throwing up, everyday. I didn't understand how a man would want to do something that makes you sick. It turns out that he just came from the hole a few days before I did. That meant to me that the cell I was in was about to get out of control. In my short time in prison, I learnt that people in prison get raped and/or killed for a couple of main reasons. Gambling: dudes like to gamble with no money, then can't pay their debt, so they have to pay one way or another! Drugs: dudes like to get drugs on credit, then they can't pay their debt, so they have to pay one way or another! Now there are instances where guys just get raped because they are scared and weak, but as I said before, 'these are guys that are afraid to die!' Everyone knows that a guy who is not afraid to die, is not afraid to kill. No one wants to be killed! Not even the most vicious rapers or killers!"

He vividly recalled an incident that had profound consequences and was part of the test of wills and survival in such an environment.

"I know this guy from Pittsburgh who was tricked into giving other guys sexual favors. I was shocked because I've known this dude most of my life and also, on the streets with a gun in his hand, he was a monster! I guess the key word was gun, but anyway. A guy lets him use his radio, then has someone steal the radio from him. He couldn't pay the guy because he didn't have any income. Dilemma... get the money, die, or get raped! He chose to get raped. Soon after, he became a prison homosexual. I say "prison homosexual" because some guys get released, go home and act like it never happened or become undercover bisexuals!"

Soon, he was challenged to the max with a request from his new cell mate.

"I didn't know much about my celly, but I knew where his activities were headed. I put in a request to be moved ASAP, but before I could be moved, my celly came and told me that he was moving. A few days later, some guy comes up to me and starts telling me about the guy who just moved out of my cell. He says to me, 'I'm coming to tell you this because you're a good dude. Your celly is crazy as hell. He came to me and asked me for some credit.' When I told him that I only want cash, he turned around, pulled down his pants and said, 'I'll pay you some ass!' I told that mother fucker, I don't want none of that stink'n ass! I told the guy that he wasn't my cell mate anymore."

Incidents like this one played out in prisons. Survival or submission. Ever the warrior and in control, Rayco wouldn't allow any compromise of his own self worth to come into play. Like the gladiators of old, he had hardened into a solid albeit at times angry man who was intent on making his mark. If a situation was unacceptable, he would have no part of it. Period.

"Letters from family & friends were consistent for me. I received mail every week while I was locked up. On one of these days, I received a letter from my lil partna Ken Dig (RIP). I was always happy to hear from my young partnas. They kept me close to the streets, by keeping me current with what was going on out there. Also, it let me know that they were alright. These little guys didn't exactly have writers penmanship, so he was straight to the point, 'J-locc shot you and he snitched on you! He said he snitched on you because you snitched on him.'"

A moment of truth mixed with disappointment and pain. Loyalty was always paramount to Rayco. He would back up his friends and wouldn't think twice of the dangers and implications. It was just not a part of his makeup. Yet this revelation hurt and hurt badly. Knowing the truth now made it all the harder in the environment he was in. The noises in the joint seemed louder, the shouting seemed deafening and the odors from the cells felt more nauseating. To have a buddy, a friend, a confidant try to execute you gangland style was too much. It was also a rude wake up call. The streets still echoed here as well.

"I didn't know what to feel at that moment. I couldn't do anything. I just re-read the statement over again. Then I felt sick. It felt like I just watched my best friend get killed. I wanted to cry, but I'm too hard for that. I wanted to holler, but this would have made me angry. With this news I didn't need to be angry. I needed to stay calm. The rest of that day I just chilled and replayed every moment in me and James Guscharles Jones lives. I replayed everything! Every conversation between us. Every action he made. Everything! Even though JC was suspected as being a snitch, I wasn't sure... until now! I was hurt about him being a snitch but it killed me internally to hear that he was the one who shot me. This cock sucker was by my side 1½ years after I got shot! He was in my house. We freaked women together. We ate together, etc!"

"That night, I laid in my bed and a song by Tupac, "Ambitions As a Ridah" flowed through my mind like a cool summer breeze flows through just before it thunder storms. This whole song was like a prophecy to what was happening to me."

I WON'T DENY IT, I'M A STRAIGHT RIDAH
YOU DON'T WANNA FUCK WITH ME
GOT THE POLICE BUSTIN AT ME
BUT THEY CAN'T DO NOTHING TO A G

"That's how the song starts off! In verse two, Tupac says,"

PEEP IT. IT WAS MY ONLY WISH TO RISE
ABOVE THESE JEALOUS COWARD MUTHER-FUCKERS I
DESPISE

"The last verse touches me the most. In it he says,"

I BEEN HESITANT TO REAPPEAR, BEEN AWAY FOR YEARS
NOW I'M BACK MY ADVERSARIES BEEN REDUCED TO
TEARS
QUESTION MY METHODS TO SWITCH UP SPEEDS,
SURE AS SOME BITCHES BLEED
NIGGAZ'LL FEEL THE FIRE OF MY MOTHER'S
CORRUPTED SEED
BLASTED ME BUT THEY DIDN'T FINISH, DIDN'T DIMIN-
ISH MY
POWERS SO NOW I'M BACK TO BE A MOTHERFUCKIN
MENACE,
THEY COWARDS THAT'S WHY THEY TRIED TO SET ME UP
HAD BITCH-AZZ NIGGAZ ON MY TEAM, SO INDEED,

THEY WET ME UP,
BUT I'M BACK REINCARNATED, INCARCERATED AT THE
TIME I CONTEMPLATE THE WAY THAT GOD MADE IT

....

....

GETTIN MUCH MAIL IN JAIL, NIGGAZ TELLIN ME TO KILL
IT
KNOWIN WHEN I GET OUT, THEY GON FEEL IT
WITNESS THE REALIST

Hard as it was to swallow this devastating news, Rayco tried to overcome and forget it. But it wasn't easy. It never is – finding out someone you entrusted wanted to target you. The thought of the shooting, the deception, double-cross and hypocrisy of it all was too much even for him. It resonated in such a confined and uncaring environment with more challenges.

"This information made it very hard for me, mentally, to get through my remaining sentence without getting more time added to my sentence. I started getting into disagreements with the guards regularly, although this wasn't too hard to do. Some of these guards were worse than some prisoners. In fact, the difference between some prison guards and prisoners is so slight that if you took away the guards uniform you wouldn't be able to tell them apart. I've seen guards encourage homosexual behavior. Everyone knows that drugs cannot, with the drug detection equipment that they have today, get into the prisons without the help of the prison guards. The guard that I seen encourage homosexual behavior, we got into it because he said something to me that I didn't like. I was cleaning my cell and I had two cups of cleaning liquid in my hands. He used to pick with everyone who didn't subscribe to his standards. I dropped both cups without blinking and said, 'Say one more fuckin thing and I'ma throw you over that fuckin railing!' He slammed and locked my door. I thought I was going to the hole for threats, but I was already on E-block and would return to E-block, so I guess he let that one go. He never said anything to me after that."

This toughness and hardness was duplicated time and again.

"I started to really get an 'I don't give a fuck anymore' attitude.

Although I did fulfill a promise to myself that I would cut my hair if I ever went to the penitentiary or became a member of the TV reality show, "America's Most Wanted". I grew it back and started to wear it in a unicorn type pony tail on top of my head. A guard commented about it being too long by rule standards. I told him what he could do with the rules. He replied that he would be sitting in on my pre-parole hearing. I laughed."

Events soon unfolded and the incident with the guard came home.

"Sure enough, about a month later, that same guard was at my hearing. When I walked in, the unit manager told me to have a seat. I replied that I wasn't going to be that long. He said, 'Ok, but have a seat'. I told him again that I wasn't going to be that long. All four people in the room looked at me. That's when I said, 'I refused to be paroled from Graterford penitentiary'. Then I walked out of the room. Afterwards, when I saw the guard that sat in on the hearing, he acted as if we were childhood friends. Prison officials hang parole over the prisoners head as a means of control. I refused to be controlled by anyone. The reason that I refused to get paroled from Graterford was because, if I was to get re-arrested for anything, I would have been returned to Graterford because it's the prison that I was paroled from. That's too much for me and my family to deal with, especially after getting reacquainted."

The anger still there, Rayco soon found another challenge testing his fibre and this incident further eroded his trust in the authorities at Graterford. Like most incidents, a verbal exchange got out of hand.

"Shortly after, I got into it with another guard. This time it was a guard from Pittsburgh. He was always trying to be cool with guys from Pittsburgh, but certain guys start telling me about how he would be cool one moment, then backstab you the next. Then one day we were in the prison yard, on opposite sides of a 10 foot fence. Good thing too, he said something to me that I didn't like and I said to him, 'If you were on this side of the fence, I'd break your fuck'n neck, pussy!' I was locked in my cell pending a disciplinary hearing. At this time, I happened to be reading the Satanic Bible. I borrowed the book from this brown skinned guy that was from Pittsburgh. I had heard about this book when I was in Shuman. Although the book was interesting, it was not what I expected it to be. I thought it was going to be scary. Instead, it was like many other religious books, just different views. However, it did tell you how to conjure up demons and how to curse people. Although I don't believe or disbelieve, I wasn't willing to find out if the chants worked."

The rage inside was still with him and as fate would have it, he again encountered the same prison guard who had reported him.

"I went to my disciplinary hearing and was given 60 days in the solitary confinement. On my way back to my cell, handcuffed, I saw the guard that I got into it with. I told him that when I come from the hole, I got his number and I'll be sure to give him a call. I got 60 more days for that. 120 days in the hole! Didn't matter. I was on a downward spiral. It was probably for the best."

Unlike most individuals, faced with the prospect of 23 hour solitary confinement, Rayco decided that he would utilize his time productively. He set out to reform his outlook. It would begin with himself. A time that would have been stressful and painful instead became a period to reevaluate himself and begin anew. He knew he had to change. And change within started. A time to delve into books, reflect on his life and a time to set goals. He was ready.

"Being in the hole was uplifting for me. It helped me develop a certain set of skills that I was lacking in. I've become a very patient person. I can turn my emotions off at will. I never get bored. I've learned to think before I act and listen before I speak. I read a lot of books while in the hole. I also had a subscription to a local Pittsburgh paper. I read every page of the paper. I learnt how to play chess with another person by both men setting up a board made of cardboard, with game pieces made of soap, and calling out the letters and numbers of the chest board to each other. Me and Chuck Afrika who was also put in the hole, use to battle all hours of the night."

Challenging himself further involved keeping his taut physique in prime shape. He didn't need fancy gym machines or weights. He would do it the old fashioned way, disciplining himself in the one hour that he was let out of his confined space. That hour would be his and he set out to use it to the max. First, he had a more pressing problem.

"When I was placed in the hole, I had a cell mate. This dude had a terrible body odor and he snored! He had to go. I made up my mind that

I was not letting anymore prisoners be my celly while in the hole. My time in the hole was going great, despite being locked in the cell 23 hours a day. When they called me for the 1 hour rec period, I'd hit the yard. As soon as the cuffs and shackles came off, I'd start my workout of 500 push-ups, five days a week. 2500 push-ups a week. I would also do 300 reps of various stomach exercises before I ate breakfast."

This strict regimen would be his life saver and his determination to not give in. It helped him ease the stress. That coupled with the safety net of a steady partner to play chess, the books to let him escape and the isolation from the general population, actually helped him. He started writing more. But another incident soon followed and the latent anger emerged. Yet the steady, determined Rayco held his ground and emerged from it stronger and more respected.

"One day they brought another prisoner to my cell. When they opened my door, I was standing right in the door way, blocking his entrance. I had a pen & note tablet in my hand because I was in the middle of writing a letter. When the guard saw that I was not moving, he told me to do so. I told him that I wasn't taking a celly. In his best training voice he ordered me to back up to the wall. I dropped what was in my hand and said, 'For what? He's not coming in here.' The guard then ordered me to turn around so he could hand cuff me. I told him, 'No! I'm secured in my cell. I'm not putting on those hand cuffs.' He hit the radio and about 10 more guards came with sticks, ready to throw down. The lieutenant also came. When the lieutenant got there he just looked at me. I said to all that could hear me, 'I don't mean any disrespect and I'm not trying to cause any trouble, but I'm not taking a celly. I have to be in this cell 23 hours a day for I don't know how many months. That's too many hours to be locked up with another man.' The guard that started the situation said, 'Lieutenant, it's your call.' The lieutenant looked me in my eyes, and vice versa, puffed his cigar, then said, 'Close his gate.' He saw it in my eyes that I was willing to fight for mine. After the incident, the guard that started it apologized to me, then start giving me extra food. The other prisoners seen this as the guard fearing me. I saw it as more respect than fear."

He got his way and finished his time free of the distraction of another cell mate. He utilized this period as he had set out – to find himself. The two month confinement was a defining moment. When faced with challenges he always was ready. His behavior changed. His routine in the one hour stretch in the yard and the time spent alone in the cell allowed him to face his own demons. He started to relax. It was soon noticed by others. But when it came time to face the review board and return to the general population, he held firm.

"After being in solitary confinement for 2 months, I went to my review hearing to determine if I would be let out of the hole. The guard that sits in on the hearings, stated that I met all the criteria to return to population. He told the review board how my behavior was excellent, etc. They denied my release. They scheduled my next review in 30 days. Once again, I was called for my review hearing, but this time I refused to go. They sent me notice saying that I received 30 more days. At this point it didn't matter anymore. I made up my mind that the hole was best for me at that moment. Shortly after, I was called to see the parole board to determine if I would be sent home on parole. I refused to go and also gave a message to the guard to give to the board, 'Tell the parole board I said, kiss my ass!' The guard laughed and said, 'Rayco, you're crazy.' About 2 months later, the parole board came again. This time I told the guard to tell them to kiss my ass and I'll see them on the other side of the wall."

Rayco's attitude made him a unique case. Life had been difficult growing up, losing his mom and never having a dad around. His defiance of authority from his early years on the streets of Pittsburgh cemented a resolve and distrust that when confronted, he would stand his ground. Even when given the chance to escape the isolation of confinement, he chose not to. He had his reasons. He knew he was framed and he wouldn't give in. The toughness never left. The pain never left.

"Shortly after, I received my green sheet from the Board of Probation and Parole. It stated, 'since you feel so negative about parole, you are ordered to serve your unexpired maximum sentence of...'. I laughed at these fools. Being that they didn't get the chance to make me beg and plead for them to send me home early, talk bad to me, deny me and laugh behind my back, they were upset! They had to get a word in some how! So they put the "personal" comment on my green sheet! I wasn't going to give another man a chance to tell me when I have to be in a house that I pay the bills in, for something that didn't even happen. Further more,

I'm a grown azz MAN! I never had a father and my mother has been deceased since I was eleven years young! No one tells me what I can or can not do. So rather than give them the opportunity to TRY to dictate to me, I chose to serve all of the time.

"I received notice from the prison that I was being transferred to SCI – Mahanoy. Here I was in a level 4-5 maximum security prison, in solitary confinement, about to be transferred to a level 3 medium security prison. 'I love the way things in this country work backwards!' If I would have knew this is what it took to get transferred to a prison, closer to home and with more resources to better ones self, I would have stabbed someone or done something drastic when I first got to Graterford! We live and we learn though."

CHAPTER 16

Mahanoy State Correctional Institution is located in Frackville in Schuylkill County in the eastern part of the state of Pennsylvania. A medium facility, it houses prisoners transferred from the maximum facilities, such as Graterford. It thus serves as a conduit, preparing men to eventually assimilate back into society. But it's still a prison with all the limitations and rules that the commonwealth places on its inmates. The day of his transfer is etched in his mind. It began in the early hours during a torrential downfall.

"The morning of my transfer, it was raining harder than I've ever seen it. All of the transferees were shackled and handcuffed. We had to go to this other building where we would get into the van and be on our way. We're on our way to this other building, moving very fast through the rain. We went up a flight of steps in single file. When we reached the top of the steps, I never thought to look up. My concern was to get out of the heavy rain. BAM! I'm sliding back down the steps upside down! The other prisoners who are behind me, although they are handcuffed behind their back, are trying to break my fall and slow my momentum with their bodies! After a downwards slide, which seemed forever, I finally stopped! The rain is hitting me directly in the face because I am on my back, hands cuffed behind me, looking straight up into the sky. The guard finally comes back and picks me up. My side was bruised and hurting, but I declined medical treatment because my transfer would have been postponed until I was cleared by medical to leave. About an hour later, I was on the van, headed to SCI Mahanoy."

What awaited him at the new venue was a repeat of Graterford. Despite the fact that it is a medium prison, the rules were harsher and the treatment more severe. Rayco was soon to find out what life in solitary at Mahanoy was really like. It began the first night. A reality check soon emerged.

"When I got to Mahanoy I was put into solitary confinement, because if you are transferred from a solitary, you must be placed in one until your review, which usually takes place in 7 days. I quickly learnt that it was a little different here. This solitary was designed to inflict mental and physical torture. They used a tactic in this hole that I read about in books, explaining different ways that the CIA, use to break people. The cell room lights stayed on 24 hrs a day! My first night there, I got up to turn the lights off so I could go to sleep, and they didn't go off. So, I hollered to another cell and asked about the lights. I was told that they never go off, and if you cover them up, the guards write you up for breaking the rules and you get more time in the hole. I immediately recognized this tactic... sleep deprivation! I tried to pull the covers over my head. Didn't work! The blankets were so short, that when you pulled them over your head, your feet were exposed, and the cell was too cold for that. I ended up tying my socks together, then tying them around my head and eyes to block out as much light as possible. I didn't sleep well at all during that seven day stint and my bad dreams came back, so I found myself sleeping less and less."

The lack of sleep and the lack of reading material gave him time to reflect. His anger, ever simmering at the surface, was back. He began to think of the person who had set him up.

"I didn't have any books to read, so I thought a lot. I thought about everything. I mostly thought about JC, a.k.a. James Jones, a.k.a. J-lock, a.k.a. Snitch Lock! It's wild too because Jay-Z came out with the Hard Knock Life vol 2, album in late 1998, and on it he has a song called "a week ago" featuring Too Short. So everyday all day, I'm singing this song:"

Growin up in the hood just my dog and me
We used to hustle in the hood for all to see
Problems, I called on him, he called on me
We wasn't quite partners, I hit him off my P.
Let him unlocked doors, off my keys
Yeah we spoke, much more than cordially
Man he broke bread with me, my business spread swiftly

The Feds came to get me, we both fled quickly
Wasn't quick enough to jump over the hedges with me
Got caught, and that's when our relationship strayed
Used to call me from the joint til he ran out of change
And when he called collect and I heard his name
I quickly accepted, but when I reached the phone
he's talkin reckless, I can sense deceit in his tone
I said, "Damn dawg, what, nine weeks and you're home?"
He said, "Main man, you think shit's sweet cause you're home."
I just sat, spat no more speech in the phone
Them crackers up there bleachin your dome, you're reachin
I said, "The world don't stop I've got to keep keep on."
From there I sensed the beef was on
I ran to the spot, store to add some more features to my phone
To see if I had bugs and leeches on my phone
Can't be too safe cause niggaz is two faced
And they show the other side when they catch a new case
It's on

Chorus: Too $hort, Jay Z

It was cool when you had hella weed to smoke
And you bought a new home where you could keep the folks
I don't see how this side of you could be provoked
(Uh huh, uh huh, it was all good just a week ago)

Funny what, seven days can change
A stand up nigga, now you sit down to aim
Used to have a firm grip now you droppin names
Uh huh, uh huh (It was all good just a week ago)

Verse Two: Jay Z

Like I put the toast to your head and made you sell

We both came in this game, blind as hell
I did a little better, had more clientele
Told you put away some cheddar now you cryin for bail
Seventeen and I'm holdin on to around a mill
I could bail out and blow trial and come around on Appeal
Had niggaz thinkin I was from Uptown for real
I had so much hustle plus I was down to ill
Like a Brooklyn nigga, straight out of Brownsville
Down and dirty, down to fight the round thirty
Freezin on them corners still holdin my crack
Lookin up and down the block, the fuck is the dough at?
Came from flat broke to lettin the dough stack
You tell them feds I said I'm never goin back
I'm from Marcy, and Marcy don't raise no rats
You know the consequences of your acts, you can't be serious

Chorus

Verse Three: Jay Z

The lawyer I retained you said you leakin some things
All this after a week in the bang
I'm mad at myself cause I didn't spot the weak and lame
I woulda bet the house you wouldn't speak a thang
Nigga this was the oath, to the top of broke
Even pricked our finger, anything that got between us
we sposed to cock the ninas, what happened to that?
Instead you copped out to a misdemeanor
Fuck it, the same thing make you laugh make you cry
That's right, the same game that make you mad could make you
die
It's a dice game, and sometimes you crap
Who woulda thought you'd get popped one time and rat?
Now you know that's bad when your sister is mad

and your son gotta grow up like, "This is my dad?"
The labelling of a snitch is a lifetime scar
You'll always be in jail nigga, just minus the bars

Chorus

[Too $hort]

Shit is crazy man
All these niggaz out here snitchin
We was one step away from takin this crack money
and recyclin it through the ghettoes
and buildin back up our own hoods
Now all you niggaz start snitchin on each other
I got partners doin 15 20
Wouldn'ta been doin SHIT
if you didn't snitch
Beyotch!
It's about time y'all check that shit out man
It ain't all good
Shut your mouth
Just watch the game
And don't snitch
It sure will do a lot for you
Believe that baby
Jay Z, Short Dawg's in the house main
You know I got it
Got it goin on
We got the money
Ain't got nuthin to do with crime baby
But I'm recognizing

[Jay Z]

You rat bastard!

"The more I sung this song, the more I seen the signs that Snitch Lock was guilty. I had to get out of the hole. I needed to get back to working out."

He knew he had to abide by the rules. He wanted out of this nonsense and he decided to cooperate up to a point! He was still the old, defiant, iconoclastic rebel. It would soon show.

"I was called for my review. They told me that they were letting me out of the hole. I asked them would my long hair be a problem, because if so, they could just leave me in the hole. They told me that it wouldn't be a problem. The first thing that I did was go to the property room and get my things. I haven't watched boxing, Martin or G-String Diva's in six months. I couldn't wait, now that I was out of solitary confinement! Although I haven't celebrated Christmas in years, since I found out that it was all a lie, I got a similar feeling as I did when I was a child on Christmas morning, when I got my T.V. back. When I got to my new block, there was a note from the guy that told me that my hair was not going to be a problem, instructing me to get a hair cut. I immediately told the guard on duty to send me back to the hole! This coward didn't have the heart to tell me this to my face! I guess he thought that when I got a little taste of being out of the hole, I would do whatever to stay out. WRONG! They didn't understand that I was at peace in the hole. Furthermore, I was on my way back down the mountain of my sentence. Making it hard for me would just further create what I have become to be!"

But Rayco didn't want to be confined in solitary devoid of books and a modicum of some 'luxuries,' such as sleeping without a constant din of the light bulb to test your resolve and serve as a constant reminder of your confinement.

"The female counselor overheard what was going on and told me not to worry about it. So I didn't. I settled in, bumped into a few dudes that I knew from the streets and got familiar with the dos and don'ts, the who and who nots."

He decided to immerse himself once again as he had at Graterford and soon was taking classes. He did find changes at Mahanoy that were vastly different than the maximum Graterford.

"SCI Mahanoy was much more geared to handle short timers than Graterford. I immediately got into school. They did have a waiting list for some classes, but the criteria to get on the list wasn't as drastic as Graterford. I signed up for a few classes and was immediately put into the typing class. I was hoping to get the "Computer Aided Drafting" class first but I was cool with typing. I thought that I would have a lot of difficulties with this class because I have some nerve damage in my right hand that makes it difficult to feel. I passed though and got a certificate. Mahanoy for the most part was incident free for me. You still had your asshole guards which every prison had. Other than that I just let my time count down."

Yet Mahanoy was still a prison and soon he was called in for a review. Part of that review involved signing papers acknowledging his wrong doing. It would not be a pleasant encounter.

"When I got close to my day, I got called into the counselor's office. He wanted me to sign some papers. I refused. He told me that if I didn't sign these papers, I would get more time in prison. The papers had something to do with probation. I never had to sign papers for probation before and I wasn't going to start. My theory on everything, is that if someone needs you to sign some papers for something to take effect, it can't take effect if you don't sign! The counselor threatened me with years and more years but I still didn't sign. He was mad as hell! Then one morning I get woke up for court. Court! Now I'm nervous! I always worried about a FED case popping up on me, but whooo! It was about the papers that I did not sign. They took me all the way back to Pittsburgh about a signature! To the people that are reading this book... if they NEED you to sign something, DON'T SIGN IT!

"Judge Durkin said to me, 'I don't even know what to do. No one has not signed before.' She asked me why didn't I sign?

"I said, 'I've had probation before and I've never had to sign anything. Also, this crime never happened! I can't just participate in these proceedings like it did.'"

"I couldn't believe that I was the first person to refuse to sign the probation papers. The judge and everyone else probably couldn't believe it neither. After the judge sweet talked me, I will confess, I did sign. I wasn't threatened or anything. She just did her womanly thing and made everything seem alright. Got me! Sucker'd me right on in."

CHAPTER 17

Freedom. At long last, Rayco Saunders was a free man. A free man? What does it entail to come out of the system with a record? Freedom? For some, it's a chance to immerse oneself back into the community, reacquaint with family and friends and start anew. You could almost smell it in the air. Freedom! It was now Rayco's – he would deal with it on his own terms. He always did and yet somehow it was different now. Freedom. Not just a word. He was ready! And, true to form, Rayco would not disappoint anyone as he reemerged onto the stage of life. He was Rayco after all and no one would be in his way! It began immediately.

"January 21, 2001, I was released from prison. I was picked up by my partna. Although I was on some type of fraudulent state probation, we went straight to New York. When I got to New York, I still had on my prison clothes. The people that worked in the stores were laughing at me. I was laughing too. It was all love. I bought some clothes – a leather coat and some boots – from one of the stores in the garment district. I went up to 125th street, to the legendary Apollo Theater.

"Growing up watching the shows on TV, I wanted to see it. I took a few pictures, then headed to Pittsburgh." But, this wasn't the end of their quick venture to the Big Apple. Their car with out-of-state license plates, aroused a few locals, resulting in an encounter he recalls to this day.

"Before we could leave New York, a car with two guys in it pulled up beside our car. The guy in the passenger side said to us, 'I got chickens for 25! Follow us!' He was telling us that he had kilograms of cocaine for $25,000! I found this amusing being that this was my first day out of prison, and also the fact that I used to get them for $20,000 to $22,000, four years before. I wondered why and how something like that could happen so openly, and was told it was because we had a PA license plate on the car. That was funny. I guess profiling goes on in all walks of life!"

Rayco had time on his hands to reflect on his long ride back to Pittsburgh. The episode in Harlem was still fresh in his mind. The first day of freedom and to have it nearly upended! He had to get back home and he was ready. Freedom! Soon, the skyscrapers and noise and smells of the big city gave way to the idyllic countryside of Eastern Pennsylvania as he and his partna drove westward on the Pennsylvania Turnpike.

The January cold and the accumulated snow was for him an awakening. The trees, buildings and adjoining landscape reminded him that he was at last a free man. Freedom. A different outlook on the world. Those same trees, laden with heavy snow, an occasional bird flying or perched above them and the bitter wind would be for him, a part of that freedom. So different now. How very different!

"Driving back to Pittsburgh was a beautiful thing. I got a chance to see the world again. Even though everything was covered in snow, I was free! I drove us home. I didn't know that driving could be so much fun. I guess after being locked up 4 years, most things would seem fun."

For Rayco, the quick New York trip, however illegal by parole standards, got him ready for the reality that was to set in once he arrived in his hometown.

"When I got back to Pittsburgh, the first thing I did was see my family, and when I say family, I mean "blood relatives." This was a happy time for me. Locked away 350 miles across the state, I haven't seen any of my family in 4 years!"

Knowing the pain of not having a father there for him, Rayco knew that he had to start bonding with his son. Despite the distance both geographically and personally, he was ready for the responsibilities that came with being a dad. He was ready. He wanted to be part of his world. Like a good detective, he would find out what his son was all about. Yes, he was ready to be the father to his son.

"I immediately resumed being a father to my son, Li'l Rayc. Growing up without a father, I knew how important this was. I went to his school and got to know his teachers, etc. When I was sent to prison, Li'l Rayc wasn't of school age yet. When I came home he was in the 2nd grade. I learnt that he was held back in the 1st grade and was now failing the 2nd.

The teachers told me that being that he was already held back, they didn't want to hold him back again. I assured them that he would get it together."

He set out to change things immediately. He began by a visit to his son's mom.

"Me being a firm believer in "all blame for a child's missteps falls on the parent", I questioned his mother about him failing school. She said to me, 'I have my education, it's up to him to get his!' There was no need for anymore conversation after that. I knew what I had to do!"

Part of his job was now to free his son from those who had not given him the attention any young person needs. He thought of his days in school and didn't want his own son to be left out. He would be an advocate. He would be a responsible parent. He would connect with his son. He would be there for him. Freedom – yes, it involves making decisions, too, and Rayco was ready to make some firm commitments to ensure his son's chances at a better life.

"My theory is that schools are there to give the students guidance on what they should know at a certain stage of their lives. It's the parents' jobs to make sure that his/her child learns and knows these things. When your child is in the 2nd grade or grade school period, it's the parents responsibility to make sure that the homework is complete and turned in, the child knows all of his/her colors, shapes, how to read, write, etc!"

Rayco set off at once to change things and make the home environment a learning one. He would not only get enrichment books for his son but also be there for him and interact and learn as well. Absent four years of his son's life, he was steadfast and undeterred as they both set out to explore. No one would be in their way. Freedom, for sure. To learn. To explore and grow. Rayco liked this new role and he became stronger for it. Father, teacher, mentor and best friend – all rolled into one nice packet. He would soon see striking results.

"I went to a certain retail store and purchased some activity books that were a grade ahead of my son. We worked on them everyday for the entire summer. I taught him different methods to do math until we found the easiest method for him. I taught him how to spell words the same way that I was taught. I was taught the "phonic" system which is the sounds and syllables of the English language so you can put them together like building blocks and be able to read big words. In the beginning, it was hard and I was impatient so I hollered a lot. It took me a minute to understand that my son along with most children now, are being taught "whole language", which is guessing at whole words from pictures on a page, skipping over words you don't know, substituting words that seem to fit (e.g., pony for horse, holiday for vacation), predicting what you think the word could be based on the context of the story. In whole language you do not learn the letters, sounds and syllables, you just look at the configuration of the whole word. The typical 1st grader already knows the meaning of thousands of big words, such as hamburger, football, birthday, toothbrush, and even ridiculous. But the child will not be able to read those words unless he/she is taught the skill of sounding out the syllables. That is called phonics. The child who is taught bad habits, instead of how to sound out the syllables, will never be able to read big words or become a good reader. My partna tried to tell me that hollering was going to scare my son into not doing his work. He told me how his brother use to do him, which made him shut down. This was not an option for my son. My son was and is not allowed to be afraid of anything, short of something life threatening!"

The results of these efforts started to show. The teacher Rayco and the father Rayco would soon show his teachers and anyone else what a lot of hard work and love could do.

"My son made honor roll on his first report card of the 3rd grade. His teachers were elated! On his second report, he made honor roll again! When I attended teacher-parent days, every teacher told me of how they couldn't wait to meet me! As a father who never had a father, this felt great! I was helping my son achieve what I wanted the guy who slept with my mother to help me achieve... intelligence, knowledge, success, etc.! My son continued to make honor roll and high honor roll throughout the rest of 3rd and 4th grade. Everything was good."

While Rayco was attending to his son, the lure of the boxing ring was not neglected. He had just one month after his release to hone his skills in the ring for the upcoming events. Like everything he did in life, nothing would deter him from achieving his goal. He was ready. Ready to sweat in the gym, preparing for the bouts. Ready to smell the leather gloves – even the putrid odor of the locker room! It was his time now and yes, he was ready! He was ready.

"In the meantime, while catching up with my son and my family, I continued boxing. The amateur Golden Gloves tournament was starting in February. I returned to Chuck's gym, in Brookline. I couldn't wait to try my new skills that I learnt from being on the Graterford boxing team. My first day back to the gym, I was asked to spar. From what I've heard after the fact, certain guys that didn't know me thought that I was going to get beat down. I sparred the guy who was considered the best in the gym, "Shane". As I said, WAS considered the best in the gym! After that sparring session, there was a new best; Rayco 'WAR' Saunders"!

Rayco, determined as ever, was about to make his reappearance in the boxing world. The zeal that he had shown for the sport was clearly evident to anyone and he was now back in his niche. And the efforts now were starting to show.

"I was heavier now, 198 lbs of chiseled muscle, so I was fighting in the 201 weight class. A lot of my buddies from my neighborhood were happy to see me fighting again, so they came out deep and showed me a lot of support. One of my most memorable fights was when I fought in Punxsutawney. It was one of my most memorable fights because Punxsutawney was known for its Ku Klux Klan activity, but after my fight, which I won, I received a lot of love from the crowd. A lot of people came up to me to congratulate me and shake my hand."

With his victory behind him, it was now time to move ahead.

"I made it to the Golden Gloves championship. I was fighting the guy who was picked to win. His corner men were Eddie Chambers, Sr. and his son, current heavyweight contender at the time of this writing, Fast Eddie Chambers, Jr. I didn't know father and son at this time. Not that it mattered."

Rayco goes on to describe what happened in the ring from the outset. Ever the analyst, he sized up his opponent and started noticing something that would affect the outcome.

"The first round started out a war! At the end of the round, I felt it was pretty even. I noticed that my opponent kept dipping down towards my right side. So as I'm sitting in my corner getting instruction from Chuck, I started replaying the Iron Mike Tyson vs. Buster Mathis, Jr. fight in my head. In less than 60 seconds, I replayed the moves of both fighters that resulted in a knockout for Iron Mike Tyson. I made up my mind to do exactly what Iron Mike did, because Ray (I think that was his name) was doing exactly what Buster Mathis, Jr. was doing."

Rayco, knew how to approach his opponent and what moves to take. That dipping to the right would be used to his advantage and he set out to take advantage of his opponent's weakness. Rayco clearly remembers what transpired next.

"At the start of the 2nd round, we met in the center of the ring, just as we did in the first. This time I was waiting for him to dip to his left. He did it! As soon as he dipped, I pivoted on my front foot away from his move. My back foot swung towards my left. Right upper cut, right on the money! He stood up in what seemed like slow motion. Left hook! He crumbled to the canvas. The ref starts counting, 1-2-3-4-5-6- he's getting up, but his legs betrayed him. He crumbled back down. Fight over by Knockout! I became 2001 Pittsburgh Golden Gloves Champion!"

CHAPTER 18

Victory! A champion that would be recognized. An upset victory at that. People would start to take notice and ask where to next. It was a question that Rayco demanded an answer from the newly crowned champ. He knew what to do. As he had in the past, he took control and set out to show himself and everyone else that he was in charge. Now that the Golden Gloves were over, he had to make his move.

"Unfortunately, Brookline didn't train or fight outside of this tournament, so I started training with my partna, Rick Manning who trains fighters at 3rd Ave boxing gym, owned and operated by Jimmy Cvetic. Me and Rick had some memorable moments of my amateur career. The most memorable was when I fought James Lowe. There was a boxing show out South Park. The fights were going to take place outside under the sun, at a fair. I didn't have a fight that day, but Rick told me to come anyway. We are sitting in the dressing room, Rick is wrapping my hands. The fight coordinator calls out, 'Does anyone in the 201 weight class want to fight Rayco Saunders?' After 5 seconds of silence, a deep voice came out of nowhere and said, 'I'll fight him!' Everyone in the room looked up in silence! The fight coordinator asked his name and the guy said, 'James Lowe'. James was of Euro decent, about 6'2", 200 lbs. It was announced that he had 10 fights to my 5. Rick asked me (already knowing the answer) if I wanted to take the fight, because at 10 fights you are considered an open class or expert fighter and at 5 you are considered a novice."

Rayco was ready as always despite the odds. People training him could offer some measure of support and tell him what to expect. Yet it would be up to him to perform. Being Rayco meant that he wouldn't back down and he started to strategize.

"Now that the fight was made, three people offered me advice that I neither asked for nor wanted. Jimmy Cvetic told me to get in and get out on this guy, because he's not going to come after me. Another person told me that he's going to come after me, so I gotta bang with him. Brian Noel caught me in the mens room and said, 'the kid James that you are fighting… I used to train this kid. He's sharp, but you stay sharp.'"

As fate would have it, his bout was the one that would draw the most attention. It would be a fight that Rayco would never forget. Equally important, it was the fight that made Rayco known in Pittsburgh. He was on his way.

"We were the last fight of the day. The bell sounds the first round. We meet at the center of the ring and James Lowe, hits me with a three punch combination in my head. I jabbed a couple of times and he hits me again with a combination. He's being aggressive, too! So I turn it up! Double jab, straight right hand to his face! He wobbles a little. He's hurt! I go to finish him but the ref steps in and gives James an eight count. He asks James is he alright. James nods yes. We continue. I immediately go back to my jab. James is in retreat mode right now. He's trying to clear his head. I throw a straight left right, combination. James backs up to the ropes. I follow him and keep him on the ropes with a continuous volley of straight lefts and rights to his head and face. Out the corner of my eye, I could see the ref ready to step in and stop the fight. At this moment, I throw my left hook with all my might! Bulls eye! Right on the side of his skull! His arms fall to his sides. His body slumps and James goes down! When he went down, his body language didn't look good at all. The ringside medics immediately jumped in the ring! The referee, paced back and forth and kept saying to himself loudly, 'I should have stopped it!' After 15 minutes, he finally was brought to his feet. He was escorted by the medics out of the ring to the ambulance and to the ER. I don't think James has fought since."

A first round knockout! One for the books! And a win that would catapult Rayco Saunders and get him noticed.

"I was declared the winner by knockout at 1:46 of the first round! Trophies are given to the winners of their bouts. There is also a "fight of the night" trophy for the best fight. I won both. However, I didn't get a trophy for either. I was told that they ran out of trophies and that I would get rewarded at the next show. This to me was the start of the less than satisfactory treatment that I received, representing Pittsburgh amateur boxing and the A.M.A. (Allegheny Mountain Association)!"

Whenever a fresh face struts his stuff and shows the world that he's got what it takes, the world notices. Fresh meat, raw meat. Who is Rayco Saunders? This was his moment. The victories put his name on the boxing map and soon changes would occur.

"These two vicious knockouts that I gave out, sent word through Western PA, and the surrounding areas, that I could fight and that I had power! They were also witnessed by Eddie Chambers, Sr. who was a former boxer himself and current boxing trainer. As I said previously, he worked the one guys corner. He took me to meet boxing promoter Greg Nixon who happened to be scouting the guy that I knocked out in the Golden Gloves Championship. When I got to his gym located in Steubenville, Ohio, the guy that I knocked out in the GG championship was there training. There were no hard feelings so we spoke and joked about a few things."

Nixon soon became interested in the upstart Pittsburgh boxer and saw a raw talent that needed to be nurtured. He would make him a professional and make him known. But Rayco, ever the skeptic, came away uneasy at the first meeting with Nixon. He goes on to explain:

"Me and Greg Nixon spoke one on one. He told me how he wanted to turn me professional. He said, 'Rayco, you are knocking these guys out with 12 oz. gloves on and headgear! You will destroy these guys with 10 oz. gloves on and no headgear!' At that moment, I seriously was considering turning pro! Until he said, 'Now, you will lose some fights, but that's expected.' I didn't know much about the business side of boxing but I did know promoters of any kind are about progression! Losing is regression! This was not a good sales pitch! Also, I was undefeated as an amateur. I didn't want to hear anything about losing. I turned down Greg's offer to turn pro. I told him that I wanted to see if I could become a Golden Gloves State Champion and win a National amateur title, which I really did. Before I left, he told me to look up a trainer named Brian Noel. He said that Brian would be a better trainer for me because Eddie, Sr. was only focused on his son."

Shortly thereafter, Brian Noel emerged on the scene. Immediately, he made a lasting impression on the young pugilist. Not entirely a favorable one. One episode stands out for Rayco.

"I eventually bumped into Brian Noel. He became a good fit as my trainer, physically. Mentally, this guy was on something else! One day he comes into the gym with a tiny pair of boxing gloves made from porcelain or something. At first, me and my partna, Rel thought they were baby shoes, because that's what they were similar to. Then Brian starts telling us where he got the gloves from: 'I had a dream that I trained three world champions! When I woke up, I seen this bright light that all of a sudden disappeared! It was like a burning fire! When I fully opened my eyes, I looked next to me and these gloves were sitting on the table and they were smoking! When I touched them, they were still hot! It's a sign, Champ!' Then Brian says to me, 'Champ, let me get some of your sweat on these gloves!' I said, 'No thank you! I'm not superstitious!' This jigga was crazy! As far as training, I felt he was pretty good. I give him credit for my superior defensive skills. He brought a guy into our training sessions and it was here that I developed my defense. His character is another issue. The guy that slept with my mama lied to me all of my life so I don't take kindly to liars!"

Rayco's sense of trust was violated. A no-no. No turning back, no need to continue. As he aptly put it:

"Me and Brian's relationship started its downward spiral when I went to the Golden Gloves National tournament."

Then, the downward spiral continued into the new year. As with all fading relationships, there would be consequences. They came soon enough. It started in Niagra Falls and then in Baltimore.

"2002, I fought in a few different amateur tournaments, with Brian as my trainer. As I said before, I felt that he was a good trainer. I fought in Niagra Falls. It was Team USA vs Team Canada. I lost by decision. This decision was so bad, that some of the people in attendance expressed their displeasure by leaving, but first coming to congratulate me.

By the time he got to Baltimore, Rayco realized something wasn't right.

"I fought in the USA Boxing, Regional Championship, in Baltimore. I lost a decision. This fight was stacked against me when I got to the venue. At the registration, the head official asked me what I would prefer to be called, 'Ray or Rayco'. I answered: "Rayco". Nothing more, nothing less.

"That night he told Brian that I had an attitude with him. I was surprised! The next morning, weigh-ins were from 7am.-9 am. I got there at 8 am. The same official scolded me and told me that I was late! He said that we were supposed to be on site at 7 am. This was the first time that I've heard anything like that."

Rayco's suspicions soon resonated and what resulted was not good. First impressions mean a lot and to both Rayco and the attending official, ego apparently superceded all.

"One of the rules of amateur boxing is that you must have your facial hairs shaved. Being that I never and don't cut my face bald, I shaved my hairs very low. He told me to go shave and if I don't make it back to the scales on time, I'm disqualified. I went to my room to tell my team what had happened. I didn't touch my face! Then I went back to the weigh-in. The official looked at me and said, 'that's better.' I knew what it was then. I was fighting their pick to win."

Rayco always was fit and looked it. He immersed himself into a regimen and his appearance apparently set off some alarm bells to the opposing team. Again, his suspicions were accurate. What resulted just confirmed it.

"My physique had them scared, so they were trying to shake me. When I entered the ring, the ref came to me to do the mandatory inspection; mouthpiece, cup, correct headgear, gloves. When he inspected my gloves, he took me straight to the head official! They were really acting like I had something in my glove! The official finally waived me clear. I beat the shit out of this guy! He was bleeding from the nose and mouth!

"At the end of the 3rd round, Brian said, 'Champ, you're winning the fight! Go win this last round and it's in the bag!' The bell started and I was not going to be denied! I chased this dude all over the ring, hitting him with left hooks, straight right hands, etc! Brian was ecstatic at the end of the fight! He high five'd me. Hugged me! Congratulated me. Everything! When the decision was read, anger and disappointment took the place of joy. Every coach from our team wanted to see the score cards. A guy from Baltimore that had something to do with the venue, told us who to see, to look at the cards and appeal the decision. The guy ended up going to Las Vegas to fight in the National finals. He got knocked out in the first round."

Never one to give up easily, he became Rayco the Realist and set out to prove that he was the best. Before long, he had his chance. It would occur in his hometown, Pittsburgh.

"I won the Pittsburgh Golden Gloves Championship. Then I won the Golden Gloves State Championship, in Scranton, PA where I tied for fight of the night with a guy named Rasheem Jefferson. They gave him the award though. I agreed with the decision and was honored to be tied in the voting for fight of the night with this dude. Rasheem won the Golden Gloves National Championship, three times in a row at 119 lbs, including 2002! He was nice with his hands."

Yet, despite these impressive wins, he felt that his hometown had let him down. This was obvious to him from City Hall to the professional boxing associations of Western Pennsylvania. Did they still harbor a deep seated grudge from the former drug dealer?

"When I became a 2002 Golden Glove National Team Member, I didn't receive any recognition from the city of Pittsburgh media or amateur boxing associations. It's as if I didn't even matter! It didn't faze me though, because I was already used to it, being that every amateur fight that I went to outside of Pittsburgh, I paid my own way. I'm talking transportation, hotel and food, with the exception of the Golden Gloves Nationals. At the State finals, I went to check into the hotel that was supposed to be paid for by the people that ran the Western PA boxing, but was told that there was not a reservation for me. When I gave them the other coach's name, I was told that the reservation was cancelled! I wasn't fazed by this though. I already paid my way there. The hotel room was in the budget also."

Rayco knew what hardships life had dealt and he wasn't going to give in now. No, especially not now with so much at stake. He would persevere and show anyone who wanted to challenge him that he would not back down. Never!

"About a week or two before the National tournament, Iron City Pro

Boxing, which is headed by the director of the Western PA P.A.L., had its first professional boxing show. I took my son, Li'l Rayc, who was 9 yrs young. I purchased two $20 tickets to get in. One would think that since this was a P.A.L. tournament I would be introduced to the fight fans of Pittsburgh, PA, since I was the current, amateur heavy weight champion, but I wasn't mentioned at all. Instead, a buddy of mine who was also an amateur at the time, Verquan Kimbrough, was introduced. A few months prior, he won the title in one of the other amateur tournaments, at one of the lighter weight classes. As usual, I wasn't fazed by this. It was a small thing."

Yet, was it? Or was it another chance for the city to snub their native son? Maybe not such a small thing after all.

CHAPTER 19

Ever the optimist and the one in control, Rayco set out for his next bout. This would be a big event. A national one that would further give the boxing world a look at Rayco Saunders. Everyone would have to take notice. The destination would be far-off Denver.

"Me and my team prepared for the tournament like it was a world championship. Being that my trainer, Brian Noel, was not invited to the tournament, just as he wasn't invited to the other tournaments that I fought in, even though he was my trainer, I paid for his transportation to and from, as I always did. However, this time, he had to cover his lodging & food. We had two months to get everything in order.

"Everyone's plane ticket was purchased weeks before the flight date. I personally purchased the four tickets for my brother; Wachi, my woman, at that time, my brother's girlfriend and Brian. My flight was purchased by the tournament and was scheduled to fly out of Pittsburgh, to Denver, earlier than the others."

As expected with Brian, nothing went according to plan. Rayco's frustration at the person in charge is clearly evident as he recalls:

"When I arrived in Denver, I paid for a hotel suite for one week and waited for the other four to get there. They were scheduled to meet up in Pittsburgh and fly out together. I received a call informing me that Brian was a no call-no show. When I tried to reach him, I was unsuccessful. I instructed the others to leave without him. I received a message on my phone from Brian, telling me something about him having to watch his grandchildren, so he couldn't make it. I respected that. Anything that has to do with the caring for and security of children, is a first priority!"

But, it was a phone call from a friend that led Rayco to suspect that

Brian's family issues, however sincere sounding, were not on track. Once again, Rayco knew the deal.

"I received a call from my partna, Terrell. He questioned me as to why I didn't call Brian and left Brian in Pittsburgh! I was both angry and confused! It turns out that Brian lied to everyone. Why? Who knows! One can only speculate that he didn't have his food money together, as he didn't on previous out of town trips that made us return home much earlier than expected. Terrell informed me that he was called by Brian, and told that I didn't call him! That he was ready and waiting for me to pick him up, but I didn't show up! So I replayed the voice message that Brian left me, for Terrell. Terrell was upset. Neither of us could figure out why this dude would lie like that. This tournament was too important for me to have to deal with petty stuff like that!"

The trust issue. Coming back. Trust. What to do next? Dwell on it and let it stress you out or concentrate on the matters before you. Rayco knew what direction to take.

"I pushed it to the back of my mind. I had a job to do. I was scheduled to fight a guy named Rob Jacobs. It was his 6th straight time there. He was also ranked #6 in the country. I was prepared though to deal with anything. This was evident by my physical appearance. When it was almost time for my fight, I asked the team appointed coach, Barry Stumpf, for some mitt work to get warmed up for my fight. He told me he didn't have any mitts. Imagine that! A coach without one of the key components of boxing training! That's like a car without a transmission!"

The trainer a no show, Rayco now had to prepare for this latest setback. He hated liars and felt that he was lied to by Stumpf. Another way of trying to undermine him? He wouldn't let him have the day. But he kept thinking about these bizarre actions. It stayed with him.

"I would have preferred Barry to just say, 'I'm not giving you any mitt work! You're from Western PA. Our rival! I don't know you! You're not my fighter, so I don't care if you win or lose!'"

Regional rivalry aside, he was in Denver to fight and didn't want any part of the theatrics to stop him from getting his just due. He began, as he always did, with the training regimen that he knew worked well. He began to shadow box and concentrate.

"I shadow boxed and warmed up as best I could.

"In the fight, my opponent showed that he was going to try to out box me rather than bang with me. He constantly moved away from me and he was a southpaw (left handed) fighter. He was difficult to catch up to. The instruction from the team coach was worthless! He told me everything but the right thing. Me and Rob had one exchange. He landed one punch to the face. I landed none. My punches landed to the body. At the end of the 3rd round, I head back to my corner knowing I'm losing! I'm telling myself that it's all or nothing in the last round! Rob is walking to my corner with me! The coaches are on the ring apron like the fight is over! I'm confused now! In the open division, we fight 4 rounds, not 3! So I thought! It turned out that in the Nationals, all fights up to the semifinals are 3 rounds. Something else that the "team coach" didn't tell me! I lost."

Rayco was able to reflect on his loss and yet he knew there were issues. A large part of the problem lay with Barry Stumpf. Sooner or later, he would have to confront the harsh reality at hand.

"I stayed in Colorado for the remainder of the tournament. The day after I fought, I'm sitting in the stands with my woman, on the far end of the arena, up and away from the crowd, when I see Barry walking to the back with mitts on his hands! He was going to warm up Jason Gavern! He came to this end of the arena, because he thought that no one from the team would be over there! He felt my gaze and looked up right into it! He was so busted that he couldn't even break eye contact with me! The wall that him and Jason went behind is what finally broke our stare!"

Rayco couldn't let him go without knowing what he felt. The adrenaline set-in, but he contained himself. Was it worth a confrontation? Would it have any residual effects upon his career? He thought twice and made a quick decision.

"I started to run down there and do something to him, but I didn't want to mess up the nice time that I was having with my folks. So I stayed in my gentleman state of mind.

"Me and my folks enjoyed our six days in Denver, Colorado. It was a real nice city. The people were cool. I have some great memories of some great fights and good fighters. The 2002 Nationals had warriors in it. I can't name all of them but some of the guys that stand out in my head as I write this are Curtis Stevenson, Allen Green, Jaidon, Rasheem, Rock and Tiger, The Dargan brothers, Lajuan, Nemo and of course Rob Jacobs, because he was a smart fighter. He boxed me but banged with everyone else, until he got disqualified. 2002 had some bad boys! We didn't have all the flash of the Ray Leonards, but we were gritty fighters like the Marvin Haglers, my favorite fighter!"

Yet, it was decision time. So much had passed during his stint of four years in the Pennsylvania prison system. Much time passed. Four years! A lifetime to a fighter. It was again decision time for the Pittsburgh native. He knew what needed to be done. And like everything that Rayco did, he gave it his all.

"I made up my mind to turn professional. I was behind 4 years for being sent to prison for something that never happened! It was time to play catch-up, although I could never actually catch up! I called Greg Nixon and informed him of my intentions. After a brief conversation he said that he would call me back that Sunday. He never did!"

Disappointment? He wouldn't let it get in his way. He had a goal and like the hungry tiger, he set out to find his prey. No one would get in the way!

His search led him to Jimmy Cvetic.

"I heard that Iron City Pro Boxing was putting on a show soon, so I decided to go talk to the boss, Jimmy Cvetic.

"When I got to his office, I put my cards on the table. I said, 'I hear that you're having a show and I want to fight on it.'"

Cvetic sized up the fighter and liked what he saw.

"Jimmy said, 'Can you sell tickets?' He said that I had to sell approximately $1000 in tickets. This to me was not a problem. I was some what famous in Pittsburgh, inside of the urban communities! I use to have parties, etc. A lot of people followed my amateur career. This would be easy! Our conversation lasted all of 5 minutes and at the end of it, Jimmy said, 'You want on the show, it's done!'"

A man of his word, at last! Someone who would give him an opportunity to show his capability. He was ready and he would prove to everyone he was a class act.

"I may not agree with everything that he stands for or does, but for the way he handled that day in his office, I will always respect him for that! If I don't have nothing else in this world, I have my balls and my word! I respect any man greatly that stands by his word!"

Up to now, not all was going Rayco's way. Then, this conversation led to his introduction to the professional world of boxing. He was on his way!

Rayco's professional debut was electric. The gladiators were ready in the newly constructed arena and were eager for blood. Rayco would not disappoint the crowd. What happened next made the world, at least in the eyes of Western Pennsylvania, take notice. And notice they did!

"I made my pro debut on 03 August, 2002 at the David L. Lawrence Convention Center. Although I personally sold $3000 plus in tickets, I was paid $400! I fought a guy named Wayne Holloway. I actually told the match maker to get this guy. My partna Rick Manning, saw him before I did, and I think he was a little nervous, because he instantly started talking about how this guy was built.

"He said, 'I seen this guy Holloway! It's going to look like a body building contest when you two get in the ring!'

"Jimmy also showed me that he was nervous too, when he said to me, 'the word on this guy is that he's durable. He's going to take you the distance, but you should be able to handle him!' When my ring walk song came on ("Down for my n***as", by C-Murder & Snoop Dogg), the crowd went crazy! To this day when I watch the film of that fight, I feel the electricity! I knocked Wayne out 1:46 into the first round!"

Rayco Saunders had officially arrived! But there was still the issue of Brian.

"Brian was still my trainer up until my fourth pro fight. He, like 98% of the people associated with boxing in Pittsburgh, was greedy, possessive and selfish! He told me that he wanted a contract. My career as a pro fighter wasn't even secured yet! Further more, unless you have and are contributing to my career financially, you are hired on a fight to fight basis! He showed me, by not coming to the gym for weeks, that it wasn't about me, it was all about him, so I moved on!"

The attitude and the trust issues wouldn't deter Rayco. Yet, he

178 | Rayco Saunders

wouldn't give in to those just out to use him. He had been through enough in his young years and he wasn't about to allow just anyone to tag along for the ride. He knew that boxing was a brutal sport. He also knew of fighters that had been conned into contracts and, after being bloodied-up in the ring, were forced to let their hard-earned dollars fall into the hands of greedy promoters. The warning flags were there for Rayco. He always had a suspicion whenever anyone wanted a part of him and he wouldn't let the avarice and greed get out of control. He had his reliable and faithful pals – Rick and Terrell. He would allow them to be part of the upcoming career of one Rayco Saunders.

"I was doing a great job at managing my own career. I still had, and still have currently, two of my closest partnaz, Terrell and Rick, in my corner. I traveled to different cities, such as, Philadelphia and Detroit to spar with their best. I was undefeated at 6-0. I just knocked out an undefeated fighter named Jeff Fox, my last fight! I was getting calls everyday from people in the fight game! People were meeting with me, etc! It was a beautiful thing to be a free agent! I told the promoter and match maker to get a guy named Greg Wright, from Detroit. It was time for me to step it up. While I was in prison, I wrote down a few names of guys that I wanted to fight, when I would watch them on TV."

It was time to square off with Greg Wright. If he could defeat him, he would get the respect and recognition he needed.

"Greg Wright was the former N.A.B.F. champion. He was a good fighter, but I knew I could beat him. Beat Greg Wright, and I would have got a deal with a major promoter! Although this was probably the most boring fight of my career, I won the fight! Greg ran and jabbed the entire fight, except for the final round.

"At the end of the 5th round, Jimmy Cvetic, came to my corner and instructed my corner men to tell me that I was winning the fight on all score cards and not to do nothing stupid! I wasn't going to back off! I'm not a back-off type of fighter! At the sound of the bell, I was on the attack. In a flash, Greg caught me with a veteran move and hit me with a good upper cut! He hurt me, but I had sense enough to grab him. For some reason, my whole face was burning and my vision was distorted! Towards the middle of the round, my vision cleared up and I was back! I re-took control of the round until the final bell. While we were waiting on the decision, Greg came over and congratulated me on the win. He told me how strong I was, etc."

What happened next came to Saunders as a thunderbolt! Was his past coming back to haunt him? Even in Pittsburgh, the tough, no-holds-barred city!

CHAPTER 20

"It was announced that it was a split decision! I won hands down! This couldn't be! Not in my city! All of the judges were from PA. Two of them went against me! 'Til this day, I feel that their decision was based on my past and not the fight! But as I've shown over and over again, I can't and won't be held down!"

Yet, afterwards, some questions lingered with Rayco's partners. Was he really in his best form? Was there something in his character that just didn't sit well? His partners approached him and began to address some concerns. It centered on a trip just a few weeks before the bout.

"One of my partnas questioned my readiness for this fight, because we went to South Beach, Florida, just three weeks before the fight. This was paradise! I'm talking women, from what seemed like every corner of the country! I never seen anything like this! There were parties everywhere that didn't end until almost sunrise! I partied hard, too! I had the pleasure of meeting a few women. I really enjoyed some of their company, too. I went with both of my younger brothers, Raymont and Wachi, and also, a few of my partnas. We stayed in one of the premiere hotels for a week. There were a lot of celebrities at this hotel, too. I was about 4 feet away from Lisa Ray, one time. If she didn't have two big body guards with her, I would've said something to her. I didn't want to have to kick no ass though! One of the highlights of the trip for me was when me and Wachi went to hip-hop artist, Fat Joe's pool party."

Rayco enjoyed the taste of the good life. Fat Joe's party stayed with him. He liked what he witnessed. The good life?

Fat Joe's party. What an event. As Rayco explains:

"It was at one of the hotels on South Beach. There were people dancing everywhere! I filmed the party from the time we were there, 'til the time that we left. They had a few contests that night, but the best one was when the DJ announced that the first female that takes off all of her clothes and jumps into the pool wins $1000! I think most of the girls in the party got naked!"

Quite an incentive, no doubt. Yet, there was still a fight coming up.

"Although I knew that I had a very important fight coming up, the temptations of Miami, over came me! Did this trip have something to do with my performance in the fight? Maybe, maybe not."

His trip over, it was now high noon for him. He had a defeat. He was ready now for another fight.

"Exactly fourteen days later, after I suffered my first defeat, I fought at the Pittsburgh, Expo Mart. I was actually asked to carry this guy for a few rounds! I carried him all right! I knocked the him out in 32 seconds! He stayed down for about 15 minutes! I didn't care, just as the people that took the fight away from me two weeks earlier didn't care!"

The boxing world finally took notice. He was ready to appear on nationwide TV.

Great exposure but at a price. Literally.

"This knockout gave me the opportunity to fight on ESPN2. This opportunity came with conditions though. I had to pay my opponent and my pay would be based on how many tickets I sold! If I couldn't pay my opponent, then I couldn't fight and if I didn't sell enough tickets, then I would not get paid. I was given enough tickets to pay my opponent and myself, providing that I sold them all, which I did."

His opponent would be Steve Fischer.

"Steve Fischer was my roughest fight to date! It lasted about 5 minutes, including the minute rest, which resulted in a knockout victory for me, but I received a major concussion! It was so bad, when I tried to laugh, it hurt. Against the advice of my doctor, I accepted a fight scheduled to take place 3 weeks later. It was a rematch between me and Greg Wright. Since the ESPN2 fight, I had a new addition in my corner. Cool Norman. He was in his late 40's, a Muslim and had a couple children close to my age. Me, Norm and Rel, did most of the traveling out of town to the other gyms. We had a lot of fun. Our best trip was when we went to Detroit! I'll just say this; the strip clubs were open at 2:00 pm every-day!"

The boxer, the party-goer got what he wanted – a rematch. Ignoring his doctor's advice – a concussion just three weeks prior, he prepared, as he always did, for any fight. Sparing, jump roping and sparing again.

"So we're getting ready for the rematch. My team had a great plan, 'Every time I punch, throw a combination!' We also worked on a counter move for Greg's overhand right. It was the miscalculation of this punch that ended my night. After the first round, I was winning the fight easily. I was executing the fight plan masterfully! I seen Greg's right hand, as if it was moving in slow motion. Therefore, it never landed. I decided to go into the overhand right, let it slide over my left shoulder and hit Greg with a counter right uppercut! Here it comes! There I go! Boom! Vibration! No sound! People are telling me to sit down. I don't want to sit down!

"Everything was happening so fast. People were asking for pictures and autographs! When I finally made it back to the locker room, I asked Norm, what happened. He gave me the details. I asked him did I get knocked out? He told me that I got hit, but I fought on, even harder than before, but I was hurt!

"About a minute after the first punch, I got hit with another good shot and went down. I beat the ten count, but the ref stopped the fight, with one second left in the round! When I spoke to the referee days later, he told me that if he knew that there was one second left, he wouldn't have stopped the fight."

Disoriented, a bit confused and no doubt still suffering from the concussion, Rayco headed for the locker area. With little time to reflect, he realized he had signed one too many autographs! The result was soon apparent.

"I was so disoriented and everything was happening so fast in and out of the ring, that I received my check when I got out of the ring. By the time I made it to the dressing room, I lost and never found it! I think I autographed it and gave it to someone! I was later paid again though."

A real wake up experience! Stubborn to the core and not listening to medical advice, he emerged luckily enough to keep the fire burning inside him. But this was one tough episode and one not soon to be forgotten. Like most experiences in life, good or bad, he dealt with it and then dusted himself off for the next bout. Yet, he would not soon forget this night.

"This was a learning experience for me. I moved on. I went on to fight and continued winning! Out of all the Pittsburgh fighters, I picked and fought the roughest fights. I was even questioned by the promoter, of why I was picking such tough fights. My response was, 'Fight the best to be the best!'

"In between time, I was still trying to enjoy life! I just completed a four year prison term and definitely was trying to make up for the time that I lost! To me, when I went to prison, I lost my life! When I was released, I was resurrected! As all men, I had many fantasies! While in prison, I decided that once I was released, I would make them reality! Every man that I know dreams about making love to two women at the same time! I made it happen... a few times! There is nothing better to watch than two soft, sexy, beautiful women, touching, caressing, kissing and pleasing each other! Yes, this is my only bias in life... I love sexy women that love sexy women! Threesomes, foursomes and moresomes, I done'm! I gave and attended orgy parties! Me and my brothers made many consensual sex tapes with different women! With my younger brothers, Raymont & Wachi by my side, the new millennium was the start of a new beginning! Some people will look down on some of the things that I speak on. I say two things to them: 1. When you are 20 something, enjoy it! 2. Check what you are doing before you check someone else. How one chooses to live life is between them and the creator!"

Conquest both in the ring and in the bedroom made the local boxer a celebrity. Soon he was noticed and got the attention of the media. And the women! Oh yes, the women!

"I did an interview on a show called Black Horizons. In the interview, I stated that I would win a title in in my second year as a pro. On 2 August, 2004, I accomplished just what I said that I would. I won the North American Boxing Council, cruiserweight world championship! I beat James "Hurricane" Walton, in a decision. But before I could achieve this goal, I went through more hardship, some almost fatal, but I came through it, as I did and do everything else!"

It happened on a cold, wintery day. Much like the days of his past when he peddled his wares in the neighborhoods of the Steel City. A wintry mix of wind and cold that made the face freeze up and had everyone who ventured outside take a few minutes to secure a hat, scarf and gloves to combat mother nature's wrath.

The weather was the least of Rayco Saunders' worries that cold February day. The news that awaited him would make him rethink the past and wonder where he was headed. The news was about to be delivered to him at of all places – the neighborhood barbershop.

"On 12 February 2004, I'm at my partna, Calvin's, Unisex Hair salon, getting my face trimmed. I'm in the barber chair when I get a call from Jimmy Cvetic!"

It was a call that would change him.

"He says, 'Rayc! Where are you right now?' I found this question to be very odd, reason being: the tone of his voice and he was an ex cop who still dealt with a lot of cops! Also, if anyone calls me and that's the first thing out of their mouth, I'm cautious! I answered carefully, 'Chillin! Why? What's up?' Jimmy says, 'I need you to come to my office right now! I mean right now! Be very careful! Watch your back! Watch everyone and everything around you!'

"I get to Jimmy's office, which is located in downtown Pittsburgh on Ross St. Instead of taking the elevator to his 3rd floor office, I take the stairs. I didn't know what he had in store for me, but I wasn't going to take the usual route! At every floor, I looked around cautiously, expecting the unexpected! Nothing happened though. When I got to Jimmy's office, he was there with another guy, who was in a suit. Jimmy introduced him as Detective Steve Hitchings. After the brief introduction, Hitchings got right down to business! 'Rayco, there have been two attempts on your life!' I didn't flinch. This was not a shock or surprise to me. I was interested to know how in the hell does this cop know this and who was behind it, so I listened! 'Someone tried to take your life at your residence and at the gym! Do you know of anyone or why someone would want to hurt you?' I went through the reasons of why people want to harm other people and could only come up with one reason. I haven't wronged anyone. I don't owe anyone any money. It has to be about a woman!

That's the only reason that I can think of! Then I asked who tried to take my life. Hitchings told me that they were still investigating and that they should have the final guy in custody soon!"

The past was coming full circle.

"I went home and immediately took the necessary precautions! Although I had a selection of bullet proof vests hanging up in my closet, I wasn't wearing one when I got the call from Jimmy. Flashbacks of 1995 came to me! When I was shot in my chest, I had a bullet proof vest, at home, laying on my floor! I swore not to repeat that! I made the necessary phone calls and informed the necessary people! Now it was a waiting game!"

The old Rayco – cautious, ever vigilant and suspicious set in. It had sustained him before and it would be his strength again. But he wouldn't let these circumstances take over. He would still be in charge. He knew what to do next.

"I went on with my day-to-day activities. A couple of my partnas have permits to carry firearms, so I was rarely unprotected. A bullet proof vest became and still is a part of my daily dress code. It didn't take long for Hitchings to get back to me. The next day I get a call from Jimmy telling me to come to his office. Again I went and again there was Hitchings. This time he told me everything... well, almost everything! 'Rayco, you were right! It was about a woman! Do you know a Julie?' I said, I did. Hitchings went on: 'Our plain clothes detectives pulled over a stolen car in Beltzhoover. In it were two guys, Arthur Paul Smith and Jason Korey! The cops found some guns and some heroin! When they arrested them, Arthur started telling them that he knew of a planned hit on someone! Arthur said, Keilan Walls, payed Jason Korey a kilo of cocaine to kill Rayco Saunders, because Rayco was messing around with his girlfriend Julie! Shawn Davis, a.k.a Fat Grim, provided the AR-15 assault rifle and showed us where Rayco lives and what gym he goes to! Jason walked past Rayco, while he was sitting in his car at the gym and tried to shoot him, but the gun didn't fire! We also waited for him at his house, but he never came outside!' I just listened! Then Hitchings, says, 'Our boys raided Shawn Davis's house and the AR-15 was there! He was arrested on the scene! Shawn Davis made bond and came in with his lawyer Mark Lancaster, and gave us a nice statement and agreed to testify against Jason and Keilan!'"

It all became clear to him now. Past events, however trivial at first, made an impression. He started to recall some of them. It started with that night outside the gym.

"I started replaying certain events in my mind while Hitchings was talking. I recalled the night when Jason was outside of the gym. He actually walked past my partna, who also had a white Cadillac and was sitting in it when Jason tried to do his walk by! I was still in the gym. My partna Rel, who is licensed to carry and was fully strapped, called me on my cell phone to tell me about these strange individuals outside of God's Gym!"

Yes, outside the gym. He started to recall what had happened.

"The day that they were sitting outside of my house waiting for me to come out, I was at Julie's house! I went to a fight that evening in West Virginia and when I returned to Pittsburgh, I stayed the night at Julie's! Lucky for the would-be hitmen, though! I informed Hitchings, if I would have been home that morning, and the would-be hitmen would have been sitting outside my house, they would still be sitting there... in a deteriorated form! Dead! Gone! Deceased! No more! Regardless of man's law, one of God's laws is 'self preservation'! That supercedes any of man's laws! I will protect and defend myself when necessary, by any means necessary!"

The anger, ever rising inside, he knew not only that his life was in jeopardy but also his young son. A son he was raising as a single parent.

"Although I didn't show it, I was furious that these individuals had the balls to come to my house where my single child at that time, laid his head and to the gym where I trained 10-15 year young, boys and girls how to box! I didn't know these characters, Jason Korey, Keilan Walls or Arthur Smith, but this cocksucker Shawn Davis, I knew well! He was all sissy in a fat man's body!"

He let the detectives explain. When it came to family, it was clear to Rayco that his top priority was to ensure their well-being. As a good father, he wouldn't let anyone compromise him.

"I paid attention to everything that detective Hitchings said, especially when he started telling me the names of certain individuals that were selling drugs for other certain individuals! I found it not surprising but amazing how he knew exactly what was going down! He was running off so many names, that I thought for a second that he was trying to draw a reaction from me! He touched on specific situations that I knew about, but was myself trying to get all the details of!

"He shot the name, 'Greg' at me but I didn't flinch. The last name of this person threw me off. I assumed that he was of Euro decent, because of the last name. It was when he started talking about how Greg got caught with 6 kilograms of cocaine coming from California, that I put a face to the name! I knew that this individual got caught up, but I didn't know to what extent! I knew Greg well! He used to buy from me heavy, before I went to prison! He was the guy that I did the deal with over the phone from the Allegheny County Jail in 1997. Out of nowhere, he would pop up on me and tell me to get with him on some business! Before I got the confirmation about Greg from Hitchings, I knew something wasn't right because he disappeared. He never missed a Pittsburgh fight! I asked him where he's been. He said, 'Man, I was down in Florida, laying low, enjoying that good weather!' This confirmed that something wasn't right! Word had it that he got busted! He says he was on vacation! I haven't seen him since Hitchings gave me this information, but I hear that he's around. Just like rats, they never go away once they're around!"

Rayco had to be there for the arraignment proceedings. He couldn't miss this. He had to see them up close. The people who wanted to snuff him out. He had to be there.

"A few months later, all of the would-be killers are scheduled for court. Being that I didn't know Jason or Keilan and haven't seen Grim since the incident, I wanted these guys to see my face! I wanted to see their faces! I thought that being that I was the victim in this case, I would receive some form of notification, informing me of the trial date. Didn't happen! I had to use my various resources to get this information."

The target of a 'hit,' he felt that he was entitled to know when the court date was scheduled. A public trial. An event that any citizen could attend. Why wasn't he notified of it?

"They say what you do in the dark will come to the light! It came to light why I was never notified of the court proceedings, even though I was the victim!"

Rayco didn't flinch when, arriving in court, he came face-to-face with his would-be assassin. His anger got the best of him and he tore into the suspect, Keilan Walls.

"It was fate that I would bump into Keilan Walls in the hallway, outside of the courtroom. The first thing that I wanted to do when I seen him was whoop his ass! Had we been in the restroom, only one of us would have walked out! I immediately confronted him! While I was asking him about the situation, I called him every derogatory term that I could think of! He wouldn't respond. He just kept his distance. Finally, he spoke.

'What do you want to do, fight me?'

I said, 'yes muthafucka!'

He said, 'Do what you feel you need to do!'

I said, 'I got you on my radar! I'ma see you!' I knew not to do anything stupid in the courthouse! Once we got outside was different story!"

It was during this heated courtroom hall exchange that Rayco heard something from Keilan that would explain it all.

"Then Keilan says something that brought me to full attention. 'What you heard is wrong! I didn't do this! Grim is putting this on me because he's trying to protect some dude named JC!' The mention of JC made me very interested and willing to hear Keilan out! I told him to start from the beginning. 'Before I went back to the halfway house, I rode pass Julie's crib and saw your car. When I went back to the halfway house, I was upset. Everyone knew that I was upset because I didn't speak to anyone. I usually kick it with Jason and Grim, so they kept asking me what's wrong! I said, Rayco is messing with my girl! Jason says to me, I don't like him anyway. My boy JC told me and Grim to kill him before he gets out of prison! Do you want me to handle that for you too? I said, yeah, because I was upset, but I didn't agree to pay him anything! Grim is the one that came to me saying that they wanted a whole chicken (kilogram of cocaine)! I didn't even respond! I just looked at him. Grim told me about you and JC's feud. I ask Keilan how do I know that he is telling the truth. He says, how do you think that I know you and him are feuding or that he's locked up? I don't even know who JC is! Grim is trying to use me as the scapegoat and now he's testifying against me and Jason!' When Keilan saw that I wasn't too convinced, he offered to get the preliminary transcripts for me.

"Keilan took me to his lawyer's office and instructed the secretary to get me a copy of the transcript 'OTN G 273340'. Sure enough, there it was! Shawn Davis, witness for the Commonwealth!"

Suddenly, it became apparent to Rayco what all this was about.

"I would be lying if I said I wasn't surprised! I was shocked, disturbed, then upset when I got to pages 124 & 125 and read (DA, Lisa Pellegrini): 'Mr. Davis, prior to today's proceedings, had you made arrangements to be interviewed by Pittsburgh detectives, in particular, Detective Hitchings?' (Shawn Grim Davis): 'He picked me up.' (DA): 'Did you know you were going to be interviewed by him?' (Shawn Grim Davis): 'I knew from a prior number of years ago to go and talk to him!'

"A prior number of years ago!!! I read the transcripts over and over again, and kept thinking to myself, 'Shawn 'Grim' Davis has been dealing with Hitchings for years!' Furthermore, Hitchings played me! He made it seem like he never knew any of these guys! Here it is the whole time, he's been knowing Grim for years!"

It all made sense now. So clear and yet so disturbing.

"After reading the transcripts and doing a little investigating myself, I summed it! Jason Korey & crew had been set up. They were given the drugs! Then the police were notified! That's how the police knew what car to surround, with guns drawn, despite the absence of a traffic violation! I am even further convinced being that Shawn Grim Davis, despite being caught red-handed with the AR-15 Assault Rifle, was only convicted of criminal mischievous for that offense!"

CHAPTER 21

Rayco's life now seemed to take a different direction. The issue of trust once again came full circle. Who to trust? What to do? Added to the mix was his boxing career, a career that had been put on hold due to imprisonment. And now the possibility of a hit. Anyone in his situation would be stressed out, yet Rayco, ever the one in control, decided to take matters into his own hands. He felt he had no choice.

"As I said before, my title fight almost didn't happen because of issues that were going on surrounding this failed assassination attempt. I got word that Shawn Davis was riding around with an AK-47 assault weapon with two 30 round clips, looking for me. If I hear that you are looking for me, I'll make it easy for you to find me!"

It didn't take long for him to find out.

"I got a call from one of my spotters, letting me know where Shawn was. I immediately made myself present. When we saw each other, I could smell the fear coming out of his skin! An altercation followed and Shawn ran away like the coward he was!"

What happened next only added to the drama and made Rayco ever more vigilant.

"I received two abnormal phone calls that day. The first was from Shawn, via my woman at that time. She phoned me, a little distraught because Shawn called her, in hopes that he could get her to convince me to forgive and forget our issues! As he told her, 'I grew up under Rayc, I know how he gets down!'"

An even more bizarre call came from the detective investigating the case.

"The second call was from Detective Steve Hitchings. He asked me did Shawn shoot at me? I would not answer that. He told me that he would revoke his bond if I said yes. I still didn't answer the question. If you do something to me, I don't want the cops to get you. Men take care of themselves!"

Shortly afterward, Rayco would find the police were not going to let him off the hook. Too much had transpired and he had a history with the police that was well known.

"Being that my car suffered a few gun wounds, I drove around in a different car for a week. When I switched back, the police immediately pulled me over, despite the absence of a traffic violation! I was asked for my driving information, which I produced. While I'm waiting, a lot of other police cars started pulling up. This didn't bother me until a cop, that had nothing to do with the stop started talking shit to me! I really dislike pussy-type individuals that get tough when they feel they have the advantage over someone else. A truly tough person is tough 365 days of the year, like myself! This dude doing all this talking was a coward!"

Keeping his cool, Rayco was ready when the police began to approach the vehicle. But he sensed something was about to happen. He didn't have to wait very long!

"Now the lieutenant and sergeant were all up on my driver side window, as if they were going to try to snatch me out of my car! So I leaned to my right and asked them, 'What's up?' They repeated it back to me. In my side mirror, I could see police with dogs approaching my car. The cop that was talking shit was still talking shit! The lieutenant was now reaching for something! I decided it was time to go! Did I have something on me... maybe... maybe not! When I turned to look at the lieutenant, he sprayed me in my face with pepper spray! I started my car and pulled off! I couldn't see nothing! I couldn't even breathe properly! The Creator was with me as I drove as fast as I could to get away! When I was caught, in the surrounding area where I was caught, the police found a bag of marijuana. The report said I was seen throwing it! This was not true! I had probation, so a detainer was placed on me. I was scheduled to fight at Heinz Field, for the N.A.B.C. title in a month, so I had to get out. My probation officer, Dave P. was understanding. He lifted the detainer and I made bail."

At court, Rayco, aware of the seriousness of the charges, decided to confront the officer who had issued the report. Never one to back down, he was ready to face off.

"I hate being lied on. If I did it, then I did it! Don't make up something that didn't happen! When I saw the arresting officer "Able", at court, I immediately approached him and asked him why did he lied. He admitted that he didn't see me throw anything. He also told the judge that he didn't see me throw anything and it could have belonged to anyone! The judge still held it for trial!"

He had an important fight coming up and, like most professionals ready for the big event, he had trained hard. He was ready and the legal issues were a constant cloud that he had to address. Yet, he was ready and wanted to get into the ring. Any other person might capitulate or try to postpone the bout, but not Rayco Saunders. He wanted to show his home town and anyone within earshot that he wouldn't give up and wanted the opportunity to prevail. And prevail he did! He describes the night of the fight in his hometown.

"My journey to this title fight was long and hard, but I made it. This fight was historic in Pittsburgh because 53 years prior, the Rooney's hosted an outdoor, no-roof fight at Forbes Field. Jersey Joe Walcott vs. Ezzard Charles! Now I was fighting at Heinz Field, under the lights and the stars! It was a interesting fight for many reasons First, I contacted the sanctioning organization to inquire about their various title belts. I was told that I could fight for the biggest title, but that the promoter had to conduct the business. I introduced them. I was arrested a month before the fight. I got cut on my left eye lid, while sparring, three weeks before the fight. 18 stitches!"

Despite it all, Rayco was as relentless in the ring as he was in life. This was his time to shine. And he came through!

"Through the first seven rounds, I was in control. My trainer was telling me to take off and rest a few rounds, but I was very confident in my conditioning, so I kept working! As the fight went on, the ring became very slippery from both our perspiration and the humidity in the air. It was hard to throw a meaningful combination and maintain your balance at the same time. In the 8th round, my left leg started to cramp bad! I couldn't put any pressure on it! Then my right leg started to cramp!

When I threw any power shot my legs felt as if they were going to collapse! I felt very confident that I was winning the fight. I couldn't take any chance of slipping and it being ruled a knock down, so I moved cautiously. My opponent, James "Hurricane" Walton, sensed that something was wrong and got aggressive! I kept my composure and when the final bell rung, I knew that I was the new N.A.B.C. Cruiserweight World Champion!"

Standing there, with all eyes on the announcer awaiting the results of the judges, Rayco knew this was his moment in the sun. Despite the chaotic often desperate and unimaginable existence he had experienced, it all came down to this night. He was ready.

Seminal events have a profound effect upon us. Rayco knew this was one. He would get the recognition and the stature that befit a champion. Respect, admiration and the knowledge that he was at his prime. It was indeed his magic moment. He wanted desperately to fit in and finally the boxing world would have to give him the respect he deserved. It was his time. Things were changing in his life.

"At that moment, everything negative in my life didn't matter. This was a time to cherish. I was surrounded by family and friends. I had the Fathers' Coalition there, which was one of many organizations that helped children, that I invited and paid for to see a live professional fight. It was a joyful time.

"After my next few fights, which I won, I was ranked #26 by the WBC (World Boxing Council). I showed the monthly rankings to the Pittsburgh promoter, but got the feeling that he didn't understand the ramifications of this position. I was offered a contract to fight exclusively in Pittsburgh. As I read through it, I laughed. It stated everything in detail what I was to give to the promotional company, but stated nothing what I, the fighter, was supposed to get. It promised not one fight, and more importantly, it failed to state what I would be paid for the 6 years that I was to sign for! I kindly handed the contract back and said, 'No thanks'. I was told that it would be revised. I was never asked to a meeting about signing a contract again, in Pittsburgh."

Ever vigilant and suspect, Rayco turned down what he knew would be a locked in contract with no avenue to move. Yet, he was a proven terror in the ring and was in demand. Despite the recent series of triumphs, he still felt shortchanged. He could smell a rat a mile away and this was one of those moments. His past made him strong and this event was another niche that only contributed to his inner toughness.

"I fought all but one fight in Pittsburgh up to this point. I drew crowds over 2000 people. I always fought the hardest fight out of all the Pittsburgh fighters. I took pennies for fights that I should have been paid way more to fight! I did a hell of a lot to prove that I was willing to work with everyone around me! For two years, I done this!"

But, something else was about to happen. Rules are rules in the boxing world and everywhere else. Rayco was soon to find himself once again embroiled in a new challenge. This not did not occur in the ring but as a result of it.

"One day I received an email from the N.A.B.C. asking me did I fight on a certain day. I answered that I did. I was emailed again that, 'You are being stripped of your title. When the promoter pays the sanctioning fee, you will be reinstated as the champion!' Once a fighter wins a title he has to defend it in a certain amount of time. When he defends the title, the promoter has to pay a sanctioning fee! This is how the alphabet soup organizations make there money, in exchange, the fighter gets recognition. Thus I was stripped!"

Refusing to give in, he decided to go it alone. His pride intact, he moved on. Fight when offered the chance and go wherever the offer took him. Another journey for a fighter who had been through it all and, with more hurdles to conquer, it made him all the stronger and determined.

"With this, on top of the other things that happened too, I felt no support, so I moved on. I started fighting all over the country. The money was way better! I didn't have to sell tickets and I got a chance to travel around the country for free! The downside was I wouldn't have much time to prepare for the fight and if I didn't knock out my opponent, no matter how convincingly that I beat him, I wouldn't win the fight!"

Yet, his past was quickly catching up with him once again. Old grudges apparently won't die and soon a new challenge, far greater than the boxing ring, once again emerged. This happened during a workout while training for the next bout.

"One day, I'm training at 3rd Ave Gym. Detective Steve Hitchings and his partner stop in. Hitchings tells me that James Jones, a.k.a. "Snitch Lock", is coming home from prison. I tell him that I'm looking forward to seeing him! It's been 8 years since the last time that I saw that Bitch! Hitchings purposely aggravated the situation by saying how big Jones was, etc! I ended the conversation with, 'Jones was a bitch before he got muscles! Jones is a bitch after he got muscles!' Then I continued to work-out. Rick Manning, who was present, asked me who the police were talking about and why they would instigate trouble. I said, 'because they like trouble.'"

Rayco, always the iconoclast, was now ready to demonstrate his disdain in the courtroom. His attire said it all. He was ready to face those who tried to have him killed and he was determined to get noticed. And he did just that! His appearance sent a powerful message for all to see – it got the attention he wanted.

"In 2005, the trial was supposed to start for the guys that tried to assassinate me. Although I was the victim in this case, I wasn't notified of this trial by neither the district attorney or the police! I had to find out through my sources, that a trial was taking place! I usually would never show up as a witness, but this was a special occasion! I wanted to watch Shawn Davis "snitch"! I wanted to see everyone of these guys faces and I wanted them to see mine! I even got dressed for the occasion! I wore a black T-shirt with a big red stop sign on the front of it that said "STOP SNITCHING" in white letters, and a matching baseball cap!"

Never one to shy away, he immediately caught the eye of a young district attorney. The assistant DA approached him immediately and the following confrontation ensured:

"While I was looking in the court room where the trial was supposed to take place, an assistant district attorney named Lisa Pellegrini approached me and told me to turn my shirt inside out. I refused of course! She then threatened me with jail if I didn't take my shirt and hat off. I laughed at her! So she went and got the sheriffs to escort me from the building, stating that my clothes were worn to intimidate witnesses! When I told her that I was the victim/witness, she changed her statement to, 'Those clothes are not allowed in the court house!' So much for the first amendment of the US Constitution! I put my hand up in a halt position, made an about-face and walked away in the middle of her sentence!

The sheriff that escorted me from the building, told me that she agreed with the stance that I was taking against these guys being allowed to commit crime after crime and remain free just because they give up information on other people."

His courtroom theatrics didn't go unnoticed by the press. Both the local and national papers ran a feature story on him. The <u>Pittsburgh Post Gazette</u> and <u>USA Today</u> both featured the defiant pugilist in the courtroom drama, complete with a picture of him in his rebellious garb. Rayco sent forth a message and the word got out. Demand for interviews started and his name became at once a source of controversy and curiosity. Who is this fellow that would dare appear in a courtroom defying the rules and not yielding an inch? It was classic Rayco and it was the real deal. Theater, drama with a right to be heard. He wanted his way. He got it. His name was now out there.

"Shortly after, the 'Stop Snitching' campaign took off I was on the front page of USA Today! I did interviews on MSNBC while I was in Florida. BET, while I was in Atlantic City. PBS, NPR radio, just to name a few! I was asked to do "60 Minutes", but at the advice of my management at the time, I declined."

Rayco knew that the controversy wouldn't let up and he needed to define himself and in the process let the world know what the 'Stop Snitching' campaign meant. Normally anathema to law-and-order folks, Saunders knew he had to come full circle and explain his actions in the Pittsburgh courtroom. He said it best:

"As always, the haters tried to misconstrue my words. They tried to make it seem as if I was against everyday ordinary people reporting crime if they were witness to it. This was not the case! I always said that if you were an everyday law abiding citizen and something happened to you or you witnessed something, you have every right to go to the police. But if you were gang banging, selling drugs, shooting at people or doing anything that is classified as criminal activity, get caught and tell on someone else or something happens to you and you go to the police... YOU ARE A SNITCH!"

Hating the hypocrisy of it all, he knew that his action would not make him popular and people would look to his past. They would criticize and ridicule him, but he knew he had to come to terms with this issue. Yet, he was determined to have his voice heard and he felt the venue that best served that avenue of discourse was his unscheduled appearance in court with the message on the shirt and hat. He set out to show Pittsburgh and anyone else what he meant. Regardless of their station in life, be it law enforcement gone awry or street thugs, hustlers or associates, everyone was subject to the wrath of Rayco. Indeed, it was classic Rayco and he set out to expose the mess. He was a man on a mission and, like everything he did, he gave it his all.

"Before, while and after the 'Stop Snitching' campaign, I exposed a few of Pittsburgh, PA's high profile snitches! Some police hate me for this! Not because I exposed the snitches to other people that are classified as criminals, but because I have exposed their shady practices to the law abiding citizens! Law abiding, tax paying citizens have the right to know that murderers, child molesters and some drug dealers roam the streets unrestricted, and are paid up to $60,000 a year, given housing and cars, on the tax payers dollar, because they supply information to the police that keeps the arrest quota up, even if they falsely accuse someone! In some cases, the snitch will commit a crime and blame it on someone else just to keep his or her end of the deal!"

He wouldn't give in and he was determined to be heard! In the meantime, he had established himself as a professional in the boxing world and his love of the profession didn't deter him any further. He was still a boxer and didn't lose sight of his goals. Training every day allowed him to concentrate on his love of the sport. The lure of the boxing gym with its faded posters of past local boxing events and the smells of the gym—from the leather gloves to the acrid locker area, became a place to let loose and be himself. Comfortable in his own skin, he never lost sight of his goals.

"While all of these things were going on, I still trained hard! 7 a.m., three hard miles of running! 10 a.m., 1½ hour of weight training! 11:30 a.m., 2 hours of boxing training! I also trained younger fighters, including Lil Rayco."

In the meantime, events were rapidly unfolding in his life. Rayco had to ponder his future which was now going through changes from his career to his family. His life experience, both on the street and in prison toughened him. Afraid of no one, he soon found himself in a new dilemma.

"James Jones was released from prison, just as Hitchings said. When I found out, hatred, anger and rage hit me! I wanted to walk up to him, in broad daylight, and share my feelings with him! But I was smarter than that! Prison matured me far beyond what I or anyone would have thought! Although unorthodox, prison, for me was an educational experience. Prisons are filled with experts in every conceivable type of crime. Thousands of criminal are penned up day and night with nothing to do but share knowledge amongst each other. I learnt many things. My son needed me to be here! My second child, Jelani, was about to be born in a few months! My life wasn't just about me anymore. So I chilled!"

Pondering his future and wanting to be there for his sons, Rayco decided he would be a father first. He knew what it was like growing up with a single parent and how dysfunctional families are challenged; he set out to be a dad to his sons. Yet, he had to deal with the problems surrounding his life. A life-threatening event soon unfolded.

"Snitch Lock sent me a few messages, telling me that we were older and wiser now. Our beef was when we were young guys and that he wanted to leave that in the past and just live drama free. A few months later in broad daylight, Snitch Lock shot up my car when I was driving Lil Rayc, who was 12 at that time, to his boxing match!

"We were on our way to my house to get his boxing equipment, when I heard a loud pop and felt something hit my wheel! At first, I thought that I ran over something in the street, because I was looking to my right when it happened! As I was trying to look out in front of my car, I seen him out the corner of my eye on the left side of my car! Gunfire from the muzzle! My driver side window collapses! I put my left arm up to shield my head! Gas pedal to the floor, I got less than a second to decide left, straight or right turn! I'm leaning to my right to shield my son! Left turn is not an option! If I go straight, Snitch Lock will have target practice! I make a right turn! Bullets are hitting my car! Windows are breaking! The whole time I thinking, 'I gotta get my son to safety!' As the bullets are hitting my car, I'm putting distance between us and Snitch Lock! A cop car rides right past me into the line of fire! I didn't even think about stopping!

Rayco's quick reaction saved his life and that of his son. Amazingly, neither he nor his son were hit. But the evidence of a major hit was there for anyone to see. He knew he had to take action right away.

"When I got to my house, I made sure my son wasn't hit. I made the needed-to-know phone calls. My brothers and my lawyer! The car was totaled! Three flat tires! Three windows with bullet holes! Bullet holes up and down both sides of the car!"

His life in danger, he refused to allow circumstances, however deadly, to change his role as a dad. His son, Rayco, Jr. was scheduled for a boxing match and he would be there. Yet, there was still more to the drama. Another episode would ensue.

"The police circled my house about three times, even stopping on one occasion. Then they left. I wasn't going to let this incident spoil my son's night, so I told my brother, Wachi, to pick us up and take us to the fight. A few minutes later and a block from the house, he calls me and tells me that the police have him pulled over. Being that he didn't have a license, I walked up the street to get the car. As I am having conversation with the cop that pulled him over, the sergeant pulls up and gets out of her car. We continue talking when the sergeant says to me, 'Put your hands on the car!' I reply, 'For what?' The other cop is looking, wondering what is going on! She repeats herself, then reaches for her gun! Now, I'm wondering, what bullshit now? I put my hands out to my sides and slightly in the air, then ask, 'What's this about?' She reached for my waste, touched my phone, then said, 'Oh!' I just shook my head and resumed the conversation with the other cop. When I got the ok to take my brother's car, the sergeant asked me where my car was. I told her at home. She made reference to the shooting that took place about a half our earlier, and I confirmed that it was my car. They checked it out and took a report. They asked me did I see who did it? I told them yes. They asked who? I declined to answer."

Finally, he got to the boxing match to see his son shine. All the maneuvers he had taught his son came through. The stressful night culminated in a victory for another Saunders. For his father, it was a proud moment. Considering the harrowing experiences, Rayco was able to be there and be the dad he wanted to be.

"Lil Rayc fought that night and won best fight of the night! He was very happy when he got his trophy that was almost as tall as him! I was happy for him. I tried my best that night to not show what was really on my mind."

CHAPTER 22

"2006 was a new, but rough year for me. Being that my son was caught in the middle of a war, due to my cockiness, bothered me greatly! I had problems sleeping! It was so bad that I wouldn't go to sleep until the sun came up! I will never forget the fright on my son's face when the smoke cleared!"

About to make changes in his boxing career, Rayco set out in the new year to make his mark in a new weight category.

"I let the boxing world know that I was dropping down from cruiserweight (200 lbs.), to fight at light-heavy weight (175 lbs.). My first fight at this weight was against a top 10 guy named Danny Santiago, in Coral Gables, Florida. I had to force myself to get rest for this fight.

"At the weigh-in on my way to the gentlemen's room, I spoke to Danny and his friends. He gave me a 'don't speak to me' look! That was fine with me. The ass kickin' he was going to get was business. Now it was personal! When it was my turn to get on the scale, I removed everything but my spandex shorts. You would have thought that I was a movie star on the red carpet! The cameras went crazy! They've never seen a fighter built like me! Before I could get all my clothes back on, a representative from Danny's team came to speak with me. He said, 'We'll pay you $1500 more to fight this other guy, 2 rounds less.' I said, 'I'm supposed to fight Danny 8 rounds. But you will pay me $1500 more than what you were going to pay me to fight 6 rounds with this easy opponent!' The rep said, 'Yes.' I said, 'Let me talk it over with my team.' I already made the decision, but wanted to show some diplomacy. When I returned to the rep, I told him that I didn't come for the money, I came for Danny's rankings!"

Further surprises awaited him just as he was about to enter the ring as a light-heavyweight. Something was in the air – he could smell it, feel it and knew that another scene was about to unfold.

"Three minutes before I was to walk to the ring, the same rep came to the dressing room and told me that my fight was switched from 8 rounds to 6 rounds because of TV, but I still would be paid the contracted amount! I put up an argument but was told there was nothing they could do!"

The bout went on according to plan and it was all Rayco. He knew he won the fight and the fans did too. But like many of the events in the young boxer's world, this was another one for the books!

"I kicked Danny's ass that night but was given a "draw"! Everyone from the commentators to the ref, had me winning! Yet the judges sent me home disappointed again."

Undeterred and not broken, he set out for bigger and better bouts.

"This didn't break me though. I trained even harder! I went to four different training camps, three times in Florida and once in Arizona. These camps consumed 3 months of my year. When the last camp finished in Florida, I was in Chicago, Illinois, when I got the call 8 days before the fight, to fight Chris Henry! I accepted!

"I met Chris Henry at one of the camps in Florida. We were cool with each other. Now we were fighting! I was excited! I knew he was coming to fight and so was I! We were fighting in a land that I purposely avoided for 7 years of my life. Houston, Texas!"

Houston did not disappoint Rayco. It was home territory for Henry and he knew he would be on unfriendly grounds. Yet, he was ready as ever to prove to the boxing world that he was the best. What happened in Houston was yet another fateful occasion that was marred in controversy. But for Rayco, it was his night.

"This was my most enjoyable fight to date! I love when another fighter gives his all! Chris gave his all. From start to finish, the crowd was on its feet! Although an accidental head butt in the 3rd round opened a large cut above my left eye, the fight was non-stop! I felt that I won the fight. One of the Texas judges, Boxing Talk and most of the other press, had me winning the fight but we were all overruled by two of the three Texas judges. I lost by split decision."

The fight over, Saunders and his opponent both received reprimands from the boxing officials and the state of Texas.

"I received a 45-day suspension because of my cut. Chris received a 45-day suspension also, because the fight was that brutal! After my suspension was up, I hit the gym hard because my management team was working on a fight for me in the beginning of the new year, possibly on the west coast or down South!"

But it was also a time for him to let loose and cultivate a certain someone whom he had met. It was time for him to unwind, relax and take a breather. Some down time.

"Being that I knew I was about to be booked for a tough fight, I flew back to Chicago, to visit a female friend that I met on the previous trip. To give you an idea of her ethnicity, her father was a dark brown skinned guy from the United States. Her mother was from South Korea. I learned a few things about the differences in cultures, cooking, eating, etc. It was very enlightening!"

As with most events in his life, Rayco was about to encounter yet another episode that tested his fibre and nearly cost him his life. He noticed it as soon as he entered his neighborhood.

Something was unusual in the streets in his hometown. It wasn't the fact that Christmas was just two days away. There were police out in force and it wasn't the usual lone police patrol car. There was a presence! Something was about to occur. Rayco could feel it in the cold air.

"After a brief stay on Chicago, I flew back to Pittsburgh. I resumed my training schedule as planned. On the 23rd of December, 2006, I started my day as usual. However, on this particular day I noticed that the police presence on my street was far more than usual! On an average, I might see the police ride past my house once a day. I lived in a very quiet part of my neighborhood. Most people thought that my street was a dead end, so there wasn't much traffic, especially police traffic!"

Yet, the police presence. More patrol cars whizzing by. A most unusual sight and one that not only caught the notice of Rayco but the residents as well.

"It seemed as if every time that I came out of my house, I would see a police car riding past! When I came to get the mail, feed my dogs, get something from my car, etc. About 4 p.m. this day, me and my 18 month-young son, Jelani, were about to go pick up Lil Rayco, and go to Weight Masters Gym in Wilkinsburg. While I was putting Jelani into his car seat, another cop car rode by! I had to stop what I was doing and close the passenger door so the cop could get pass my car. After the cop car passed me, I resumed strapping my son in and we went to the gym. We had a good training session. I say we because all three of us worked out, even Jelani! My little man knew how to throw combinations, etc."

His session over at the gym, it was time to go home. Within a few blocks of his home, the beefed-up presence of Pittsburgh police was apparent. This time it was Rayco who was affected. He would soon find out why.

"We left the gym about 8 p.m. to go to my house. When we got to Taft Ave. in Beltzhoover, a police car sped up behind me and turned on its red and blue lights. I pulled over immediately wondering why I was being pulled over now! Then out of everywhere, other police cars start surrounding my car! I was on the phone with my neighbor, Robin Player, having one of our many conversations about improving one's self, improving one's community, etc., before the police got behind, so she was on the phone when it all transpired."

Events like the one he was about to encounter would rankle anyone. But Rayco had been through this before and he was ready. At least, he thought so! As with every encounter he had with the police, what was about to unfold was nothing short of theater.

"Police cars, lights,... more cars,... more lights! Then a voice over the intercom says, 'Exit the vehicle with your hands up!'

I holler out of my window, 'What am I being pulled over for?'

The same voice, 'Exit the vehicle slowly with your hands up!'

Now I notice that there are a lot of guns drawn and aimed at me! Jelani is crying! Lil Rayc is quiet. Now I'm getting worried, not for me, but for my children! My windows are tinted 100%! The police can't see in my car! So I start to holler, 'My babies are in the car!' The police didn't care!

They just hollered back, 'Get out the car and get on the ground or you will be tazed!' I had to think fast! If one of my young partnas would have came by and they had heat on them, there were too many places to shoot from where one could remain undetected! Shots would have been fired! So I complied with the police request. As I did this, I instructed my neighbor to come get my children. Yesterday! As soon as I said 'Laferty and Taft', a cop snatched my earpiece out of my ear!"

Keeping his cool because of his concern for his sons made Rayco vulnerable, yet he wanted to be heard.

"Once I was handcuffed, they picked me up off of the ground. The detective in charge was already searching my car at this point. They knew I didn't have any drugs on me, so I knew he was hoping to find a gun! Him searching was a waste of time. I've already let it be known that if and when I carry a gun, it's on my hip! I need to be able to access it at any given moment for ANY and ALL threats! It's 100% as my tattoo says, 'Live Free or Die!'"

The sirens, lights and shouts soon attracted a group of people.

"My neighbor Robin Player, came running to the scene. I asked what I was being arrested for, and every cop that I asked including the cop in charge said, 'I don't know.' I felt like Mandela! I was being took to jail in front of my children and noone could tell me why!"

Why? What was this all about? His thoughts clouded by the events, he wanted to focus on his sons and ensure their safety. But still the question, why is he being arrested?

"Someone mentioned something about my children walking! The temperature was about 25 degrees Fahrenheit! I told the cops that my Baby was 18 months and he was not walking anywhere! One of the cops made an allegation about my car being stolen, but my neighbor Robin quickly squashed that! She was allowed to take my car because it was not used in any crime. I also called Jelani's mother after I got off of the ground. She showed up just before they took me away. Once I was put in the police wagon, I asked one last time, 'Why am I being arrested?'

The cop in charge said, 'I don't know. It's Steve Hitchings' warrant." A little clarity came to me, but I still didn't know what I was being charged with! I was barely in Pittsburgh in 2006! If I did something that I knew I could go to prison for, I had many chances to run and never come back! I traveled around the country all year, so what was I being arrested for? I knew that Shawn Davis was working for Hitchings and I told everyone that I could! I knew that it wouldn't be long before James Jones got back to snitching, and I told everyone that I could! I knew that Hitchings was upset that I exposed his RAT, because another cop mentioned it. So this was his get back!"

Rayco's suspicions were now realized and magnified beyond proportions.

"I was arrested and took to my arraignment without being questioned by the police, like they do on television. I finally got my paperwork and found out why I was arrested! It turned out that James Jones, a.k.a. JC, a.k.a. J lock, a.k.a. Snitch lock, was shot up on July 8th, 2006! He tells the police, according to the police report, that his name was Eric Timbers, and that he was walking on Climax Ave. when he heard gunshots and was hit, but he didn't see nothing! It was also discovered that in Jones's vehicle, at the time of the shooting, was 125 grams of crack cocaine, 1000 stamp bags of heroin and a bag of powder cocaine! He left the hospital before he was arrested! 3 days after he was shot, Jones calls his parole officer and tells him, 'I didn't see who shot me, but I know that it was Rayco!' Approximately 30 days after he was shot, Jones was arrested! On his possession was a Glock 40, semi automatic hand gun! He was also charged with that gun! 70 days after he was shot, he gave his first statement, and after talking to his P.O., Jones gets a visit from Detective Steve Hitchings! After this visit, Jones changes his statement to, 'I saw Rayco Saunders shoot me!' He gave detailed descriptions of the crime scene, too! 86 days after his changed statement and 159 days after Jones was shot, I was arrested! There wasn't anything or anybody that tied me to this crime, but the changed allegation of James Jones!"

Reprimanded and now in custody, Rayco knew he was set up.

"Now I'm in jail! This is a direct violation of due process, according to the 5th & 14th amendments of the US Constitution! However, to the powers that be, these amendments, as well as most of the US Constitution were enacted way before an African, born and raised in the United States, was considered a Man or a citizen, so they don't apply! My bond is $100,000 straight! I can't pay it because I have two probation detainers on me. One is a detainer that stems from my conviction in 1997. The other stems from my conviction in 2006, which was an invalid detainer because I was sentenced to this probation 10 days after James Jones was shot up! When I addressed my detainer issues with my attorney, she told me that the two judges would not lift them, even though she hadn't tried to get them lifted. I also received information that Jones told multiple individuals that he didn't know who shot him, but was going to get me to pay him $25,000 to set me free! My lawyer said that she would interview these individuals but never did!"

Sitting in jail for an alleged crime he had no part of would make anyone stressed out and angry. He had been through this procedure before and knew the wheels of justice would be slow and deliberate. He would be patient up to a point. But like most wrongly-accused individuals, he set out to right a wrong. He wasn't going to allow the warped criminal justice system have its way. Not now. Not ever!

"From my 1997 conviction, where I was convicted without any evidence for a crime that never happened, I learnt to never put your life in someone else's hands, so I started working on my case myself. When I checked on my detainers, I discovered that the valid detainer from 1997 was lifted! This is the time that I figured out that the detainer from 2006 was invalid! I also got word from my potential witnesses that my attorney had not come to interview them. I was furious! What blew my top was when I got a letter from my attorney asking for more money on top of what I already paid her or my case would be postponed! I had no problem paying the money, but I wanted to see some action!"

Frustrated by the inaction of his attorney and confined to the bleakness of a barren cell, Rayco began to form a strategy. If his attorney wasn't up to the task, he would make some drastic changes. His years of incarceration made him something of a 'jail house lawyer.' He knew some of the major court decisions affecting the accused and set out to make his voice heard.

"I started to have doubts about my attorney when she told me that I couldn't file a "motion to suppress the identification of me, by the witness!" I knew that she was either wrong or she was working for the other team! According to "McCormick Evidence 297 (2d ed. 1972)" and some more up to date US Supreme Court cases that I can't name off the top of my head, I had a very strong argument that James Jones's statement was very unreliable and would not fall under the "spontaneous utterance" or "res gestae exception", and therefore should be suppressed!

In the meantime, his quality of life already compromised by his arrest was further tested when it came to his diet. A diet that didn't meet his rigid standards as a professional boxer.

"While I'm going through this with the people that are supposed to be working for me, I'm dealing with some other issues inside the Allegheny County Jail. They wouldn't provide me with a vegetarian meal! They kept denying me on the basis of religion, or in my case, a lack of! So for 8 months, I fed myself through the jail commissary! Granola bars, oatmeal and pistachios! $2,000 dollars! I still have my receipts! Finally, word got to the warden. I was immediately put on the vegetarian list!. However, this proved to be a little too late. My body was lacking so many nutrients that in July of that same year, a couple of months before I finally got to eat a meal, I was shooting basketball in the jail house gym! I had already played a few games before, that day, and also the day before. It was an added activity to take my mind off of my current problems!"

The basketball court became an escape; a place to let loose and a source of bonding with rules respected and cooperation replacing stress and regimentation. A temporary escape from the environment of control. It gave Rayco, the chance to let loose – a welcome refuge from the harsh life of incarceration.

It was one of these innocent past-times that would change the dynamic in Rayco's life. A simple game of basketball suddenly changed everything. For any athlete like Rayco, the simplest injury gone unat-tended can have catastrophic results on one's career. This was to be his 'wake up' call.

"The serious ball players played basketball in the evenings. My team won the first game. Being that another team always had next, the second game started immediately. I scored the first two points of the game, so my team kept giving me the ball. The next play was a screen. I run my defender from one side of the court to the other, pick and roll... I'm wide open! The ball is passed to me! I take the 15 foot jump shot... "POP!" What was that? I felt my left foot flutter like a diving board that's just been jumped off! When I came down, I went to the ground! I knew from the sound and the feeling that I ruptured my Achilles Tendon!"

Everyone sensed that something very wrong had occurred. Writhing on the ground, holding onto his shattered leg, the damage already done, Rayco cried out.

"The guys standing on the far wall, which was about 25 feet from me, had a look of horror and shock on their faces! They heard the sound of my Achilles when it snapped! One of their first questions was, 'What was that!?'"

Rayco knew he needed help immediately. Fast! But like most situations in such a confined and isolated environment, there would be a delay. A lapse of a few minutes is understandable, but this wait seemed to go on forever.

"Though I was on the ground, laying on my side, holding my ankle, I stayed calm. I instructed the guys around me to tell the guard that I needed immediate medical attention. Yesterday! This was a waste of energy. I wasn't seen by medical personnel for an hour. Once I was escorted to the jail clinic, I was seen by a Doctor Young. He was a 400 lb. brown-skinned guy that was a sad excuse for a doctor and a person."

By the time the doctor had arrived, Rayco had assessed his injury and was ready to convey the information he knew to the medical staff. A medical staff that didn't want to hear him.

"He asked me what was wrong. I told him that I ruptured my Achilles Tendon. He asked me, 'How did I know?' I told him, 'I am a professional athlete. It is my job, duty and obligation to know when and what is wrong with my body!' This dude told me that it was just a sprain and that it would be alright in a week or two. Then he tried to give me some pain medication. I refused them! I told him my reasons for not taking medications. However, I did ask for some rubbing cream. My leg was killing me! I was sent back to my pod with a cane!"

With no x-ray or follow up procedure to determine the source of the injury, the inaccurate and cursory evaluation of Dr. Young would resonate in a still worsening of Rayco's condition. Inaction and inattention led to severe pain. Yet he was still not given the proper care. With no follow-up, his condition would worsen.

Knowing the gravity of his injury, Rayco pleaded for help. Time and again his request was met with skepticism and outright neglect. Finally, Dr. Young appeared again.

"In an attempt to try to get my leg fixed, I put in numerous requests to medical, only to be seen by Doctor Young two more times within 7 seven days of me getting injured. Both times he brushed me off. As the days went on, my lower left leg doubled in size! My toes even swelled up! About three weeks later, I was called to medical and seen by a different doctor. He told me to do different movements with my foot, which I could not. He took notes. Whatever he was writing, I knew that it wasn't good. He sat with one hand on his head, in a slouched position. He told me that he was sending me to the Ortho Clinic."

Finally sent to the clinic for a thorough examination, what was known to Rayco was, at long last, recognized by the medical staff. Three long weeks had passed.

"A few weeks later I was escorted, in leg shackles and handcuffs to the Ortho Clinic. My ankle was so big the sheriff was shocked! The ankle cuff would barely go on the first notch. Because I couldn't get a MRI, due to the bullet fragments around my heart, I was given a sonogram. A sonogram wasn't like a x-ray. The results were immediately viewable as it was being done. Both doctors and the assistant who were present, simultaneously agreed that my Achilles Tendon was completely ruptured."

Able to finally be evaluated by an orthopedic surgeon, the news was as bad as expected.

"The main doctor said to me, 'If this injury would have happened yesterday, I could've fixed it! Because so much time has gone by, there is nothing I can do!'

"I asked, 'What does this mean for me?'

'You will never be able to stand on your toes! You will never be able to jump as high! You will never have full function of your leg again!'"

Anger reinforced Rayco's already cynical, albeit correct assessment of the prison system. They were responsible for his present condition. Imagine a star athlete, injured on the field and sent home without any follow-up treatment. The media along with a legion of supporters and a line of lawyers would surely fall in line and demand an explanation with legal repercussions. Unfortunately, in his present venue, little could or would be done. Anger and the feeling of abandonment were replaced by a dose of reality – what next? What could he do with his boxing career?

The blame justifiably started.

"I blamed Doctor Young for this! If he would have listened to me, my leg would be fixed! I set in my cell and thought about what this would mean for my boxing career. In order to be successful, I needed full function of both legs. This was the first time in many years that I shed tears! I blamed myself! I blamed doctor Young! I blamed the police! "What did I do so bad in my past life to suffer so much in my current life?" (Tina Marie, Deja Vu)"

To any person who had to confront what Rayco Saunders endured as a result of what happened on the basketball court, it would be understandable that the person would have much to be cynical about. That same person could withdraw into himself and make himself reclusive and brooding over what had happened and ask: 'Why me?' The tough, hardcore streets made Rayco more defiant at the system, angrier by the day and left wondering what was to become of him.

Added to this scenario was yet another completely and devastating event. One in which he had absolutely no control. It occurred on the same mean streets that he had known throughout his life. This time, the streets had their way and reigned supreme. Like a superior opponent in the ring, this time there was no way out. That event took place on a hot July night, not far from his cell.

"Man! Could things get any worse? On 24 July, 8 a.m., I'm listening to "The Steve Harvey Show", and the local news comes across the radio, 'A Northside teen was killed last night when he was shot with an AK-47 assault weapon! 18 years old.' At this moment right here, everything in my body stopped working except my ears! My heart, my lungs, anything that made sound! In a matter of 1 second, I begged the Almighty, 1000 times, 'please don't let it be Trevor!' The radio continued, 'Trevor Greer was shot multiple times last night!' I jumped off the top bunk, not worrying about my leg anymore, and ran/hopped to the door! I had to get to the phone! It wasn't yet time for recreation so the doors weren't unlocked yet. Every cell has a button and intercom so the prisoner can reach the guard on duty, and vice versa! I hit the button and watched through my cell door window as the guard on duty went to answer my call. When he came over the intercom, I tried to tell him that I urgently needed to use the phone, but before I could tell him, I broke down into tears! My door unlocked and I made it to the phone as fast as I could. Trevor's mother, answered crying! I was crushed! We had our differences through out our relationship! We had our share of ups and downs! None of that mattered anymore! She had just lost her first child! The eldest brother of my son, Jelani, was physically gone, forever!

Grief quickly turned to anger. Here he was locked up and alone. Unable to attend to Jelani and his mother, Rayco wanted to be there for them. Anger set in. He was determined to use the network in jail to find the facts. The subculture of prison is rife with information that seeps into the darkest confines of the cell from the streets. The facts relating to the murder of young Trevor soon became evident behind the walls. With the murder of Trevor, it would be no different. Determined despite his grief, to find out the facts. But, first he thought of the young man.

"I met Little Trevor in 1993 when he was just 4 years young. It's interesting because I was at his house with his mother when I got the call that my first son, little Rayco, was born! I used to call Trevor, my human alarm clock, because in the mornings he would make sure that I woke up by hitting me in my head with his plastic baseball bat!

"I was crushed that I couldn't be there for his mother! If someone ever needed any support, this was definitely the time! Yet, I had no control! No say so! I couldn't even pay my respects at the funeral without being told what to do! The county wanted hundreds of dollars to allow me to view Trevor's body, but under these conditions: I had to go when the funeral home was closed! No family members could be present! I had to go in shackles and cuffs and they couldn't be removed! And I could stay no longer than 15 minutes!

Insult added to the wounded Rayco! How callous could the system be? No time off to pay his respects and no time to bond with Trevor's mother at her most traumatic and stressful period.

"I wanted to go so bad, but these conditions were unacceptable! If it were free, yes! But for hundreds of dollars... never! So as a result, one more notch of hatred was added to my heart!

"Sadness, turned into anger! In jail, you get more information than they do on the streets! The police had names of suspects. I had names of perpetrators! I knew what gun was used, who had the gun and where the gun went! I just needed to get out of jail!

Rayco was determined to get to the bottom of the tragedy. He wanted justice for Trevor, but it was not to be. Not in his present circumstances. Now he had to harness his energy into his case and prepare for his court date. Difficult as it was for him to mourn alone, he redoubled his effort to ensure that he was ready for his day in court. He had to. He had to move on. Nothing could be done for Trevor, despite all the anger and hurt.

"I channeled my focus back to my law work and my leg! I immediately went into rehab mode! Up the steps on my toes! Down the steps! I was in so much pain, but I was not going to be denied of the use of my leg! Running! Walking! Jumping jacks! I would not be denied!

"My lawyer postponed my case without my consent. I fired her! I wrote a letter to the judge telling him that I was ready to proceed without an attorney. This letter preserved my rule 600 right to speedy trial! I also filed a motion to represent myself. When this motion was granted, the prosecution, thinking that they were about to get over on me, exposed their full hand! They opened my eyes to things that I didn't know about! Once I felt the prosecution was all in, I hired another attorney.

"Out of the three attorneys that I met with, he made it clear that he worked for me and would do what I asked him to do! Every motion that I wanted filed, he filed it! Whatever information that I didn't have, he gave it to me! When I brought his attention to a specific issue, he paid attention! I was confident that I chose the right guy!

With his confidence restored in the new attorney, it was time to get ready for his trial.

"When trial started, picking the jury was the first time that we had a disagreement! We disagreed on a juror, a brown-skinned guy, who was arrested for stalking his girlfriend! My lawyer wanted this guy bad! I didn't want him! He reminded me so much of the only brown-skinned woman that I had on my jury in 1997! I think they even wore the same kind of eye glasses! My lawyer saw something in this guy though that I didn't see! We accepted him.

The ensuing trial was a time for the bogus charges to be brought and dissected. Rayco was prepared, as was his new counsel. He would make his mark, beginning with his wardrobe.

"The trial lasted three days. The first day, I wore some greyish blue dress pants, with a similar button up shirt and my blue Alligator and Ostrich, David Eden shoes, with matching belt. I didn't know who was on trial, me or James Jones! The prosecution spent the whole day presenting and going over what James Jones was caught with! What did James Jones guns and drugs have to do with me? It was a smoke screen! There were no witnesses and no evidence to tie me to this crime, so the prosecution stalled for time by presenting all the drugs and the gun that Jones was caught with! Without this smoke screen, the prosecution's case would have took 20 minutes, tops, to present! A major blow in the prosecution's case was when their star witness, James Jones, was asked to show the jury one stamp bag of Heroin, out of 1000, that he admitted to possessing and distributing! Jones acted like, and stated that he was afraid to touch his own drugs! He should've won an Oscar!

Rayco knew what was going on with Jones. He would testify to save his own skin, even if it meant perjuring himself. He also knew he had cut a deal to lessen or avoid any jail time.

"James Jones was on parole for drugs and guns when he was busted this time. He was facing 33 years in federal prison under the career criminal statue! My lawyer asked James Jones what he received for these crimes that he was just convicted of, because we knew some type of deal was reached for his testimony. Jones answered, '10 years probation!' My lawyer, not expecting that kind of answer, was shocked and asked Jones to repeat his answer! 10 years of probation was unheard of for a guy facing a MANDATORY 33 year sentence in the federal penitentiary!

The next witness, a police officer, fared no better under relentless questioning from the now competent and dedicated attorney representing the defendant Rayco Saunders. His attorney went right on the attack.

"When my lawyer questioned the cop in charge, Steve Hitchings, he immediately asked him, 'who sanctioned this deal with Jones! Who gave the go ahead to override the federal statue, on this case?' Hitchings stuttered, stumbled and everything else with his mouth. When he couldn't do that anymore, he used the infamous words that can get you out of any question asked in court, 'I can't recall!'

The first day of his trial over, Rayco awaited the next day's proceedings and felt ever more relaxed. A new day meant he would don another eye-catching wardrobe. His taste in designer clothes was evident the minute he set foot into the courtroom.

"The second day of trial, I wore a silk tan sports jacket, a brown long sleeve shirt, tailored fitted brown pants and my Stacey Adams, brown & tan Alligator shoes, with matching belt. I was sharp as a guillotine! I was scheduled to testify this day. My son, Lil Rayc, was scheduled to testify also. Not about my innocence, but about what me, him and the baby do every Friday and Saturday evenings, which is watch fights on TV. There would be no way that my son could testify to something that happened 1½ years prior! The DA, Chris Avetta, tried to trick my son into saying that I coached him to say things that were in my favor. This wasn't a concern of mine because I never told my son to say anything! I only wanted him to speak the truth of what he knew.

After his son's testimony, the defendant himself was called to the stand. Sworn in, sitting in the witness chair, he was prepared as ever to let the court and anyone hear what needed to be said. He wanted to get the facts out.

"When I took the stand I spoke what was on my mind. But my number one rule when being questioned is 'to answer what I am asked as truthful as possible'. The less you say, the better off you are! Unless you can turn the question into a positive! I was asked by the DA, 'Do you want to see Jones dead?' I replied, 'The only people that I want to see dead is rapists, child molesters and serial killers!' The real answer to the Jones question was, 'I want to see him suffer!' But given the circumstances, my reply was the 'politically' correct answer.

His testimony over, his defense attorney called upon three other character witnesses to take the stand. They performed marvelously.

"Three other people testified on my behalf. My brothers from another mother, Malik "Dripp" Cobbs, Thomas "Train" Darwin and Jelani's mother. Dripp and Train were eye witnesses to the shooting! The DA asked them why they didn't go to the police? Both answers were, 'We don't go to the police!' When Jelani's mother testified as to my where abouts, all the males in the court room were spellbound! I don't know what it was on that day, but she was super sexy! Everything about her! Her walk! Her movement! Her voice! Very soft spoken. She reminded everyone of Sharon Stone in the movie "Basic Instinct", when she was being interviewed by the police.

The last day of the trial was the most momentous. It also had its share of surprises.

"On the third and final day, I wore a crème sweater, crème pants and my three tone Umberto Pellegrini, square toe shoes, with matching belt. The judge on the case who used to be a homicide district attorney, addressed all of my motions while the trial was going on. He denied everyone of them! My rule 600, "right to speedy trial", although violated, was denied. My motion to suppress the obviously "unreliable and unduly tainted identification by James Jones", although praised by the judge as, "very well researched", was denied. So the case went to the jury.

"This was it! Do or Die! I was took back to the bull pen. I went to the restroom and soon as I finished, my name was called to go back upstairs to the courtroom. The escorting sheriff said, 'jury's back quick!' I responded, 'either they love me or hate me!' After I was unchained and seated, my lawyer whispered to me that I am going home. He told me that he ran into the two alternate jurors in the hall and they told him that we won. They also told him that the jurors didn't even sit down before coming to a decision.

Much is said about a jury when they reach a verdict and report back to the courtroom for the decision to be made public. Would they look at the defendant? Would the DA look at the defendant? Would the jury have a poker face, smile or look straight ahead?

"When the jury entered the court room, the assistant DA, Chris Avetta, didn't even look their way. He was as white as Casper the Ghost. I thought he might fall over in his chair. The jury read the verdict, 'not guilty.' My lawyer hugged me, and told me congratulations. I was still furious! Another year of my life, took away from me, just like that! Took away from my children, because another MAN said so! I don't appreciate that at all! I will have the last laugh though! One way or another!

"After I was found not guilty, I wasn't immediately allowed to go home. The frivolous probation detainer that judge O'Toole had on me and refused to lift, still was holding me. I didn't get released until two days later. While I was being held, illegally, the medical brains of the Allegheny County Jail found out that I was cleared of all charges so they tried to rush me into surgery the morning I was to be released! I knew that if I got the surgery done, that I would not have been able to go home until I was medically cleared. In other words, if I would have had the surgery, even though I would have been a "so-called free man", I still would have had to remain in jail until I was medically cleared to leave. Knowing surgery can't be done if you eat, I told the guards in the intake that I had eaten. The surgery was canceled. I was released later that day.

His freedom won, Rayco felt yet another setback when he arrived at his home. Knowing that he was incarcerated and possibly spending years if found guilty, vandals took advantage of the vacated premises. The house ransacked and its contents strewn about, he looked around and assessed the damage, aware of what was stolen. The robbers knew what to take and did a thorough job of upending his home.

"When I got home, I went to see my little men. I missed my sons so much! I missed being the father to them that I never had! I picked up my life where I left off, partly! I say partly because while I was locked up, someone broke in and robbed my house! They even took the copper pipes out of the walls! It bothered me, but not that much. I'm not a materialistic guy! If I had something once, I can get it again! Also, I can't change the fact that it happened, so I move on. I will find out who did it eventually! When that time comes, I'll deal with it then!

Yet, nothing would deter him from his family and his career. He wanted back in the ring and began to explore possibilities of future bouts. A series of unproductive phone calls plus his daily regimen of training, albeit with the recent injury of the torn Achilles heel, the loss of Trevor and the break in at his home were tough setbacks. But, he was determined to get back into the mix and soon his routine set in.

"I missed a lot of fight opportunities while I was gone, so I had a lot of ground to make up. I immediately started training. Sure enough, opportunities start knocking. The first was a show being held in Pittsburgh, PA, the city where I was born and raised! It was also an ESPN TV fight, featuring, Monty Clay as the main event! This would be great to come home and fight on TV as the co-main. Didn't happen though! Two guys from who knows where, got the co-main spot. I didn't even get put on the off TV fight card! The people in charge wanted to pay me pennies to fight! They said that being that I just got out of jail they were doing me a favor. I laughed at this! Once my fans in Pittsburgh heard that I was back and fighting, the fight venue wouldn't have had enough seats! However, I was willing to compromise! I'll take pennies for an easy fight. No, they wanted me to fight a guy that was in a higher weight class and had been training for months for this fight! Come to find out that his people were paying for the fight! Meaning that the promoter in Pittsburgh wasn't spending a penny! Also, the promoter, (World Class, who went bankrupt) was being paid by ESPN, so he/they were just being greedy! Small time thinking for small time people, though! Didn't faze me. I didn't and don't need them!

Still undeterred, he made more calls, resulting in a few bouts.

"I made a few calls and hooked up a fight on ESPN a week later! The fight in Pittsburgh happened on 1 February, 2008. I fought in Delaware on 8 February, 2008! The people in Pittsburgh wondered how I did that! I was the co-main event against a guy that was closer to his home then me. The judges were even from the same city he was. Even though I wasn't as strong as normal and I wasn't in my best shape, I was the aggressor the whole fight! I and others watching felt that I won the fight, but I lost a close decision. It was a real shame that I even had to fight in another city on another show when one was held in the city I lived in, just 1 week ago! It was cool though! I don't want any favors!

Fate was about to intervene and give him a new opportunity. An opportunity that he had never envisioned. When it presented itself, he jumped at the chance.

"Another opportunity presented itself soon after! This opportunity was amazing to me. I was called to go train in Germany! I always dreamt of traveling overseas to Afrika! I promised myself that I would do it in my lifetime, after I found out where my family was from! But here I was being offered an all expense paid trip to Europe! I didn't hesitate to take it!

His first transoceanic flight was not only a chance to hone his skills at a new venue but also to witness, take part in and appreciate a totally new environment devoid of the stress on his home turf. It was like a flight of the Phoenix, a chance at self-renewal. With each passing mile separating him from his hometown, he felt more and more relaxed and eager to meet the challenges.

"The first thing that I want to reflect on is the flight! 9 hours in the air was crazy! It was a beautiful thing though! Every time I fly, it is amazing to me, but this was something special! Looking out the window, I never saw so much water! Beautiful!

"When I landed in Germany, I can't describe the feeling I felt! B White, my homie/big brother describes it best, "a young guy, from the projects, who lost his mother, never had a father, been stabbed, shot and been to prison, is not just in another country, but is on another continent!" I will always cherish that experience! Most of the people there treated me well! Very few still had the old ways, but that didn't faze me! I had experience in dealing with people with hatred in their hearts in the USA! My solution to that was to Act like they're invisible! And hope that they want to get noticed!

The accommodations, cuisine and boxing program became for Rayco, a chance to reacquaint and immerse himself back into the boxing world. Meeting people from different parts of the globe, exchanging stories of their careers and where the program would take them, he bonded with his fellow pugilists and was at once made to feel at home. He learned from it and enjoyed it.

"The boxing program there, from what I've seen in the USA, was more efficient! Every one of the house fighters trains together! They all attend the training camp! They are all catered to, from the Champ to the guy/girl making their pro debut! Also, damn near the entire country supports the fighters, regardless of where they are from. Some of the top fighters that I met weren't born Germans, they were from other countries! In the USA, it's hard for some to get "a neighborhood" in a "city" to support an individual! I came away with the thought that you can be totally talent-less in the sport that you want to pursue, but will be taught, groomed and fashioned into the best athlete that you can be if you are determined! Here in the USA, I haven't seen or heard about this happening! I am a living example! I've been on a national level in amateur boxing. I turned pro and ran to a 6-0 record as a hell of a fighter! Got ranked #26 by the WBC! I was always supported by my family, friends and the fans, but the people that could have made me bigger, such as promoters, media, etc., didn't really support! Why? A lot of this book already covered that.

The venue where he stayed was state-of-the-art. And why not? It was used to train Olympic athletes and built to make their stay comfortable while trying out for such vigorous events to represent their nation.

"We all stayed at the Olympic Training Center called Keinbaum. This facility had everything: a pool, weights, a gym, hot tubs! Sport teams, such as the track team and the volleyball team to the rugby team were training there! This was a nice place. And the food was good! It was all you can eat too! You were responsible for your weight. The rooms were like hotel rooms. They had cable TV, couches, refrigerators, etc. You could come and go as you pleased. There was also a sports type of bar on the premises. Nice place too! It had free access computers, TVs... it was also co-ed! I enjoyed it.

His training over, it was time to travel a bit, see the capital, Berlin, and mix it up with the locals. A few of the people he met decided to go to a club that would further offer some new possibilities.

"When it was time to go back to the USA, I was took to Berlin. Me and a couple other fighters went to the night club. We met two brothers from Mali, Africa. They showed us the spot to go to. When we got off the train we had to walk quite a distance so I didn't know what to expect. My friend from Mali kept reassuring me that we would have a good time. When we got there I was very surprised! First, the music choice was the same hip-hop that I listened to in the USA! Second, there were a lot of brown people in this club! They were from all over the world! My friend from Mali smiled when he seen the smile on my face, then said, 'I told you that you would like this!'"

CHAPTER 23

The club in Berlin. It was here that he would meet her. He couldn't take his eyes off her. She was perfect.

"Then I saw her! 5'4" – 5'5", about a size 4 or 5 and weighed about 125. Light brown skin, with her hair down her back! Was it all her hair? I didn't know but I was going to find out! I didn't move immediately. I watched her. I wanted to see if she was with someone. I wanted to see if she drank, smoked, and any other piece of information that I could get.

"I noticed almost immediately that she was with another female. I was trying to assess the situation. Were they friends or were they FRIENDS? Or were there guys in this picture? I watched her some more. Closer now! I paid attention to every movement. I was trying to read her body language, follow her gazes, etc. After about 10 minutes of watching, I concluded that there was no guy. I couldn't get a read on the girl she was with though. So I moved closer to them, but far enough from them not to be noticed. The whole time that I'm watching her, she's dancing. Sexy! Exotic! My buddy from Mali saw me looking at her and followed my stare. He turned back to me, smiling and said, 'go get her.'

"I went to the other side of the club where I could get a better view. Her and her friend were still dancing, not with each other, but by each other. I've been to a lot of states and cities in the US where I've seen women dancing "sexy as hell", and now here I was in Berlin, Germany, watching this female "do her thang!" I wouldn't have believed the whole club experience, if I didn't see it for myself!

Always observant, always vigilant, Rayco wanted to make his move. The opportunity finally presented itself.

"From what I could tell, no alcohol. This was a good thing. And no cigarettes. Even better! I decided it was time to make my move. I've never been shy or scared, so since she was dancing by the stage where the DJ was set up, I leant on it, made eye contact with her, but wanted to and let her keep dancing! I kept my eyes on her now. Occasionally she would look at me to see if I was still looking at her. This is when I would bring my eyes back to her eyes. As soon as she would look away, my eyes would wander back to her body movement. Erotic! Once she was certain that she had my attention, all the brakes came off! After about 3 songs of this silent flirting, she stopped dancing and her and her friend starting talking and laughing with each other. I approached.

'Excuse me, are y'all together or are y'all TOGETHER?'

The female that I was watching spoke with an accent. 'Do you mean like lesbians?'

I answered, 'Yes.'

She spoke again, but this time angered. 'No, we are not lesbians! Do you think two beautiful women could be lesbians?

I apologized. I didn't mean any disrespect. I was actually asking out of respect. In the US, there are a lot of beautiful lesbians.'

She spoke again, still irritated. 'Well we are not lesbians!'

"After explaining why I asked that question and making peace, I asked what her name was. "Jelena", pronounced like "Helen-ah", but the "J" has a "Y" sound like in "yellow". Once I got the spelling of it, I seen that it was similar to my son's name. So I pronounce the vowels as they do in Kiswahili, "Yay-lane-nah". She corrects me when I pronounce it my way.

"We went to the lounge area in the club so we could talk. I asked her what her ethnicity was, and was bothered by the answer that she gave me: 'I'm Black.' I could have overlooked it, but that word really bothers me! So I said, 'You're not black! You are light brown. That word "black" tells me and anyone else, one thing about you! It has one meaning – a brown person who was a descendant of a slave, who doesn't know what his ethnicity, culture or heritage is, who is usually born and raised in the US! Where were you born? Where are your parents from?'

"This is when it came to me why she's a great dancer. 'My mother is from India and my father is from Africa. I was born in Croatia, and now I live in Germany.' Wow! Afrikan, Indian, mixed! Wow!

After meeting Jelena, Rayco learned much about the beautiful woman's background. Her beauty was matched by her intelligence and her insights into areas from geopolitics and culture to language and fashion. He was smitten!

"Jelena went on to tell me what places in Africa and India her parents were from. I explained to her why she should always say, when asked, that she is African and Indian, and never take away from her ethnicity, cultures and heritage by saying, she's black! She understood. We talked more and got more acquainted. She spoke six languages, English being one of them. Beauty and brains. I liked this girl! Although the clubs in Germany don't close 'til 7 a.m., me and the other fighters that I went with had early flights back to the US, and had to pack. I tried to get Jelena to come back to the hotel with me but she wasn't going for it. We exchanged phone numbers and emails, and said our goodbyes.

The chance encounter also got Rayco to think of his ethnic heritage. He was ever so curious to find out where in Africa and any other places his ancestors may have come. He had to find out. The trip to Germany and meeting Jelena capped his desire and upon arriving home, he set out to find out.

"Bothered by the fact that I knew my color but not my ethnicity, when I got back to the US, one of the first things that I did was arrange to have my DNA tested to see if I was Afrikan, and if I was, what country and ethnic group was I and my family from.

The DNA test would open up still another chapter in his life.

"I first heard about the DNA test on television. After researching all the companies, I feel that I chose the best one to do my test. Since the guy's ancestry that slept with my mother and made me, was not important to me, I had my "Mitochondrial DNA" that is inherited exclusively from my mother, which was inherited from her mother and her mother, etc., tested! Waiting for the results almost killed me. Because in the contract that you must sign, it states that there is a possibility that you may not be of full Afrikan descent! You could be of European decent, Native American decent, etc., or you could be mixed! It tells you that if they can't find you in the Afrikan data base, they look to all the others until they find all 100 percent of your DNA!

He was eager to share his finding with all – family and friends alike. But first he had to tell his skeptical grandmother what his findings were.

"This made me a little nervous because me and my Grandma used to have small disputes about whether we were Afrikan, Native American or both! Small things that were apart of my past started to bother me now. When I spoke to the lady on the phone, that was telling me about the test, she said, 'about 30 percent of the people who get this test done, find out that they have European DNA!' Being that I was born light – light skinned, or what some would call white, I didn't know what to expect! When my test results came I opened it immediately. As I read the results, a calmness came over me. Not because of what I was, but who I was! I could finally feel the satisfaction of knowing who I am, the same as those who can say, 'I am 'Chinese' American' or 'I am 'Italian' American' or 'I am 'Irish' American', even though we live in the 'Country' of The United States of the 'Continent' of "North" America! Which would actually make us 'United Statesians or United States citizens!' I guess 'United Statesian' didn't sound right, so the powers that be, took the entire continent name, both North & South as their country name and forgot that Mexico, Canada and the southern countries were 'AMERICANS', too! That's another chapter though! According to the signed 'certificate of ancestry' that I received from this company that does the test, my DNA sequence similarity – measure, shares ancestry with the Tikar people in Cameroon today, "100 percent"! This means that I, who inherited it from my mother, who inherited from her mother, and so on, DNA sequence is 100% the same as DNA sequences from the Tikar in Cameroon, today! Being 100% means so much to me because many people get mixed results, such as 30% Ghanaian, 30% Nigerian, 40% Cameroonian, DNA! Although that is still great news, being able to trace one route is far greater!

Like the ancient explorers finding new vistas and routes to travel, Rayco had come full circle and found himself. He felt at once relieved and overjoyed. He now knew for certain his roots.

"This mystery in my life was finally solved! It felt and feels great! Cameroonian! It sounds good. They say you don't know where you are going if you don't know from where you came. Well, it looks like I know where I'm going!

In the meantime, Jelena was on his mind and he was determined to go back to Germany not only to train but also to expand his contact with the beauty from the Berlin club.

"Me and Jelena stayed in touch. When I went back to Germany the second and third time, we spent some time together. We got to know each other more than just cordially. Knowing her and spending time with her has opened my eyes to a lot of things that I was blind to! One day we were watching "The Justice League" cartoon on a DVD that I took with me to Germany. The Green Lantern and crew are smashing and bashing their adversaries. Jelena says, 'this cartoon has such violence!' At first, I didn't even flinch to this statement. It was a cartoon! I asked her about the cartoons in Germany. After a brief conversation, I started watching it from her perspective. She was right! In almost every frame someone is getting hit, shot, crushed, slammed, etc! I grew up as a child watching this cartoon and others like it such as Spider-man, Superman, Batman and my all time favorite, The Incredible Hulk, just to name a few! My 4 year young son, Jelani, watches all these cartoons now. As I watch him grow, I can see the mental programming that he is receiving from these cartoons! When he plays with his toy men and/or cars, he makes them bang, crash, fight, slam, etc.! I will admit that I do not discourage this! I grew up like this! I've also seen how most young men that were born in the mid to late 80's and the 90's act, mentality wise... they are not so tough! Yes, I said it! They don't do what we did growing up! We used to play pick-up games of tackle football with no equipment! We used to play this football game called "free frog"! Twenty guys on the grass where we played. A guy would throw the ball in the air and whoever caught it had to run to the end zone. Then he had to try to reach the other end zone! This continued 'til he got tackled. The twist to the game was that once you caught the ball, the twenty on the grass turned into 19 against 1! This is how I grew up! That's why there'll never be football teams like there were in the seventies, the decade of the Pittsburgh Steel Curtain! There'll never be 15 round boxing matches again! Etc.!

Jelena provided a beacon for Rayco to look at and reexamine himself. Her insights provided him with a new direction when it came to his sons' upbringing. Perhaps the games are too violent. And yes, they may well imitate these crazy antics at their own peril. Jelena was indeed a beacon as well as a source of wonderment much needed in the hungry, young man's life. "When I left Europe I had a totally different outlook on certain things. Illiteracy was one of those things! Here was a female that spoke six languages better than some people spoke one! But if you didn't know all of these things and you read her emails to me, which are in English, her worst language, you would think that she was not to intelligent! This changed my thought process! There are those that say, "people died for you to learn how to read and write!" I disagree with this greatly because before, during and after, we were bought to the United States in chains, my ancestors knew how to read and write perfect! Just not in English! There are people all over the world, who are Genius, and can't read or write English! So my conclusion on people that can't read or write English, is not that they are illiterate, but that English is not for them!

CHAPTER 24

2008 witnessed the transformational presidential election of the first African American to the nation's highest office. With a record number of voters, Barack Obama, the Democratic junior senator from Illinois won 28 states with 53% of the popular vote. His election, a seminal event to be sure, catapulted the Democrats into the White House with a clear congressional majority to enact his legislative program that called for universal health care, an end to the wars in Iraq and Afghanistan and a restoration of trust by the American people in their Chief Executive. His victory was the first time a Democrat won with a plurality since Jimmy Carter's close victory over embattled President Ford in 1976. For Rayco and many others – African Americans, Latinos, young, first time voters, it was the culmination of a race that captivated the country and was all the talk from the barbershops to the union halls to the college campuses to the workplace. Rayco, like most people, got involved for the first time and cast his vote.

"Back in the United States, the presidential election between Barack Obama and John McCain was heating up! Knowing how the "electorate" voting process works, I never thought that I would witness the day when the United States of America elected a brown-skinned President! When I was in Germany, I was surprised of how many Germans wanted Barack Obama to win! Every where I went people would ask me about the election! I was excited about this election! This was even the first year that I registered to vote and voted! I felt that Barack Obama would win and I couldn't let my personal feelings towards the voting process, which is determined by the electoral vote and not by the vote of the people, keep me from being a part of "this story", a.k.a. "history"! Of all of the proud things that I can tell my children I was apart of, I couldn't and wouldn't exclude the presidential election of the first brown-skinned President of the United States of America!

"When it was announced that Barack Hussein Obama was the President of the United States of America, it was a proud moment for me, my children and all those that considered themselves to be Afrikans, born and raised in the United States of America! It was a fact that Obama's father was from Kenya, Afrika. So it couldn't be denied that Barack was Afrikan by calling him black!

"When pictures of the Obama family would be shown, it would bring a smile to my face each and every time. Whenever I think about this election, something that I read comes to mind, "The world no longer belongs to one race or another. It belongs to the young and the strong and the brilliant!"

January 20, 2009, an historic inauguration day in the nation's frigid capital. The cold winter wind didn't deter the crowd estimated at over one million, from spilling into the mall adjacent to the Lincoln Memorial to the Washington Monument. As the noon hour approached, the President-elect walked down the capitol steps and took the oath from Chief Justice Roberts and history was made. Rayco made sure to savor the moment.

"I kept my sons home from school so we could watch the inauguration ceremony together. This was a beautiful thing to be able to share this moment with my children. One of the moments that I will cherish forever.

"2009 was looking to be a good year. I was witness to a historical moment in US history, as the first Afrikan, born and raised in the United States of America, became President. I was working on establishing my own company, "RAYCOWAR PROMOTIONS LLC" and promoting boxing events. I was working on the completion of this book. I was working on the advancement of both my sons' education. Then at a routine check-up, my mother [grandmother] was diagnosed with cancer. It was a sad moment but we didn't dwell in the negative. We immediately prepared to beat the illness.

After all the tests were done, it was determined that she had to get a hysterectomy. Being that her age was 82, my family held on and hoped that everything would go smooth. Me, I knew that everything would be alright. I always think positive.

"After the surgery was over I went to visit her. I was very upset because I had just come from a custody hearing about my son, Jelani. His mother had me in court again trying to change our previous agreement because the change was convenient for her new schedule. This was not the time! When I saw my mama laying there in pain with tubes running in and out of her, I forgot about the custody hearing.

"Our visit went well. She was recovering great. I went to see her every day until she was released from the hospital. There was talk about radiation treatment but I was against this greatly. However, it still was a necessity. She had to get a minimum dose and everything is well now. I don't know what I would do if she was to leave me right now. She is my rock, my glue, my foundation that held and holds everything together for me.

There is a song by a guy name Marvin Sapp, called "Never Would Have Made It":

> Never would have made it,
> Never could have made it,
> Without you I would have lost it all,
> But now I see how you were there for me

And I can say Never would have made it, Never could have made it, Without you I would have lost it all,But now I see how you were there for me and I can say I'm stronger, I'm wiser,

I'm better, much better, When I look back over all you brought me thru I can see that you were the one that I held on to And I never Chorus – Never would have made it Oh I never could have made it Chorus – Never could have made it without you Oh I would have lost it all, oh but now I see how you were there for me I never Chorus – Never would have made it No, I never Chorus – Never could have made it without you

I would have lost my mind a long time ago, if it had not been for you I am stronger Chorus – I am stronger I am wiser Chorus – I am wiser

Now I am better Chorus – I am better So much better Chorus – I am better I made it thru my storm and my test because you were there to carry me thru my mess I am stronger Chorus – I am stronger I am wiser Chorus – I am wiser I am better Chorus – I am better Anybody better Chorus – I am better I can stand here and tell you, I made it. Anybody out there that you made itI am stronger Chorus – I am stronger I am wiser Chorus – I am wiser I am better Chorus – I am better Much better Chorus – I am betterI made it, I made it, I made it, I made it, I made it, I made it, I made it, I made it And I never would have made It Chorus – Never would have made it Never could have made it Chorus – Never could have made it without you I would have lost my mind, I would have gave up, but you were right there, you were right there

I never Chorus – Never would have made It Oh I never Chorus – I never could have made it without you. Someone needs to testify next to them and tell them I am stronger, I am wiser, I am better, much better. When I look back over what he brought me thru, I realize that I made it because I had you to hold on to, now I am stronger, now I am wiser, I am better, so much better. I made it. Is there anybody in this house other than me that can declare that you made it. Tell your neighbor, never would have made it. Never would have made it. Never could have made it. Never could have made it without you. Never would have made it. Never would have made it. Never could have made it. Never could have made it without you

"I dedicate each and every word to her because I never would have made it without her! I know that she will be called home eventually, but I want her to see me get married. I want her to hear me say, 'I made it!' I want her to be around when The Creator decides to bless me with a baby girl.

"I have my sons: Lil Rayco and Jelani. Lil Rayco, mimi mojo (my heart), who is my first born. Although me and his mother didn't see eye to eye, concerning his conception, her pregnancy and his birth, the first time that I held him, even though I was 19, I felt the love of a father and I vowed not to let him grow up without his daddy as I grew without mines!

"Jelani, mimi roho (my soul), who is my second born. Planned, conceived and then born when I was 31, is special. Me and his mother were together before he was conceived, during her pregnancy and when he was born. Being that we both had a son each from previous relationships, we wanted a baby girl, but we got a baby boy. Seeing this little guy born was the most amazing thing that I've witnessed thus far! Holding his mama's hand, telling her how to breathe so she wouldn't pass out or get fatigued, (even though me and the doctor disagreed on breathing methods), telling his mama what I could see when he started to come into the world, such as his hair, filming his birth, (even though the doctor told me I couldn't)! Going through the pregnancy with his mother was a beautiful thing also. Watching him grow inside her made me love her more. Kissing her stomach before going to sleep, putting headphones with R&B music playing, on her stomach to calm him down when he would move around and waking up rubbing & holding her stomach and seeing & feeling him move, were all moments that I cherish, even though the relationship stagnated and died because of dishonesty!"

"Although I love my brothers, Raymont, Wachi, Lil Ray, Dooby and my brothers I don't know and sisters, Paris, Bonnie, Mia, and my sisters I don't know, (the only gifts ever given to me by Arthur, with the exception of Raymont & Paris), my mama and my little men mean everything to me! My mama is my Queen, my guardian Angel! She has stood the test of time. When she goes home, I know that she will prepare a place for me.

"This is my first 35 years. Am I Blessed or Cursed? You call it"

CPSIA information can be obtained
at www.ICGtesting.com
Printed in the USA
BVOW08s2343141117

500277BV00002B/202/P